Supporting Early Mathematical Development

Supporting Early Mathematical Development is an essential text for current early years practitioners and students, offering an excellent blend of theory and practice that will enable you to provide successful mathematical education for children from birth to eight years old. Charting the delivery of mathematical development in playgroups, children's centres, nurseries and primary schools, it forges links between current practice and fundamental early years principles and makes suggestions for creating effective pedagogies in maths teaching.

Promoting mathematical development through play-based learning, this book presents:

- a wealth of practical multi-sensory teaching strategies
- instructional methodologies
- activity id   incorporating play, books, songs, cookery and the outdoors
- exampl   nildren's work
- advice   slating theory into practice
- questio   effective practice.

Throughout th   Caroline McGrath breaks down the complexity of teaching and learning math   into simple steps and guides readers through possible gaps in their knowledg   ing fresh enthusiasm to teaching mathematics. This is an invaluable resource   ctitioners and trainee teachers wishing to strengthen their mathematical teach   professional practice, or for students on a wide range of early years courses.

Caroline McG   tes from first-hand experience, having worked as a Nursery and Reception clas   er both in the UK and for The British Council in Spain. She is programme m   or the Foundation Degree in Early Childhood Studies at the City of Bristol Coll   partnership with the University of Plymouth. Her MA research includes views   xperiences of trainee and qualified practitioners working with children's earl   matical development.

Supporting Early Mathematical Development

Practical approaches to play-based learning

Caroline McGrath

Routledge
Taylor & Francis Group

LONDON AND NEW YORK

This edition first published 2010
by Routledge
2 Park Square, Milton Park, Abingdon, Oxon, OX14 4RN

Simultaneously published in the USA and Canada
by Routledge
270 Madison Avenue, New York, NY 10016

Routledge is an imprint of the Taylor & Francis Group, an informa business

© 2010 Caroline McGrath

Typeset in Helvetica by
Saxon Graphics
Printed and bound in Great Britain by
TJ International Ltd, Padstow, Cornwall

British Library Cataloguing in Publication Data
A catalogue record for this book is available from the British Library

Library of Congress Cataloging-in-Publication Data
McGrath, Caroline.
   Supporting early mathematical development : practical approaches to play based learning / Caroline McGrath.
      p. cm.
   Includes bibliographical references and index.
   1. Mathematics—Study and teaching (Early childhood) 2. Early childhood education. I. Title.
   QA135.6.M3937 2010
   372.7—dc22   2009037321

ISBN13: 978-0-415-49162-4 (hbk)
ISBN13: 978-0-415-49161-7 (pbk)
ISBN13: 978-0-203-85556-0 (ebk)

Contents

List of tables

List of figures

Acknowledgements

I would like to thank all the children and adults who contributed to this work. Each and every one has shown a great generosity of spirit.

Particular thanks to the students at the City of Bristol College who contributed to research and in doing so led to change, development and this book. A special mention to Nina Romagnoli, Tina Martin, Mel Hutchinson and Carley Pugh.

Colleagues, particularly Mary Dooley, Kate Hulm, Isobel MacDougal and Emma Richer. The librarians at the City of Bristol College, Janet Simpson and Olaf Raetzel, who find what you are looking for and sometimes more. Olaf, who sourced much material and provided sound mathematical knowledge.

A special thanks to Ashley Down Infant School to children and staff. Susie Weaver for orchestrating so much; Gerry Satherley for encouragement and support; Ben Lloyd (aged seven) for his wonderful drawings 'Topology', 'Spider', 'Seahorse' and 'A spaceship lands'.

A great insight into playgroup work was gained with St Matthews Playgroup and children. Sue Last, who has contributed both as a reception class teacher and play-group leader. Parents in discussions have also contributed.

Shani Ali and Paul Bradley, artists in residence, Room 13 Hareclive, Hartcliffe, Bristol. The work by Chloe Neate (aged 11) for 'I'm Not Stupid' (Acrylic on Canvas 2009) and Spider drawings. Thank you for sharing the work.

Lisa Townsend, Special Education Needs Co-ordinator Butcombe, Clifton College, for her knowledge and continued support. Esther Willets, Speech and Language Ther-apist, for creative ideas and practical support. Catherine Howie, Project Manager, for guidance on managing such a challenge.

Cassandra Wye, who as a professional storyteller, inspired students and willingly gave ideas and suggestions.

Frances Borrego, Early Years Advisor, for helping to steer the ship with comments such as 'think of your audience'. Jane Stirling, Early Years Learning and Teaching Scotland, for clarifying and explaining points relating to Scottish curriculum.

Dr Nick Pratt, Senior Lecturer in Education at Plymouth University, inspiring useful, pragmatic research which led to this book. Dr Julia Morgan and Dr Robert Cook of Plymouth University for support, humour and setting new heights.

Dr Toni Wing for research evidence and Numicon materials. Dr Peter Elfer, Roehampton University, for conversation, papers and making connections. Dr Sue Gifford also at Roehampton University for direction to valuable research. Dr Steve Chinn for down-to-earth suggestions.

Elizabeth Carruthers, Leader Redcliffe Children's Centre, Bristol, for emphasis on new but manageable ideas bringing people together through the National Redcliffe Early Years conference. Paul Goddard, Emeritus Professor, University of the West of England (UWE), for explaining how mathematics and music connect.

Margaret Edgington for her inspiring lectures over the years and Pamela May for setting me up for a career in early years education.

Stephen Atkinson, for working so hard in the background on many different planes including doubling up on parenting for little Orna. Michelle Mildiner, for all her help with diagrams and technology, delivered from Brussels. Jane Crisp for wise guidance. Nora and John McGrath, for instilling me with determination.

The words of *PEEPO!* are reproduced by permission of Penguin Books Ltd and were originally printed in Ahlberg, J. and Ahlberg, A. (1981) *PEEPO!* London: Penguin Books, © Janet and Allan Ahlberg.

Figure 5.5 'Squiggly patterns with closed spaces and junctions' and Table 6.2 'The table square alongside a number spiral' were originally printed in Merttens, R. (1987) *Teaching Primary Mathematics*. London: Edward Arnold (Publishers) Ltd and has been reproduced by permission of © Edward Arnold (Publishers) Ltd.

The children's poems 'The Moon' by Ki Ellwood-Friery and 'The Hill Was Steep' by Raj Tanday were taken from *Poems for the Very Young* selected by Michael Rosen, illustrated by Bob Graham. London: Kingfisher. All effort has been made to trace the copyright of writers in this book, and permission to publish has been granted. However in the case of these poems, this has not been possible, however, and we would welcome correspondence from any individuals or companies whom we have been unable to trace.

Stone Soup by Heather Forest and illustrated by Susan Gaber was paraphrased with kind permission of August House LittleFolk Books (1998). The retelling of 'Munna and the Grain of Rice' by Rosemarie Somaiah is from *Indian Children's Favourite Stories* by permission of Periplus Editions, a member of the Periplus Publishing Group, Singapore.

The summary adapted from *The Giant Jam Sandwich*, story and pictures by John Vernon Lord with verses by Janet Burroway © 1972 by John Vernon Lord, is used by permission of Houghton Mifflin Harcourt Publishing Company. All rights reserved.

The excerpt from *The Sneetches and Other Stories* by Dr. Seuss, ™ and © by Dr. Seuss Enterprises, L.P. 1953, 1954, 1961, renewed 1989, is used by permission of Random House Children's Books, a division of Random House, Inc.

The words of the *The Doorbell Rang* © 1986 by Pat Hutchins is used by permission of HarperCollins Publishers.

The Marks and Spencer Jigsaw is used by permission of Marks and Spencer.

The Listeners by Walter de la Mare is quoted from by permission of The Literary Trustees of Walter de la Mare and The Society of Authors as their representative.

The Francisan Order in Chile authorized the use of the work of Gabriela Mistral. Equivalent to copyright is given to the Franciscan Order in Chile, for children Montegrande, according to the will of Gabriela Mistral.

Introduction
Bring the future forward

Many of the things we need can wait.
The child cannot. Right now is the time
his bones are being formed,
his blood is being made
and his senses being developed.
To him we cannot answer 'tomorrow'.
His name is 'today'.

Gabriela Mistral (1889–1957)
Chilean Winner of the Nobel Prize for Poetry

What has led to this book

This book differs from other books on mathematics. It is a unique blend of experience, exchanges and chance, coming together serendipitously. It takes on the challenge of gaining insight to supporting mathematics for children from birth to eight.

The book is about young children's mathematical development and how to support this with sound early years practice. The practitioner takes a strategic position in mathematical development for the very young child up to children aged eight years old. In order to truly support learning, practitioners need a sense of the progressive nature of mathematics. The intention is that the reader will see ahead of the age or stage of a child's development, making connections which otherwise could be missed.

A Foundation Degree student supporting a numeracy session in a primary school was struggling with this. Her difficulty revealed a realization that there can be a gap between a practitioner's own understanding and what the curriculum requires children to learn. This episode made a particularly strong impression on me.

The individual's honesty following the observation sparked research for a Masters degree, with the involvement of students across a range of training programmes. The result was a greater focus on supporting mathematics with a play-based approach as part of the Foundation Degree programme. The outcome has been a shift in attitude away from fear or anxiety towards enthusiasm and excitement for these trainee practitioners.

Playgroups, children's centres, nurseries, nursery schools and primary schools in England, Spain and Sweden have contributed to this work. Observations of qualified practitioners and students, conversations and exchanges of ideas, revealed important insights which found ways into the book. The parents of children attending these settings also contribute to the content. A little person, 'Orna', born at the early stage of the research, has added a further dimension to the work. There are small accounts of her mathematical development, which come from everyday incidents.

Three themes run through the book: avoid making assumptions that children know what went before in mathematics; revisit a mathematical concept at least three times; teach all children in a multi-sensory way as one would for a dyslexic or dyscalculic child. What works for those with mathematical difficulties works for all children. Pattern, place value and practical work run through the content. Ideally having read the book you will rarely use worksheets; a colouring-in sheet maybe, but a flawed worksheet probably not.

The book will also underline the value of provision and how it is presented. The view held is that less is more. There is a deliberate focus on simple materials such as buttons and boxes. The valuable resource offered by Information Technology (IT) is not a main focus, as I believe practical three-dimensional work needs to happen first.

The book emphasizes the value of striking a balance between child-initiated and adult-led activity in the Early Years Foundation Stage (DfES 2008). As educators we have a responsibility to educate children; as practitioners we can practice the craft of teaching mathematics, a complex curriculum area. This view is shared by Griffiths when she says 'it makes sense for early educators to reclaim the word "teaching", to include a range of planning, provision and interactive strategies' (2005: 10) and Siraj-Blatchford who argues that just facilitating is neglecting civil duty to teach 'in a society where there is social injustice and inequality' (2004: 137).

Current situation

There is a need to raise attainment in mathematics. The Every Child a Chance Trust (2009) informs us of the detrimental effect of poor mathematical attainment on future employability and health.

The Rose Report (Rose 2009) advocates a new primary curriculum model with six components. 'Mathematical understanding' is one of the strands and the report advises real contexts, investigative problems and concrete over abstract experiences. These desires are the essence of this book.

If we think of the proposed curriculum as a giant jam sandwich, some components of the curriculum will be delivered discretely (the bread) and others will have a more cross-curricular spread (the jam). Literacy, numeracy and information, communication and technology (ICT) will form the new core of the primary curriculum, requiring discrete teaching. There will be a need to think creatively, connecting these to the other curricular areas. Focused teaching needs to spread outwards to reach other areas. The Report wants 'thematic, creative teaching'.

The Report also focuses on learning in different contexts, outside the classroom and within the wider community. In order to achieve this, educators will need to think differently. Where else can children learn mathematics? Who else uses mathematics in the working day? How would a chef set about making 50 banana loaves? How many eggs make a litre for this mix?

Raising expectations for young children means practitioners need to know a lot more mathematically.

Moving forward

It is advisable to keep a blank notebook open as you work through the chapters of the book. In this way you can make notes of the points that particularly strike you, or ideas that come to mind. This will also provide a record of the work you have put in to further your development in a challenging area. A good tip is to record the date along with a log of the time dedicated. These records contribute to professional confidence and are evidence of commitment to developing your role as an educator of young children.

The journal can be a dialogue, a self-reflective account, a summary of knowledge gained, a source of new ideas. This record will bridge knowledge of both mathematics and early years practice. It is a type of research itself. It is interesting to note that 'involvement in teacher research has also been identified as impacting on classroom practice' (Carruthers and Worthington 2009). Connecting knowledge to practice is a rich resource for crafting and polishing your practice. It might be that you share your findings with colleagues as part of a local network (see Children's Mathematics Network Chapter 10).

Employability is a central theme at a time of writing when the world is shrouded in a recession. Trainee practitioners or qualified practitioners wanting to return to the workforce can strengthen their position by bringing a summary of the approach they will take to teaching curriculum mathematics to interview. What prospective employer will not be interested in a maths enthusiast, with an open attitude to further learning? Students who take evidence in the form of activity plans, samples of children's work, tell me later that this helped them secure sought-after positions.

I hope you enjoy the challenge this book brings. Enjoy teaching and learning mathematics with the small children you meet over the course of your career in early years education. Children need good mathematical experiences 'today' rather than 'tomorrow'; we need to bring the future forward for children.

Section 1

Fear, anxiety and other emotions

'No passion so effectually robs the mind of all its powers of acting and reasoning as fear'

Edmund Burke (1729–1797)

The aims of this chapter are to understand:

* Fear, anxiety and other emotions of trainee practitioners
* Children's changing mathematical disposition
* Mathematical influence of parents or carers

Introduction

As early years educators, if we can continue a balance between that spark of our own childhood and the smoulder of our adult hopes and fears, we can keep the fire alive. We can experience what educator really means behind qualifications and planning and like steps going back up the track of our dreams, we get higher and nearer seeing further and wider inside ourselves and the children we teach.

Mathematics is a hard subject. It relies on the links of a chain joining up; a weak or missing link changes the strength of the chain before and beyond it. Mathematics is both magical and delicate. Mathematical delicacy can be difficult to see inside as we peel back layers to find the birthplace of ideas.

Boaler comments that 'far too many students hate mathematics and that for many it is a source of anxiety and fear' (2009: 5). A colourful spectrum of emotions is associated with mathematics, ranging from sage green satisfaction, to mid-red fear, to dark black dread. The early years experience determines where we find ourselves on this spectrum later in life; so it is important we ensure children experience early success.

Trainee practitioners have a difficult task supporting early mathematical development, as not only must they tune into the thinking of qualified practitioners, but they also depend on the knowledge of those they model, attaching this to their own subject knowledge, which may be stronger or weaker than either the children's or adults' they are with.

Children are born mathematical (Pound 2008) and we will explore why some children lose their initial positive disposition towards mathematics and how we can enable them to retain a positive belief in themselves.

Parents' or carers' attitudes towards mathematics will also influence the children we work with and they too need to be guided to support their children's mathematical development in order to nurture their self-esteem and motivation.

Questions to reflect on:

Why is it important to realize my own attitude towards mathematics?

How will I ensure children keep a positive disposition towards mathematics?

What emphasis can be placed on parents supporting their children's mathematical development?

Mathematics

The magic of mathematics can surprise or mystify us. There is satisfaction in solving a mathematically based question. Mathematics of the real world is different and surprisingly engaging (Boaler 2009). A Foundation Degree student excitedly explained how mathematics helped with the task of measuring up for curtains, realizing the need to visualize more material than for just the width of a window; when mathematics filters into everyday life, 'its appeal for us lies in the intellectual or aesthetic satisfaction that we derive from it' (Liebeck 1984: 13).

Mathematics is a subject in which a majority of the population lacks confidence (Pound 2008), perhaps owing to having an 'inherently judgmental nature' (Chinn 2009). It is perceived by many as difficult and not rooted in reality. Pound acknowledges that 'the abstract nature of mathematics and concern for accuracy make mathematics a hard subject' (2008: 12). There is a hierarchy of abstractions to build and abstract language to learn which constitute a unique challenge. The exposure of correct or incorrect answers distinguishes it from other subjects.

Unfortunately it has become socially acceptable to admit to being 'no good at maths'. This attitude needs to be weeded out, as it is not conducive to creating a future generation of competent mathematicians. The balance needs to tip to realizing that 'not being comfortable with numbers is as disempowering in our society as not being able to read' (Pound 2008: 5).

Government statistics show that every year around 6 per cent of 11 year olds in England leave primary school with very poor numeracy skills (below National Curriculum level 3 in mathematics). The Every Child a Chance Trust (2009) indicates that this failure to address numeracy difficulties incurs a £2.4 billion cost to the country, hindering employability and contributing to poor self-esteem, which affects mental health. Boaler boldly states that 'maths classrooms need to catch up not only to help future employers and employees, or even to give students a taste of authentic maths, but to prepare young people for their lives', (2009: 9). On qualifying, trainee practitioners will be in a position to influence this 'catch–up' if they are equipped with subject knowledge, have understanding of how children learn and become enveloped in an enthusiasm for mathematics.

Foundation Degree students

Before Foundation Degree programmes were Higher National Diplomas (HNDs), with an optional module dedicated to Curriculum Mathematics. I was nervous of teaching the Curriculum Mathematics module; I had taught mathematics in nurseries and primary schools, but I had not taught older students how to do this. Initially the students lacked confidence and competence, but on completion of the module, students' comments were encouraging:

> 'I have enjoyed carrying out this assignment, although my initial thoughts were that I would not like this assignment because I do not like Maths. I found it interesting and beneficial to my learning of maths …'
>
> (Student written comment HND 2006)

Another learner wrote,

> 'I really enjoyed this module, where in the beginning I had negative views on doing maths. Now I have gained in confidence in teaching mathematics to children …'
>
> (Student written comment HND 2006)

The final comment shows the value of learning how to teach early years mathematics,

> 'This module has given me a completely new outlook on maths. I feel more confident with maths in placement. Moreover, this module has brought to light the importance of giving children opportunities to develop their mathematics in a meaningful way …'
>
> (Student written comment HND 2006)

The delivery of the HND Curriculum Mathematics module identified that students had variable levels of confidence and benefited from learning how to teach mathematics in a 'meaningful way', something Hughes (1986) highlights the need for.

When they started the module the students were asked to keep a journal for a week, recording their mathematical experiences. A fabulous collection of car journeys, rounds of drinks, cookery, sleep, and haircuts were documented. The students realized they 'already know and can do, a great deal of mathematics' (Cooke 2000: 1). This broke down initial resistance to what was a threat for some and, over time, they embraced and even enjoyed this module.

The Foundation Degree programme, which replaced the HND, does not include mathematics even though learners are studying at a comparable level. Teaching the HND students elicited the emotions and subsequent satisfactions of tackling what was an area of anxiety; the Foundation Degree programme does not necessarily meet this need.

A placement visit brought this shortfall to light. Sarah was supporting a numeracy session; her role was to reinforce the class teacher's message to a small group of children. As the lesson progressed I sensed Sarah's almost tangible lack of confidence as she struggled to demonstrate the task or answer children's questions. Group work was difficult for her, as the children had not grasped what was to be done and Sarah herself could not express the ideas or guide the children.

This is an uncomfortable position to be in; students naturally want to help children and knowing that you can't when the expectation is that you will, creates a negative state. Afterwards Sarah was honest, expressing her anxiety and this led me to research the views and experiences of other students. Initially, I expected students would resist admitting a potential weakness, but they were in fact relieved to discuss the issue. As part of the research the students were given a questionnaire about their memories of mathematics as young learners.

Students were asked to comment on their best memory of mathematics:

'My Dad used to play with me doing mental calculation. It was fun and very helpful for me in practical life'

'Playing snakes and ladders in the playground'

'Counting snails in the outdoor play area'

'Winning a times table competition'

Students were then asked to comment on their worst memory of mathematics:

'Just not understanding something and having a teacher who was unable to find a way of making it make sense'

'Being stuck on work in class and not having the confidence to ask for fear of being laughed at for being "stupid"'

'Being made to chant the times table in primary school. It did not help in my learning, did not capture my attention. It just made me anxious that I might not remember a certain number'

'Double maths first thing Monday morning. Realizing that I did not have a clue what was going on. Fractions'

Other responses revealed that the majority of respondents lacked confidence with maths, making statements such as 'I lack confidence and assume I am unable to do it' and 'I find it really hard to teach and therefore try and steer away from it'.

In order to offer students some mathematical experience, I set about integrating mathematics into the Work Based Learning module of the Foundation Degree programme. This seemed an appropriate place to start, as the nature of the course is such that a close relationship extends from the module to the workplace, with students spending time in nurseries, children's centres and schools.

As part of this project a local primary school teacher, Susie Weaver, became involved and agreed to be interviewed. During this interview she commented,

'I think mathematics is one of those subjects where there is some anxiety ... I personally found mathematics challenging at school and I find that helps me support children because I can empathize with the difficulties, for a start; also I had to work at the process and I think often with maths it is the process, so you can take it back a step and back a step.'

The idea of her difficulty with mathematics as a young learner being turned to advantage as a teacher is very powerful; the point she makes about mathematics being a process and going 'back a step and back a step' is important for us to consider so we can take children back to the beginnings of concepts.

At the conclusion of the interview, Susie agrees to deliver a session on Number Stories from her year one class (children aged 6), to Foundation Degree students at the college. This offered a different experience for students, as they could observe placement best practice in a college lecture context.

Summary of Susie Weaver's session for Foundation Degree students

The main theme of the session is how do we support children from a very early age? The aims are to consider vocabulary associated with number operations, create number stories and to see mathematical possibilities in everyday resources.

Which mathematical operation?

Students look at the words, 'total', 'sum', 'take away', 'product', 'group' discussing in pairs the operation these words trigger. Students thinking about the words we use as practitioners and how these words relate to the four operations in mathematics, that is, addition, subtraction, multiplication and division. The difference between 'number sentence' and 'word sentence' is highlighted. The need for clarity and accuracy of word choice is discussed, for example, 'sum' could be confused with 'total', or 'take away' in a child's mind could connect to food on a Friday night.

Number stories children create

This part of the session relates to the food the caterpillar eats up to Friday in *The Very Hungry Caterpillar* by Eric Carle. A PowerPoint slide with fruit, numbers and a blank number line show the addition opportunity in this story with 'how many pieces has he eaten altogether?' The story is then adapted to consider 'what if a greedy fly came and took some of the strawberries away?' The story creator determines the interchange of addition or subtraction as operations.

Children's creations of number stories are shared with students who describe what the child presented pictorially. The benefit of the open-ended task these children completed is discussed. Samples of children's work include 'bottles on a wall', 'balloons popping', 'cakes eaten by children', and 'fish in the sea'. Susie expresses the view that blank paper rather than worksheets should be given to all children up to year 6.

What number story are you going to make?

Students create their own number stories, as the children did. Students' drawings include 'trees in a garden', 'cars in a car park', 'petals on a flower', 'snails', and 'a tiger drinking tea'. The possibility of extending the work using number lines or bead bars and interactive teaching programmes (ITPs) are discussed.

Everyday objects to support the teaching of mathematics

Everyday resources including a small box of raisins, a bar of Toblerone, stripy socks, a pair of pants, a tin of baked beans, biscuits, a small handbag with money and other items were given out to the group. Using materials in this way draws out the point that children can learn mathematics through everyday experiences. Students think of ways these items could be used and the mathematical possibilities.

Susie skilfully interacted with the students on two levels: as a practitioner teaching and a child learning. When asked to draw and compose number stories the students were unsure about the expectation to be creative. As an adult it is important to present ourselves with the same expectations we have for children. The activity of constructing number stories gives an insight into how we respond, particularly to open-ended tasks.

Student comments following their experience of number stories:

'I really enjoyed this session, I feel it has provided me with the confidence to be able to plan a maths session using daily recognizable resources'

'I very much enjoyed the session. Lots of useful points and performing activities designed for children made the situation more real and relevant'

'Remember that resources are essential as well as a clear understanding of mathematical vocabulary (by both practitioner and child)'

'By linking resources, children would then be able to make connections themselves in their everyday lives. This can encourage children to have an enthusiasm outside of the classroom for mathematics'

'Give children plain paper instead of worksheets – provides more possibility'

'Open ended tasks and blank paper gives children's imagination scope'

'From today's session I really realize how we can bring attraction and fun into mathematics'

'The practical aspects really enabled me to grasp the subject'

'How difficult it is to learn mathematics, so you must be very simple with your instructions'

I'm not stupid

Figure 1.1 'I'm not stupid' by Chloe Neate Room 13.

As confidence grew, the students began to reflect on snippets of good and poor practice from their early years and primary placement experiences. There was a realization that how we communicate ideas to children, visually and verbally, is critical. The students began to see that the fault was not their lack of understanding, but the way the information was communicated.

As a child, word problems caused great anxiety for me. The context of the problem was often remote, disconnected from my experience. Some parts of the problem were important, other parts were to be ignored (Boaler 2009). Strings of words such as 'if it takes', 'how long will', 'if there are' wrapped up some mathematical operation, which then needed to be unwrapped. 'Why?' I wondered, 'why don't they give you the numbers on their own?' Even at a young age we sense the deliberate mystification of word problems; they seem to put mathematics in a different domain, divorcing it from reality and making it difficult to relate to.

Brown paper bag and dinner dress dance

Many years ago my mother was getting ready to go to a dinner dance. There was a problem sum for homework, which had not been done yet. My father, already dressed in his smart suit, started on the problem, writing with a pencil on a brown paper bag. He became frustrated as he could not solve it. The doorbell rang and a classmate was at the door asking for help with the very same problem.

They went to the dinner, problem unsolved. It transpired the next day at school that no one had come up with an answer because there had been an omission in the description. Where does that leave a child fearful of word problems, or an adult under pressure to go out, or indeed an adult with nowhere to go that evening?

Word problems need to have a meaningful context for the child and be of sound structure. Problems are best presented with a purpose or expressed in very little context; The four-colour map problem holds barely any context at all (Merttens 1987, Boaler 2009).

Foundation Degree students' submission of final Work Based Learning modules includes the following extracts:

'If we pay attention to our ordinary activities it is possible to affirm that mathematics takes part in almost all things we do'

'It is believed that children build their maths foundations by experiencing real situations and then solving problems which are part of their routine. Considering that "the child's work is play" one can argue that maths has to be learnt through play'

'If children learn maths in a playful way, they probably will be equipped to build up knowledge going towards more abstract concepts in a smooth and pleasant way'

'The Work Based Learning lessons contain ideas of how to engage children in activities that will support and promote children's learning in this area of the curriculum. This includes using children's stories such as "The Three Bears" and singing songs like "One in the Bed" or "Five Little Ducks". In addition using every day objects was an activity that was actually carried out in a lesson at college. Some of these objects were wooden pegs, conkers and pebbles. Each person who attended the lesson had to write down an activity for each group of objects. This will influence future practice when planning mathematical activities.'

'It is also important for all early year's practitioner's to acknowledge that this may be a difficult subject to teach, in which peer support would be valuable'

When I met one of the students in her placement she told me, 'I have gone crazy for mathematics. I used to hate it and now I can't stop'. This shift in attitude represents that of the group of students experiencing mathematics as part of their programme of study.

Self-esteem and confidence

Self-esteem and confidence are fickle emotions, fluctuating between high and low. This can potentially cause a triad of tension between mathematics, children and us as educators. A little anxiety can be a good thing, sharpening our minds, but too much can destroy us. Anxiety inhibits some individuals' ability to achieve their potential in this subject (Haylock and Thangata 2007). The reflective activity of intelligence is most easily inhibited by anxiety.

Fractions often cause anxiety which can result in people developing a conviction that they cannot do mathematics; they expect to do badly and this becomes a self-fulfilling prophecy. A useful consideration for educators is that 'confidence comes from knowing what you're doing and also knowing that you know what you're doing' (Butterworth 2005).

Qualified practitioners

Insecurity associated with mathematics is characteristic of many teachers (Haylock 2006). This is understandable given the complexity of the subject, the length of time from when we were learners of mathematics and the emotional baggage weighing us down. It is reasonable to state that a 'teacher's mathematical content knowledge has an impact on the effectiveness of their teaching' (Rowland et al 2009). A sound knowledge of mathematics is required if the role of early years practitioner is to be fulfilled.

Relearn what we know

Taking the view that we need to relearn mathematics allows us to empathize with the child's perspective and 'revisiting ideas from a slightly different angle and working on them from an adult perspective can reduce anxiety and enable you to move forward with increasing confidence and enjoyment' (Cooke 2000: 1). The benefit of 'engaging seriously with the structure of mathematics ideas in terms of how children come to understand them is often the way in which teacher's own understanding of the mathematics they teach is enhanced and strengthened' (Haylock and Cockburn 2008: 7). If we can conceptualize our learning in much the same terms as those we use when thinking about children's learning, we become effective as teachers.

The Foundation Degree students began to hear mathematics in stories, songs and rhymes; to see it in games, objects and experiences. They enthusiastically communicated how it overlapped with each of the Early Years Foundation Stage (DfES 2008) and primary curriculum areas.

Boaler describes how 'the creative mind at work will see mathematical questions and discussion points everywhere – there is always something mathematical that can be brought into focus, if we only remember that this is what we should be doing' (2009: 171). This way of thinking becomes contagious, tuning us in to things otherwise missed; 'thinking of mathematics as a vast web of related ideas that can provide a way of solving practical or abstract problems can help the process of making connections and developing understanding' (Cooke 2000: 2). This connective approach eases tension as we spot opportunities in different contexts and 'many teachers and trainees in nursery and primary schools are helped significantly in their teaching of mathematics by a shift in their perception of the subject away from the learning of recipes and rules towards the development of understanding of mathematical concepts, principles and processes' (Haylock and Cockburn 2008: 7).

Our role as practitioners

We have established that 'what happens in the early years supports or undermines future development' (Pound 2008: 9); this places great responsibility on us as early educators. Chinn (2009) says clearly that what and how you learn the basics will have a huge influence on future learning.

Our job is to assess children's prior knowledge, build upon their strengths, facilitate their learning and enjoy the process (Copley 2000). The practitioner needs to follow the interest of the child and as 'teachers we have to adapt ourselves to these if we want our children to reap the full benefit' (Isaacs 1932: 70). The starting point is to 'begin by enabling young children to like mathematics' (Pound 2008: 9). The point before this is to enjoy it ourselves.

The adult really needs to take a strategic view point, lifting their head up, looking out across the landscape, securing knowledge about the whole mathematical curriculum not just the content of a particular age level (Pound 1999). We need to go back to the beginning and see ahead to the horizon, in order to be confident mathematical educators.

Suggestions for development of mathematical practice

Record learning

Write about the feelings you have towards mathematics in a reflective way; this will help anchor down straying thoughts and emotions. Record struggles and difficulties with understanding to identify gaps in your knowledge.

Write down what you have learnt when working through this book; this should contribute towards your continuing professional development. Record your own reflections while you work as documented learning to be acknowledged at appraisals, reviews or interviews. Summarizing key points learnt will help secure these in memory.

Personal dictionary

Build up a personal dictionary of words or terminologies to act as a reference source and secure meanings in your mind. Some examples include:

A *square* is a special rectangle with all sides equal.

To define the difference between 'weight' and 'mass': when children are finding out the heaviest by comparison then this is weight. Mass is when they are measuring using another object as a counterbalance (Tucker 2005).

A *prime number* only has itself and 1 as factors e.g 3, 5, 7 and 11.

A *perfect number* is a number which is the sum of all its factors e.g. 6 (factors 1 + 2 + 3), 28 (factors 1 + 2 + 4 + 7 + 14).

Palindromic numbers are symmetrical in that they read the same forwards or backwards e.g. 16461.

Ordinal: order of the number in a group e.g. ninth.

Cardinal: count amount. The total quantity of the group e.g. 9.

Nominal: naming use of a number such as number 9 bus.

(Note an association with letters to help remember the last three definitions.)

The dictionary can be part of the reflective journal.

Children as born mathematicians

Babies and small children come to us with intuitive mathematical knowledge (Copley 2000). The young child is more than ready to learn mathematics and precipitates learning through interaction with others.

Small children generally come with dispositions, which allow them to be positive and confident in their maths abilities (Copley 2000). Copley describes how 'highly prized characteristics of persistence, focused participation, hypothesis testing, risk taking and self-regulation are often present and seldom acknowledged in the young child' (2000: 9). There is opportunity here to become enthusiastic through our work with young children, shedding any negativity we may have previously gathered.

Yet, somehow this disposition can be displaced. Chinn (2009) describes how poor motivation sets in with children as young as six. As May succinctly states 'self-concept is the way in which a child perceives him or herself' (May et al 2006: 50). Children need to hold onto a positive view of themselves as successful mathematically. This 'success is important as it generates self-assurance, which will in turn lead the child to develop a positive self-concept' (May et al 2006: 51).

Why children fail

The Foundation Degree students expressed emotions, which took root some time in their earlier experiences with mathematics. Early enthusiasm changes to apprehension; confidence becomes fear and 'when young children develop a negative attitude towards maths, it's extremely difficult to change this mind set in subsequent years' (Copley 2000).

Failure can be attributed to classroom issues, parental pressure, a mismatch of learning styles, learned helplessness, powerlessness, missed moments of learning captured by Isaacs as 'if he dreams for a moment and loses the thread when a critical step is being demonstrated, then all his further notions may be muddled and full of gaps' (Isaacs 1932: 64).

Isaacs perceptively informed us that failure is 'practically always due to an inhibition of understanding arising either (or both) from fear and lack of confidence or from faulty teaching in the early stages' (1932: 67). Copley (2000) isolates inappropriate teaching rather than intellectual inadequacy as the reason children fail at mathematics.

Rate of learning

Children learn not only in different ways but also at different rates (Liebeck 1984). When under pressure the older child 'resorts to a rote-learning mode, relying on memorization of rules and recipes, rather than on understanding' (Haylock and Thangata 2007: 13).

Anxiety

Anxiety is akin to desperation (Liebeck 1984). High anxiety, as for adults, impedes learning for children. Children will learn mathematics best if they consider it as something pleasurable for its own sake, which is best achieved through play (Liebeck 1984) as one of the Foundation Degree students comments above.

Understanding

Children's understanding of mathematics is progressive. If early understanding is faulty this may impact on the point of entry of a new idea. Mathematics is such that 'the teacher's task is to lead children through this hierarchy without losing the chain of connections with the real world' (Liebeck 1984: 15). We need to keep mathematics real, going back to earlier links in the chain.

Attitude

Attitude needs to be kept positive up to the age of 11 regardless of ability. This will prevent the blockage of 'I can't do maths'. We need to be aware of our own emotions as educators along with the importance of emotion in learning mathematics. The attitude we have will transfer to the children we teach.

Time

Chinn (2009) considers time to be a high anxiety item. There is a culture of requiring children to do maths tasks quickly and this creates unnecessary pressure. It is important to 'recognise that some pupils need more thinking time than others, so do not put too much emphasis on doing maths quickly or expecting children to provide answers to questions instantly' (Haylock and Thangata 2007: 14).

Mind the gap: the gap between sitting on the carpet and at the group work table

When children are exposed to numeracy hours there can be a void between what appears to be well received sitting on the carpet and how this translates to written application at a table. There is a sense of 'they have got it', which is then lost whilst moving between carpet and table. The reason for this could be that,

> Sadly, children are frequently expected to write mathematics before they have learned to imagine and to discuss and those who do not easily make connections are offered more pencil and paper work instead of the vital talk and discussion. Yet in other subjects it would be unthinkable to ask children to write what they cannot say.
>
> Straker (1993: 1)

Hughes confirms that the void between imposed written method and children's informal knowledge exists, describing 'a major gap between their concrete and written understanding' (1986: 131).

If we look at how children attempt tasks which they have set themselves in an environment which is meaningful and supportive we gain a truer insight into the child's mathematical motivation and understanding. Rather than writing, children need to be doing or making mathematics. When children leave the carpet area to go to the table, could they not engage with practical rather than written applications? We will return to this later.

There are ways to overcome the barriers outlined above. They are easier to achieve in play-based settings such as nurseries or children's centres, more difficult in primary schools with a class of 30 children and little adult resource.

What children need to succeed

Multi-sensory experience through play is best. When children play, the dialogue with material objects begins (Sennet 2008). The craft of play connects to work as the child learns to conform to rules, experiment, repeat routines, and add complexity (Sennet 2008).

When children play in a charged imaginative way, they think mathematically. They find symbols to represent features of their play; for example, a book is used as the door of a car.

Multi-sensory play

Multi-sensory play which links experience to language, to pictures, to symbols, moulds mathematics into a sequence of abstractions (Liebeck 1984). Pictorial or symbolic representation happens when children see the need to record, for example, the letter, the list, or the name on the present or score for a game. This play-based approach to mathematics needs to extend to all children throughout their primary years as Isaacs (1932) wisely advised 'formal work cannot take the place of this'.

Games

Games set up a favourable attitude of mind (Isaacs 1932, Gifford 2005) and also serve to reduce any anxiety as the element of luck brings release from being right or wrong. Games establish the rhythms of repetition; repetitions establish practice; practice brings craftsmanship, which is central to the art of play. Children are artful in how they play. If they are introduced to the rules of a game they can work independently with them. Playing games also offers the important life experiences of winning and losing.

Mixed-ability grouping

Children learn from one another. We need to facilitate this by not locking them into ability groups. Boaler (2009) points out that in the Third International Maths and Science Study (TIMS), the highest achieving country of 38 countries studied, was Korea, which was also the country with the least ability grouping. Research indicates that there are no academic benefits and in fact severe negative consequences for children's development resulting from ability grouping (Boaler 2009). A greater emphasis on paired work, mixed ability, mixed gender breaks the cycle of associated group expectations.

Process of understanding

Rather than focus on what the answer is, if we draw out how the answer was arrived at, the process rather than product becomes of greater importance, preserving motivation towards mathematics (Copley 2000).

Parents

The Effective Pre-school and Primary Education 3–11 project (EPPE 3–11) findings indicate that the effects of preschool are influenced by the child's home experiences particularly the home learning environment (Sammons et al 2007). From exposure to their home environment and all the day-to-day mathematical content this brings, children gather their informal understanding of mathematics and 'it is important not to underestimate the role of simple interactions in the home, and the role of puzzles, games, and patterns, in the mathematical development and inspiration of young people' (Boaler 2009: 108).

Ironically though understandably, parents or carers do not necessarily realize the value of everyday mathematics. There is an opportunity for practitioners to make this more explicit for parents. Beyond teaching their child to recall number names we need to elicit the importance of parents' interests and involvement in order that they fully exploit their role (Pound 2008).

As trainees and qualified practitioners have developed attitudes towards mathematics, the same is true of parents. Copley (2000) describes how many parents have low expectations for their children's maths achievement. Parents' emotions stem from their own experience and they often communicate to their children that maths is not easily learnt. Unfortunately, these attitudes can influence a child at a very early age (Copley 2000) and, as with practitioners, there is a need to avoid passing negative attitudes on to children.

For some parents, previous lack of attainment is a driving force to ensure their child will achieve. For others their confidence has a positive effect on the child's self-image as a learner: these parents see themselves as having the ability to help their children (Pound 2008). If as practitioners we can find one parent with enthusiasm for mathematics this keeps the fire burning. Working with this one parent can help influence other parents and our thinking.

There are three things which parents or carers can be made aware of to support children's mathematical development:

Materials

Provide everyday materials for play opportunities such as sponges, pots, beans, kitchen utensils, bricks, stones, sticks, old keys, fabric, cushions and water. Allow the child to use whatever is available in a natural, open-ended way. If the materials are accessible, children can return to play with them repeatedly, over time.

Orna and the 'sponge train'

At 18 months Orna found her way to the cupboard under the sink, searching for sponges. She had seen these being purchased and stored. She made a 'sponge train' with these plain sponges. She came back to making a 'sponge train' aged two years seven months using coloured sponges. This time she pointed out 'blue, white, blue, white, pink' seeing a pattern.

She tested out arranging the sponges width ways asking that I look at the difference. The sponges were used a few days later as plates, lining up three in front of three toys and carefully placing three crayons on each as 'chocolate biscuits'.

Problems and puzzles

Problems and puzzles should be given to children, which have relevance to their world. How will we move the bear from here to there without letting it touch the ground? How will we carry all of this shopping? Present problems which really require solutions. Books such as *The Universe in a Handkerchief: Lewis Carroll's Mathematical Recreations, Games, Puzzles and Word Plays* by Martin Gardner will provide projects for older children to work on.

Questions

Parents can pose meaningful questions which can be their own thoughts expressed aloud. How will we get to London on Saturday? How did you make that tower of bricks reach so high? Why is it taking so long to get through this traffic?

Conclusion

As early years educators either in training or fully qualified, we are working with young mathematicians and 'the future becomes the present more quickly even for small children' (Craft 2002). What happens early on in a mathematical life influences future learning so 'it is crucial that practitioners ensure those children's early experiences of problem solving, reasoning and numeracy are successful' (Stevens 2008: 73).

We can turn our own weaknesses to strengths as we relearn from an adult perspective what eluded us as a child. There is an advantage in doing this as we see it from the perspective of the child. By going back to the beginning we relearn the story, enabling us to retell it confidently.

Enthusiasm for mathematics can be sparked as it was for the students who participated in my research. Our own positive attitude towards mathematics will influence the children and parents we work with. Parents can be made aware of the value of simple materials and allow their children to return to these with new ideas, posing practical problems and puzzles.

We can bridge between the young child's informal knowledge and formal school mathematics (Copley 2000) through stories, songs, rhymes and cookery. Play is highly motivational and enables children to develop lifelong dispositions and flexible approaches to learning (Featherstone and Featherstone 2008), particularly for mathematics.

2

General principles for teaching mathematics to young children

What he imitates he begins to understand.
Let him represent the flying of birds
And he enters partly into the life of birds.
Let him imitate the rapid motion of fishes in the water
And his sympathy with fishes is quickened.
Let him reproduce the activities of farmer, miller and baker
And his eyes open to the meaning of their work.

In one word let him reflect in his play the varied aspects of life
And his thought will begin to grapple with their significance.

Freidrich Froebel (1782–1852)

This chapter will examine certain principles of value when teaching mathematics to young children. These principles should lie at the heart of the learning experience we create. The ideas complement each other and work together to create a cohesive pattern of learning. They hold value from the newborn child to children beyond eight years. The challenge for the practitioner is to uphold these principles against the pressure of more formal curricula.

We will consider 12 principles:

- Keeping mathematics real through play
- Creating satisfying learning environments emotionally, inside and outside
- Creating an integrated spiral curriculum
- Observing mathematical schemas
- Learning in other environments
- Building working memory through multi-sensory teaching
- Using mathematical opportunities in books, songs, rhymes, music and cooking
- Learning mathematics with games, calculators and computers
- Matching learning intentions to activity content
- Looking for holes, gaps and flaws
- Crossing between home and school
- Mopping up misconceptions with explicit teaching

> **Questions to reflect on:**
>
> How can you work on strengthening mathematical memory?
>
> How would you support numeral formation when children are ready for this?
>
> What is the benefit of testing activity plans out before bringing them to children?

Keeping mathematics real through play

Mathematics is the common thread running through children's learning. Children engage with mathematics as they push their way forward, making sense of life. Mathematical learning happens naturally but is enhanced by adults generating experiences which match the child's reality.

Children learn mathematically by practising what they observe on a micro and macro level. Orna playing with a doll's house makes tea for the wooden people. The same child makes tea for the adults sitting around in a kitchen or the children in the home corner at nursery. 'Like some tea?' is imaginatively worked on in different contexts involving both miniature and large cups of tea. A child as young as two can concentrate for as long as 25 minutes making tea in their micro world.

Play-based activity prompted by an adult or started by the child allows the expression of mathematical thinking. Whether the child is using small or large play pieces, indoors or outdoors, they are learning in a physical way. Concrete learning attaches to abstract thinking, which is stored for future application. There are opportunities for structured apparatus such as Numicon or Cuisenaire rods in such play. Numicon is a fixed representation of number exploiting coupling or pairing. Imagine a plastic plate with six holes within the frame arranged in pairs to represent 6; five holes in the frame arranged in pairs with one on its own to represent 5. The paired pattern arrangement creates a clear visual image of the number in children's minds (see www.numicon.com and Figure 4.3 Chapter 4). The Numicon plates can be used with play dough, where children can press the shape into the dough or by combining a '3' piece to a single holed piece to make a '4'. Cuisenaire rods are wooden with different lengths representing different amounts (see www.cuisenaire.co.uk).

A combination of loose play pieces and fixed structured apparatus gives a varied learning experience. Rowland et al (2009) comment that there is less use of structured apparatus; perhaps this balance needs redressing. Structured materials can be played with imaginatively; Numicon plates can be biscuits. We take a closer look at provision in Chapter 5.

Play and older children

The principle of play learning is applicable to older children and should certainly feature in year one classes (Rose 2009). The 'Finding all possibilities', Problem Solving foundation stage document confirms that, 'mini-world and construction provide many opportunities for children to develop their problem solving skills' (DfES 2004). The development of these skills through play should extend beyond the early years. Play keeps mathematics anchored in a child's reality.

Projecting a play way of learning upwards will offer a deep learning experience for older learners. Sadly, children are deprived of play beyond the early years and are expected to partake in formal mathematics, relying on the abstract more than the concrete. This can be addressed by discerning educators. Year six children need concrete materials with which to build mathematical thinking; for example finding, factors can effectively be learned by laying out various combinations along a predetermined number. A number rod of, say 24 can have six representations of a four placed on top, confirming that $6 \times 4 = 24$ and that 4 and 6 are factors of 24. A series of factor layers can be built up making a wall. Arguably the connection between play and practical application is different for older children, but the principle is shared; building a factor tower is similar to building a tower.

Creating satisfying learning environments emotionally, inside and outside

The key to achieving practical play-based learning is a rich environment with quality materials. The quality of the resources raises the creative potential of the teaching and learning opportunity (Chinn 2004, Briggs and Davis 2008). Equipment or props should realistically represent those used by adults. If we take the example of a telephone, the prop should either be a real phone or a close match. It is worth testing out commercial products against these criteria, as some are over-complicated and reduce the possibility of the child imitating the adult. As a rule of thumb, less is more. The simpler, more accurate the resource, the better.

It is good practice to rid the setting of poor quality, worn resources; jigsaws should be complete, offering the satisfaction of placing the last piece. If the jigsaw or game is missing a piece, take it out of circulation, allow say a week for the missing part to be retrieved; if this fails to happen, bin it.

Every setting has obstacles to creating an ideal early years environment, particularly schools which were built with a different vision in mind to that of contemporary Children's Centres. Temperature, light, available space and acoustics may be difficult to change.

The outdoor areas of schools are often one-dimensional flat tarmac spaces. The ideal is that children can learn as much outside as inside and more. Where there is limited equipment, small-scale resources such as balls, beanbags, hoops, tyres, milk crates and planks break the monotony of tarmac space and offer stimulation.

A reception class was struggling with lack of focus at lunchtime play. Problems of rough play and bullying were setting in. The involvement of the year six children in setting up games for these reception children had two advantages: first, the reception class children had a focus in the form of games and second, the older children achieved success and, in some cases, raised self-esteem.

The project needed managing, but over time became a habit and moderated loud, directionless play. Where there is little in the way of outdoor equipment it is beneficial to provide some optional structure with games such as 'What's the time Mr. Wolf?', or 'Tags and Tails' where children with fabric tucked into pockets are chased by those without, so that freedom does not become degenerative.

Emotional environment

The emotional environment is intangible, yet something we can influence. Discussions with trainee early years practitioners suggest that it comes down to attitude. Attitude of staff to each other, to children and to change. The students went on to relate this to respect, in particular to respecting difference. The respect of the adult towards the child, with a sense of awe for their capacity to learn is central to creating an emotionally positive environment. For more on this, Elfer and Dearnley (2007) of Roehampton University have carried out research relating to the emotional dimension of the Nursery environment.

Essentially creating a satisfying learning environment means keeping resources simple, maintaining quality, overcoming limitations as best one can, while realizing that you yourself are the most valuable resource, particularly in relation to the emotional environment.

Creating an integrated spiral curriculum

The young mathematician needs to make connections within and beyond the subject of mathematics. Thomas aged four asked the connective question when, as a whole class, we were looking at number bonds to 5, pausing on $2 + 3 = 5$; 'Miss McGrath, does that mean that $3 + 2$ makes 5?' One could almost hear that connection click into place. Somehow Thomas's insight into this commutative addition point that $2 + 3 = 3 + 2$ carried weight, not just because of what was contained mathematically, but because he had stepped into thinking mathematically. The world stopped turning in that small moment as Thomas sensed he was onto something.

Children also need to sense the relationship between multiple additions and multiplication; $2 \times 2 \times 2 = 8$ is the same as $2 + 2 + 2 + 2$; division is repeated subtraction; 10 divided by 2 is 5, which means 2 can be subtracted from 10 a total of five times.

Children relate to mathematics when it holds meaning or is put into a meaningful context. The skilled practitioner integrates mathematical thinking into other curricular activities; for example, making a three-dimensional model is a mathematical process which can be connected to other curricular areas such as design and technology or science.

Mathematical creativity is extendable across the entire curriculum. At times this happens on a subconscious level, for example, when children are moving during physical activities, they are thinking about position, direction, movement, or measures of distance and height, time and speed (Straker 1993). This sense of space, pattern and position is not necessarily the main focus but is part of the process, connecting mathematical concepts.

Spiral of curriculum learning

An integrated spiral of curriculum learning can be achieved through the following activity. A child is asked to assemble a train track. Deciding how to connect these pieces to make a suitable circuit is problem solving. They can examine the pieces, draw a plan, apply the solution, and photograph a train running on the track. A predetermined number and type of track pieces focuses the problem more specifically.

The younger child can be given eight curved track pieces which will make a circle. This can be developed by providing eight curved and two straight pieces to make an oval track. If 12 curved, two long straight, two short straight and two crossovers are provided, the child can make a figure of eight (see also Chapter 9).

Figure 2.1 Boy making train track figure of eight.

Reading of stories and poems relating to trains adds to this experience, drawing out other ideas about trains, such as the number or type of carriages. Jigsaw puzzles of different complexity can also be provided on the theme of trains. The child is encouraged to paint or draw pictures of trains. Learning across curriculum areas is connected through the train theme.

This principle of connecting mathematics across curricula is relevant to older children. The themes may change in complexity but the opportunity to contextualize mathematics through physical play remains. In fact, children need opportunities to apply problem-solving skills (see Chapter 9). A possible investigation for older children could be to use structured apparatus (Numicon, Cuisenaire rods) to find out all possible factors for a range of numbers as described earlier. This opens up the possibility of exploring the features of prime numbers like 7, which only have themselves and 1 as factors. Or to explore square numbers like 4 to see the pattern of an odd number of factors (factors of 4 are 1, 2 and 4). The same investigation can be scaled up or down for different capabilities, still supported with concrete thinking.

Observing mathematical schemas

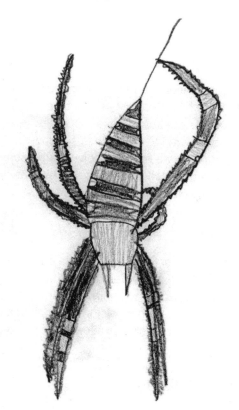

Figure 2.2 A spider on a single stretch of a web.

Very young children learn through repeating a concept or skill. They practise, for example, transporting of objects over time, applying this to more complex situations. The execution of such schemas is layering of learning as children accommodate, assimilate and equilibrate new information. They demonstrate connections which they are motivated to repeatedly test out in their play (Athey 1990).

The schema is very much the child building their web. As a practitioner, spotting these mathematical schemas, patterns or repetitious learning expressions and offering a more complex set of threads for the child to travel along, brings great benefits.

Observing, planning, scaffolding learning, extending thinking to deep under-standing is unique to the role of early years practitioners. We will look at an example of a mathematical schema which was the unexpected outcome of a student's activity.

Nina, a Foundation Degree student in her final placement, carried out a multi-sensory activity with four children in the garden area of a nursery. Children first held and played with items such as bells, stones, wood, cones, shells and feathers. These were returned to a basket, which was covered with a small piece of fabric. The children took turns, putting their hand under the cover, describing the object, but not removing it until one of the group could say what it was. This went reasonably well though the children found it difficult to apply the rule that they could not remove what they held in their hand. For some the recall of the descriptive words initially used was difficult.

The more interesting observation happened after children had moved away, leaving but one child. This child, Charlotte, spent time wrapping first one, then two, then four items from the basket in the fabric. A new idea led her to share with Nina and I what was unwrapped. Charlotte set down a clear rule that as she was in charge of wrapping we had to receive the presents and choose the item. The final unwrapping revealed two shells and two flat stones. Charlotte told us we must listen to the clouds with the shells, and speak to each other on the stone phones, saying what we could hear.

Looking out for these expressions of learning interests and harnessing opportunities is particularly relevant to the learning of mathematics. Charlotte's mathematics extended to division in this small example of a wrapping schema. A question to consider is whether we can spark schemas through provision of simple materials. The small piece of fabric combined with the shells and stones allowed for this play to happen.

Learning in other environments

A group of Foundation Degree students visited Bristol Zoo. Students were to record in journals how as qualified practitioners they would organize such a trip for young children; identify the learning opportunities offered through the education department with a particular emphasis on mathematics; perceive the value of such a trip for both children and adult learners.

The education officer used the following to prompt students' responses:

Where is the line of symmetry on the tortoise shell pattern? The line of symmetry of the pattern on the shell was found using a mirror.

How many flaps can you do in 15 seconds? Students stood and flapped their arms as many times as they could, keeping the count in their heads. They then multiplied this by four, which equates to one minute. They then kept this number in their heads. They were then told if the number is less than (a chosen number) to sit down, which was repeated several times with higher numbers. The person finally standing had a score of 84 flaps/minute.

This figure was then compared to 300 flaps/minute for a butterfly; 5,400 flaps/minute for a humming bird; 30,000 flaps/minute for a midge.

Three snake skins were measured to be 4 m 80 cm; 3 m 60 cm; 1 m 15 cm.

A snake called 'Massey' with two eyelid-less eyes had 300 bones in her body.

The following animals had to be arranged in order of how fast they travel. The picture of each animal and the speed were on separate cards which needed pairing up:

Cheetah 70 mph, kangaroo 40 mph, giraffe 32 mph, elephant 28 mph, human 25 mph, house spider 1 mph. The question then was 'how much faster does the cheetah travel compared to the giraffe?' This requires the subtraction 70–32 giving 38 mph faster.

> The next question posed was: 'if you were a cheetah and you popped your head up for a second, how many animals are in the herd in front of you?' (A picture of a herd is shown.) This requires estimation and can then be checked with counting of the herd.

Taking children outside of their immediate surroundings creates different learning experiences. Places such as the zoo or a forest provide different learning contexts for mathematics.

The exploitation of forest areas for learning opportunities originates from Scandinavia. Forest school experiences as described by O'Brien and Murray (2006) can play a critical role in child development. They state in their report that self-confidence, self-belief, motivation and concentration increase as an outcome of the forest experience. There is the additional potential benefit of the adult gaining a new perspective on the child (Maynard 2007). The forest school gives children freedom to explore using multiple senses. A regular forest experience positively influenced the speech and behavioural difficulties of children in a Bristol Children's Centre (Hill 2009).

Building working memory through multi-sensory teaching

To learn mathematical ideas children need to use their senses in practical and enjoyable experiences. Going beyond the familiar walls of the learning environment offers some experience of this, making for memorable days. Learning in a multi-sensory way is important for all children, particularly for those who show dyslexic or dyscalculic tendencies. Often strategies recommended for dyslexic or dyscalculic children are valuable for all children.

Children who are dyslexic find it difficult to retrieve letters or words and retain their meaning. One strategy is to strengthen the short-term working memory by building a mental image with a story. Buzan (1986) offers useful ways to develop memory power and encourages adults and children to use mind-mapping techniques. It is possible to improve working memory by weaving stories around mathematics, playing games, making mathematics multi-sensory.

Examples of such games include:

Kim's game

Items are placed on a tray. Children look closely at these. Placing a cover over the tray, one item is removed. The cover is removed. Children then look to see which item has been taken away. This lends itself to differentiation as items can be increased in number and similarity, providing a greater challenge.

Shopping basket game

The children are presented with a basket. Sitting in a circle each child contributes an item to the basket, which must be remembered by the others. This can be differentiated by going around the group more than once.

Recalling stories

Stories which lend themselves to memorizing lists such as *Brown Bear, Brown Bear, What Do You See?* by Bill Martin Jr, can be turned into memory games. The book can be put to one side and the children asked which animals the bear saw and in which order. This can be supported with laminated pictures of the animals attached to sticks.

A tip is to provide visual representations so that children are not solely relying on auditory input. This is particularly important for children acquiring English as a second language. Auditory and visual memory can initially be supported until the child is familiar with the words. The visual images can be withdrawn when children can rely on auditory memory.

Memory

Children need to visualize numbers and shapes and will need to have banked these in their memory. For each letter of the alphabet children need to know: the letter name, the letter shape, the letter sound, the position in the alphabet. The child acquires similar associations for numbers: number names whether ordinal, cardinal or nominal; number formation; the place the number takes in the sequence to infinity.

For children to remember information, there are two principles: imagination and association. Building a story in association with something which needs to be remembered hooks into memory, helping later recall (Buzan 1986). We will look at this more specifically in relation to numeral formation in Chapter 3.

Using a feely bag to help visualize numbers

Using a feely bag for children to visualize a number they are touching is a powerful way of strengthening working memory. The fingers tell the brain, the brain connects the information to a stored fact, the stored fact is articulated, and the articulation is verified by looking at the item in the bag.

An extension of this is to have two feely bags with matching items in both. The challenge is to find the match in each bag and take both out. This can be used with shapes, numbers, or structured apparatus such as Numicon plates or Cuisenaire rods. By closing off the other senses, that of touch is sharpened. Visualizing in the mind what the fingers feel deepens the memory connection. A student asked me to try the double feely bag, matching small three-dimensional wooden shapes and I was struck by the impact of touch on thought.

Using mathematical opportunities in books, songs, rhymes, music and cooking

There is a tendency when teaching mathematics for it to stem from adult agendas and for children to recoil from this. The teacher adopts a transmission style as they impart knowledge; the child receives a new concept as interpreted by the adult. The challenge is to be aware of the style we adopt and combine this with a discovery and connectionist approach (Briggs and Davis 2008). Our fears and anxieties about the subject may affect the approach we adopt. The child will learn best if using their senses; the teacher will teach best if they address this creatively.

Songs, rhymes and stories

Songs and rhymes, like stories, can be repeated until the child is familiar with the pattern of words. The content of the rhyme builds a picture in the mind and commits number names to memory. The pattern of number names changes beyond ten. The repetition of these is necessary when we consider the irregularity of number names 'eleven, twelve, thirteen, fourteen, fifteen, sixteen, seventeen, eighteen, nineteen'. Singing, saying or chanting allows the child to connect with adults and other children as the word pattern binds us together. *This Little Puffin* by Elizabeth Matterson is a valuable source of number songs and rhymes.

A useful strategy when counting as a group is to count one, two, three, four in a whisper and pause at five, shouting its name. Saying this number loudly adds to the excitement and creates a natural gap, allowing children less familiar with the sequence to catch up. Then say six, seven, eight, nine and pause at ten. The inclusion of more frequent pauses beyond ten will reinforce the irregularity of these number names.

Music

Music is an expression of mathematics. Musicians like Bach and Schoenberg create warm spiritual sounds using cold reasoned pattern (Kline 1953). To open a chapter explaining the connection between music and mathematics Kline uses the following quote,

> Music is the pleasure the human soul experiences from counting without being aware that it is counting.
>
> Gottfried Leibniz (1646–1716)

Professor Paul Goddard (2009) explained the connection between music and mathematics:

Three Blind Mice

The Western music major scale is often sung on an ascending scale as doh, re, mi, far, so, la, ti, doh. These notes of the scale can also be designated as 1, 2, 3, 4, 5, 6, 7, 8.

If we take the tune Three Blind Mice, it is made up of simple sections and patterns that repeat themselves.

mi   re   doh ,   mi   re   re   doh,   so   far   mi,   so   far   far   mi

Three blind mice. See how they run. Three blind mice. See how they run.

The notes of the second line repeat the first with a simple doubling of the middle note *re* (whilst halving the length of the note). The pattern of the third line is very similar to that of the other two but it has been shifted up to start on the interval of the fifth (*so*).

Goddard (2009) comments that simple melodies can be analysed and show repeating and resolving patterns which can be described mathematically. Mathematicians are often musicians. Most of the mathematics in music is understood intuitively by the musician.

Cookery

The use of multi-sensory teaching strategies employing sight, hearing, touch, taste and smell can also be achieved through cooking. Recipes for young children can be adapted to measure in cups and spoons. The use of two baking trays naturally presents addition as the child wants to know how many biscuits there are altogether (see Figure 2.3). Tried and tested examples included the following:

Jane's chocolate biscuits

Equipment

1 large mixing bowl
1 basin for hot water
1 weighing scales
2 baking trays
1 wooden spoon
1 teaspoon
1 sieve

Ingredients

4oz/100g butter
2oz/50g caster sugar
4oz/100g self-raising flour
2oz/50g drinking chocolate
A generous pinch of salt

Method

1. Grease two baking trays.
2. Preheat oven to 190°C/375°F/gas mark 5.
3. Cream the butter and sugar.
4. Add the sifted flour, drinking chocolate and salt. Mix well together.
5. Take a heaped teaspoon of the mixture. Roll in the palm of your hand, then flatten it on the greased tray. Repeat. The mixture should make 15 biscuits.
6. Bake for 5 to 8 minutes.

Note: To get the mixture to bind it is useful to have some hot water available. Place the bowl with the mixture into a basin of hot water and continue to mix together.

Figure 2.3 Orna checking baking trays to see 'how many biscuits there are altogether'.

Rock cakes

Equipment

1 bowl
1 wooden spoon
1 fork
2 baking trays

Ingredients

8oz/225g flour
2 teaspoons baking powder
6oz/150g caster sugar
1 egg beaten well
3oz/75g butter or margarine
120ml/½ a cup milk or the juice of 1 orange
2oz/50g currants

Method

1. Grease baking trays.
2. Preheat oven to 180°C/350°F/gas mark 4.
3. Sift the flour and baking powder into the bowl.
4. Rub in the butter or margarine.
5. Stir in the sugar, currants, beaten egg and milk/juice.
6. Mix to a very stiff dough. Place walnut-sized amounts on the baking tray. The mixture should make 14 cakes.
7. Bake for 10–15 minutes.

Cookery is connecting science and mathematics and the learning of both is intuitive.

Learning mathematics through games, calculators and computers

Playing games is motivational and enjoyable for children. Games are key to teaching language to young dyslexic children and a parallel lies in teaching mathematics. It is amazing how children as young as two invent games; how at such a young age rules creep in, 'No not like that. Stand up. Sit here. Like this', Orna aged 18 months. We saw earlier, Charlotte in the garden establishing the rule that she is the present wrapper so could not unwrap what was inside. There is a precision to the child's game, which does not necessarily make sense to the adult, yet the child is certain of it. This play type of game is the start of structured games where the principles of turn taking and rule making apply. There is no winner or loser, as with more structured games.

One point to note is that structured games require that the adult is available to check the contributions made so that errors are corrected. As many games involve dice, careful consideration will be given to these. Children can become stuck when playing dice-related games.

Some tips on games involving dice:

Using both types of dice, that is, those with dots and numerals, allows for translation between the numeral and the number of dots (Hughes 1986).

Hughes (1986) describes how the game of moving animals along a track between two houses by throwing a dice, exposed the mistake of children counting the square the animal was on as one, rather than moving on one. When a dice presented a one dot, they would leave the animal where it was. We need to ensure children are counting corresponding moves correctly. Another mistake was not allowing two animals to share a square and skipping over an occupied space.

Hughes (1986) found using two numeral dice caused difficulty. Instead using a numeral and dot dice allows for counting on from the numeral, counting the dots.

Hughes (1986) reflects on the possible value of attaching numerals to the dot face so that the numeral can be removed to show the corresponding number of dots. This will benefit children who find it difficult to associate the numeral with the number of dots.

Opposite sides of a dice always add to seven, that is, if the face up side shows six dots then the hidden face is one dot.

Using two dice encourages counting on from or adding two sets of dots together.

'Guess how many'

Six counters or buttons are provided. All children, but one, close their eyes. This child removes some and the others have to then open their eyes and say how many have been removed. They then count the counters removed to check the answer. This game is based on one type of subtraction (see Chapter 8).

Number box game

Provide magnetic numerals for the numbered boxes game. The number of items in the box is represented with a number on the outside. Putting two boxes together can extend the activity. How many objects does the box keeper have? Confirmation can be achieved by looking inside. The game can be adapted for young children by singing, 'What's in the box? Show me, show me what's in the box?'

The 'moneybox' game

Children put pennies into a moneybox counting as each one is dropped. They are then posed with the question, how many pennies are in the box? Children who understand the ordinal and cardinal number relationship will answer correctly. Children for whom this understanding is unclear will need to open the moneybox and recount; this game allows informal assessment of ordinal and cardinal understanding.

Games are a powerful way of teaching and 'it is surprising that they are not used more in teaching mathematics' (Hughes 1986: 135). They are a valuable way for children to learn mathematical ideas. We need to be mindful of difficulties children will encounter in games. Less traditional games need to be tested out for potential pitfalls.

Computer games have a place in supporting mathematical learning; however, they should complement real life games. Also the interactive whiteboard is a visual tool which can be used for games; however, we need to remember that it is a flat screen, very different to the three-dimensional experience of games described above.

Matching learning intentions to activity content

When planning mathematical activities one group of Foundation Degree students started by setting a learning goal from either the Early Years Foundation Stage (EYFS) or National Numeracy Strategy (NNS) or of their own creation, testing it on their peers who were asked to see it from the perspective of small children. This trialling brought out several salient points.

There can be a tendency to have too many objectives. Though a stimulating activity will have learning outcomes covering many learning areas it is realistic to focus on one objective. Sometimes it is better to have one part of a learning goal as the main focus.

The other important consideration is to ensure the content supports the learning intention. One student demonstrated this for the group when she introduced an activity with the 'Five Little Speckled Frogs' song.

Five little speckled frogs
Sat on a speckled log,
Eating some most delicious bugs
Yum, yum.
One jumped into the pool
Where it was nice and cool,
Now there are four more speckled frogs
Glub, glub.

The learning intention was 'count reliably up to ten everyday objects' (DfES 2008: 69) and though she had modified the range to five, this song is counting backwards from five, a different learning aim. We need to keep the content consistent so children receive a clear message. The ensuing discussion sharpened awareness of the need to ensure the activity matches the aim. It also raised the point that it is more difficult to find songs for addition as 'most traditional rhymes deal with subtraction' (Gifford 2005). The principle of critiquing the content so that the message is consistent with the aim adds quality to the learning experience.

Looking for holes, gaps and flaws

The idea of testing activities can be taken one step further. Taking the child's perspective, participating in the task yourself or closely monitoring other adults doing the activity, offers insights into flaws. Feedback from peers needs to be constructive, honest and accurate if practitioners are to benefit. The outcome of this is that adults serve as evaluators, a valuable contribution to practice.

Testing activities for flaws improves the fluency of words, questions and thinking when carrying out the task with children. The flow of words should be easier having tried out the idea in advance; a useful tip, particularly if one is being assessed in the workplace.

Crossing between home and school

There is positive pressure for practitioners to work closely with parents. There needs to be a sense of realism, as we will not succeed with every parent. It is not in our ability to shift damaging attitudes beyond our influence.

For those who are receptive, there are certain things which assist the partnership. We outlined three areas where parents can be encouraged to support children's mathematical development in Chapter 1. We will now consider how best to set about informing parents.

Communication of teaching themes is valuable, as parents can relate these themes to their out and about experiences. Inviting parents into the setting and facilitating their participation in adult-led and child-initiated learning gives great insight to parents as to what happens at the setting. The parents of a reception class were invited to a play workshop. They were asked to get on and play, which resulted in a vacuous silence. The temptation to intervene was overcome and they did engage, surprised at how hard it is to play. The 'Math's in a Jam Sandwich' type of workshop informs parents of the richness of everyday mathematical opportunities. For older children the parent may be retrained or reminded how to do long division the 'school' way.

We can encourage parents to talk when they are doing domestic tasks such as cooking, washing up, tidying up, shopping and explain how this casually brings out mathematics in measuring, sorting, comparing capacities of containers, estimating and calculating.

Trips outdoors allow for discussion about the pattern of numbers on doors (see Chapter 6), shapes such as squares, triangles and circles in road signs. The outdoors is rich with print. Photographs to capture outdoor mathematical print can help parents make these links.

Mathematical books can be lent as part of a home–school lending system. Each setting should have a mathematics policy and attached to this a copy of a home-school booklet describing how parents can support mathematics.

Mopping up misconceptions with explicit teaching

As practitioners we need to be aware of possible misconceptions children can have within the subject of mathematics (Chinn 2004). A heightened awareness on the part of the adult means a higher chance that we can unblock children's struggles. There are situations where it is not appropriate to let children solve the problem, where children need to be told explicitly. Misconceptions need to be removed in order that children can understand. As a practitioner it would be valuable to build up a bank of examples to inform your practice. Correction of misconceptions improves confidence in the adult and achievement in children. We need an awareness of these potential pitfalls so we can plan explanations.

Examples of some misconceptions needing explicit teaching

Multiplication makes things bigger. This is untrue for numbers such as 5 multiplied by 0.4, because the result is 2 (Haylock and Cockburn 2008).

Subtraction makes things smaller. Not always. 6– (–3) = 9 is an example of subtraction making a number bigger (Haylock and Cockburn 2008).

You cannot subtract a larger number from a smaller number. 2 – 6 = –4 (Haylock and Cockburn 2008). This is a misconception. You can but you obtain a negative number.

The word 'more' triggers the addition operation. In fact the word 'more' can require subtraction, depending on the context. For example, Amy has two *more* apples than Susan. Amy has five apples. How many apples does Susan have?

Conclusion

General principles for teaching mathematics have been considered in this chapter. The principles fit together, forming an impression of good practice. The 12 principles serve as the backbone for effective teaching and learning of mathematics, which each setting could have as part of the policy for mathematics.

A play-based approach, in a stimulating environment, with multi-sensory experiences, will create lasting mathematical memories for children. The adult will have confidence in delivery of activities which have been critiqued and tested in advance. This is particularly important for trainees who are building experience quickly.

Understanding misconceptions prevents pitfalls; sometimes children need to be told this is how it is. The link with home and school requires a greater emphasis on language as our population diversifies. The importance of precision with mathematical vocabulary will be considered in Chapter 3 and specifically for mathematical operations in Chapters 7 and 8.

Specific principles

Euclid taught me that without assumptions there is no proof. Therefore, in any argument, examine the assumptions.

Bell, Eric Temple (1883–1960)
Cited in *Return to Mathematical Circles* (Eves 1911: 165)

This chapter will emphasize the importance of applying specific principles to teaching mathematics. The ideas will help overcome children's difficulties, leading to successful learning in mathematics. The nature of mathematics is such that if you miss or don't fully understand the starting point, later learning can be difficult. Teaching and learning also rely on words, adding to the complexity of mathematics for teacher and child.

We will consider the following specific principles:

- Using mathematical vocabulary
- Repeating concepts to reinforce learning
- Moving away from ability groups
- Representing work using pictures or photographs, not worksheets
- Starting at the very beginning, making no assumptions
- Playing with place value and knowing zero
- Writing numerals
- Counting accurately with one to one correspondence

Questions to reflect on:

How would you ensure children learn to count accurately?

How will you support a child who is ready to record numerals?

What is the difference between recording on a worksheet and representing mathematical thinking?

Using mathematical vocabulary

Some children don't communicate verbal mathematics but can operate within a mathematical world, however this is unusual. Children need words to express their thoughts. For some, their thought process does not rely on word labels, but for most this is how they learn.

Mathematics is riddled with peculiar and irregular vocabulary and language (Chinn 2004). We need to accept this flexibility of vocabulary. Regular exposure and careful choice of expression is beneficial and 'fortunately most children simply absorb the information by repetition' (Chinn 2004: 94). Language becomes more of an issue when children are presented with word problems, as mentioned in Chapter 1.

Maybe we use too many words, ask too many questions. We ask questions we know the child has the answer to; 'what colour are your boots?' This is a thinking dead end with an internal dialogue such as, 'if they ask what they know I know and I tell them what they know I know, perhaps they will go'.

Pound (2008) describes how statements made by adults allow children to ask questions. Presenting a genuine problem such as 'I thought I had five black buttons, but I seem to have four now, where has the other one gone?' encourages children's natural tendency to investigate. Showing an interesting object is another way to engage in mathematical dialogue, as we will see below.

We need to be careful with certain words; the word 'fit' has at least five possible meanings. Sometimes with younger children, we should intervene and unhook the ambiguity; at other times we should let it pass, as explaining causes confusion.

Young children can find words like 'sev-en' confusing, touching one item for 'sev' and the next for 'en'. They need to know that the two syllables make one word, otherwise one-to-one correspondence is distorted as the word is stretched over two items. Attaching one numeral word to one item is best achieved by ensuring children slow down and count by touching, or putting the item to one side.

Mathematical words to watch out for

Real numbers. Does this mean some numbers are unreal, imaginary? An example is 3/7 which is 0.428571.

Irrational number. Is this a number like how I feel some days? A number which cannot be expressed as a fraction such as π.

Quotient. The number you finish up with as a result of dividing one number by another (Orton and Frobisher 1996).

Times. Multiply. But what about 'many times' or the newspaper *The Times*?

Share. Divide. But not always evenly or fairly?

Sum. Instruction to add. Describes an addition. Quantity of money. Using it to describe calculations is incorrect.

Histogram. Block graphs is a misuse of the word.

Difference. Is there something different about you today?

Similar. Shapes classed as similar have to look alike and have the same proportions.

Relation. My cousin Lucy?

Deceptively familiar words

Face. I have one, but a cube has six.

Odd. Not peculiar; not even.

Height. I am one height, though it does change the more I grow. A triangle has three heights but they don't grow.

Flat. A place where I live.

Makes. We make toast for breakfast.

Take away. Friday night, fish and chips.

Borrow. Sugar from someone else.

Carry. Someone will carry me when I am tired.

Goes into. We go into town on Saturday.

Putting two familiar words together

One. More. One more.

Children can understand each alone but not necessarily both together.

Word problems

More. The word 'more' can incorrectly prompt addition regardless of the context.

Less. The word 'less' prompts subtraction regardless of the context.

Word muddles

Not many.

A few more.

A lot less.

Children learn to accommodate mathematical language with multiple meanings but this takes time and careful, consistent exposure, as this brief exchange shows: '*Daddy's car is big. Mummy's car is a little big*', said Orna (aged two years) when introduced to the words big, medium and small. She resisted the word 'medium' as it didn't fit in place for her. Chinn (2004) offers a comprehensive list of examples of word ambiguities, based on the English National Numeracy Strategy.

Mathematical dictionaries can be made to promote word discussion. Building word banks which can be regularly referred to helps children accumulate vocabulary. Stories with mathematical language can help relate abstract meaning to physical situations (Liebeck 1984). An example includes 'Munna and the Grain of Rice' by Rosemarie Somaiah (see Chapter 9).

Everyday language and mathematical vocabulary overlap. The distinctions can be subtle and children need to step seamlessly between both. Hughes (1986) describes how children have to translate between mathematical vocabulary and knowledge of familiar things and situations. Regular contextual use of such words is essential (Orton and Frobisher 1996).

Too many words can clutter, or obstruct meaning. This is particularly important with children acquiring English as a second language. As practitioners we need to strip sentences down to simple clear structures.

Children should be encouraged to describe mathematical findings in complete sentences and to say the reciprocal; if the red box is heavier than the purple box, the purple box is lighter than the red one (Tucker 2005).

Understanding mathematical language is particularly relevant to problem solving (see Chapter 9). The mathematical language of the problem needs to be understood before the operation can be identified.

Repeating concepts to reinforce learning

Unless we demonstrate, allow children to do it once, twice, three times, their knowledge will not be secure. When we study we might explore the subject in detail, take good notes, revisit the noted information the next day, make a reduced version of notes and return to these notes the following day. We might reduce notes from A4 to A5 to a smaller memory prompt card; this means new information is visited three times, employing what we will call the principle of 'reinforcing three times'.

This principle applies when teaching mathematics to young children. The concept needs to be reinforced at least three times. This builds confidence as children respond more readily each time. The information is stored in their working memory, so it can be drawn from more easily in the future. Pressure of time, with so many curricula to cover, often means we move on quickly. Students studying Foundation Degree programmes are presented each week with new information. Though it is possible to make connections with previous learning we do not necessarily present it again in a condensed way. When delivering the module on curriculum mathematics to Higher National Diploma, as mentioned in Chapter 1, I created the habit of revisiting the previous lesson at the start of the next. This worked and responses to more complex questions became automatic. Encouraging students to look at previously taken notes is useful, as it helps both student and lecturer remember planned and unplanned content.

Investing time in revisiting what was covered previously pays dividends. The short-term working memory is stimulated by going back once, twice and three times. Ideally, revisiting new information needs to be sequential, avoiding gaps greater than a day.

Regular, repeated reinforcement, at least three times, fixes the idea in the mind. If we apply this principle to mathematics, it helps build concepts and fix them securely. This happens naturally with nursery-aged children, as they are exposed to counting, number name sequence, through milk or snack time opportunities, songs and rhymes. Older children tend to travel quickly through curricula. This principle of reinforcing previous learning is evident in teaching structures for dyslexia, where weak short-term working memory is a barrier which needs to be overcome.

Moving away from ability groups

Working groups should be as small as possible for young children; ideally one to one. The larger the groups, the higher the chance children will not engage in the work, not really deeply connect with it. A paired approach is preferable, but less easy to manage. A mixed-ability group is full of overlooked advantage. There is great opportunity for the child who has grasped a concept to discuss it with the child who needs to see it. Articulating the idea reinforces learning for one child while another is benefiting from a peer's perspective.

The Vygotskian theory that children are motivated and learn from one another can be exploited more. Most reception, year one and two classes rely on ability groups as a classroom management strategy. It is worth noting that countries such as Sweden operate differently, with an emphasis on paired work and projecting discussion to the front of the classroom. In Finland, ability grouping is illegal (Boaler 2009).

Children in groups perform to the expectation for that group. Research captured in a video the 'Eye of the Storm' shows how when Jane Elliott divided her class according to eye colour, performance varied depending on whether the child was in the 'inferior' or 'superior' group that day. When the brown-eyed children were labelled as inferior they completed a card task in five and a half minutes; when they were classed as superior they achieved the same task in two and a half minutes. The video is mainly used to illustrate discrimination, but the evidence gives insight into the effect on performance of labelling children. The advantage of mixed-ability groups is that they 'can allow children to achieve in areas that they would not usually expect to within ability groupings' (Briggs and Davis 2008: 53).

While visiting a year one class, I listened as children were given the instruction, 'the triangle children need to go to the hexagonal table', followed by 'the square children need to go to the hexagonal table; the other hexagonal table'. This made me smile and highlighted how grouping itself brings complications.

I worked at a setting in a socially challenged area, where the head teacher was insistent on grouping children according to ability, but where behind closed doors reception class children of various capabilities worked together. There were moments when I could see a child admired another and was motivated to learn. This is noted by Briggs and Davis when they comment that, 'by allowing some mixed ability grouping this gives access to potential higher order thinking skills to the lower ability children' (2008: 53). The lower-ability child looks through the window of another child's mind.

Using imaginative and original materials: Mrs Last's box

When visiting a primary school, it was refreshing to meet a reception class teacher who became animated when asked what she thought worked when teaching mathematics. Putting out imaginative, original materials which children are left to explore, standing back to see mathematics happen naturally, was her reply. She stopped what she was doing and started to show me. The children gravitated to the shiny green stones, the elephants, the bangles. The practitioner needs to be conscious of the possibilities such objects can create, and prompt mathematical thinking from this position (see also Chapter 4).

The objects here are magical, not commercial, collected over some time from life experiences. One child asked 'Mrs Last, are they from one country?' He seemed to associate what he saw with travel and a journey. These objects appeal to young children's senses and intrigue. Standing back and seeing what happens, understanding the potential possibilities, is a powerful way of working with children without fixing them in groups.

A group of children will gather naturally around such objects, intrinsically motivated to learn. An orchestra has a lead violinist, who carries the other violins along in harmony. Children do not always need to be grouped according to ability, they can learn from each other, exploring stimulating materials. A large reception class were grouped by asking who wanted to work where, generating natural groups and quality work.

Representing mathematics using pictures or photographs in preference to worksheets

There is a need to have printed numbers at appropriate child height, indoors and outdoors. Numbers are featuring more in outdoor environments, but not in every setting. Large number lines, vertical and horizontal, can be added to outdoor play. A print rich environment can be made of fixed and removable numbers.

Children need the opportunity to show their mathematical graphics (Carruthers and Worthington 2006) on boards at child height. There is a greater tendency to have boards to display children's emerging and emerged writing; the same is required to display mathematical thinking. Boards at child height both inside and out convey the message that mathematics is happening and worth pinning up. The expression of children's number writing and pictures with a mathematical theme can be supplemented with photographs of constructions. Laminating photographs protects against the elements outdoors.

More settings are taking advantage of forest school opportunities (see Chapter 2). Displaying photographs of learning in the forest back in the outdoor area of the setting brings the two learning environments together.

Worksheets

For older children there is potential for pictorial representation of ideas. Work by Carruthers and Worthington (2006) indicates that worksheets dominate from preschool upwards. They found worksheets were used by 77 per cent of their sample and that when children arrived at the age of 6 all teachers used worksheets.

Commercial worksheets are open to confusion; 'they may use, for example, lots of small print, closely spaced or fussy, confused pages with cartoons and disjointed text' (Chinn 2004: 17). I worried as a newly qualified teacher; I had difficulty understanding what a worksheet wanted, as they are not always clear for the learners and often flawed (Briggs and Davis 2008).

The worksheet, whether commercial or teacher made, requires the child to interpret what the adult wants. The benefit is in colouring, which reinforces pencil grip, builds concentration and gives adults time. So it would be better to provide colouring-in sheets rather than trying to see worksheets as mathematical assessment. Still today, I see children ferociously colouring the worksheet without application of other thinking.

Blank paper

A seven year old came up with his own way of recording how many mini sticks he uses for extending a chain of squares. Blank paper opens up originality which worksheets shut out.

He carefully placed four mini sticks on the paper for the first square writing four along with his own code inside the square; he then added three more squares to extend by another square writing seven and his own code for two squares. A pattern soon emerges!

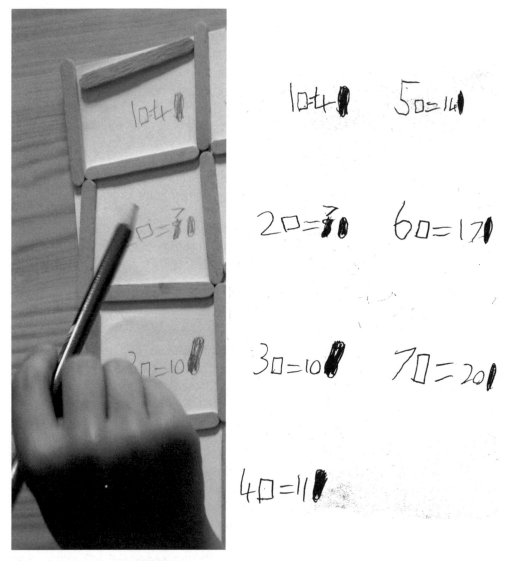

Figure 3.1 Matchstick work making squares (imaginative recording of mathematical thinking).

This imaginative way of representing mathematical thinking gives greater insight than a worksheet. Recording on a worksheet and representing in a creative way are two very different experiences.

It is challenging being a mainstream teacher; perhaps the emphasis should not be on worksheets as evidence of attainment, but as holding activities. Good games or interesting materials to explore can be used to engage children and allow the adult to work with other children.

The pressure of course is to provide evidence to head teachers, parents and other bodies, who do not necessarily see how young children learn. Practitioners are sometimes under oppressive institutional constraints. At times practice does not represent the true choice a teacher would make (Pratt and Woods 2007).

Tina, a Foundation Degree student, commented on how her daughter had learnt fractions at school through themed work with pizzas. She was surprised when another parent asked her about the 'worksheet'. This was still in her daughter's bag, forgotten. Despite convincing evidence of learning and quality teaching, she commented that there was still the pressure to provide evidence which can be filed. The irony is that, 'worksheets rarely support the mathematical development of young children' (Tucker 2005: 13). We need to ask what will be gained by requesting children to complete a particular worksheet?

We need colouring-in sheets to sustain other possibilities, particularly with large groups and few adults. We must not fool ourselves that worksheets do any more than this. Evidence of real thinking is best captured using discussion, blank paper and photographs.

Starting at the very beginning

It is dangerous to make assumptions. When a child arrives in a year two class they have travelled through the early years curriculum and experienced a year of the National Numeracy Strategy. The assumption is sometimes made that they know what went before. The focus then is on delivering a particular stage-related learning aim, but taking one specific example, 'we cannot assume that children in any age group have a thorough understanding of odd and even numbers, and work involving this classification must continue throughout the primary years' (Frobisher and Threlfall 1999: 256).

We should not assume children know what a teacher considers to be prior learning. They may in fact have gathered misconceptions along their journey. Part of our role is to diagnose and readjust these. Children can quietly move from year to year through school without fully grasping concepts such as odd and even for number work, or indeed place value. Steve Chinn (2004) comments that assumptions are dangerous.

The idea of covering what went before first will help fill gaps in a child's learning. The practitioner needs to bore down to the early learning of the concept, moving forward to the recommended learning for that stage in the child's development when appropriate. It is valuable to know where this learning leads, particularly for more able young mathematicians. The progressive nature of mathematical learning is highlighted when we look at the pattern in Chapter 6. Imagine a time line with learning mapped out; the adult needs to move backwards and forwards along the line. The significance of early learning is demonstrated when we look at place value, next.

Playing with place value and knowing zero

Number lines and squares presented to children should include '0'. Representation of zero helps to demonstrate the evenness of zero. Looking at the two number squares below, notice how the inclusion or exclusion of zero changes the arrangement of numbers. Starting with '0' changes the pattern.

Table 3.1 Two hundred squares, one starting with zero, the other without.

1	2	3	4	5	6	7	8	9	10
11	12	13	14	15	16	17	18	19	20
21	22	23	24	25	26	27	28	29	30
31	32	33	34	35	36	37	38	39	40
41	42	43	44	45	46	47	48	49	50
51	52	53	54	55	56	57	58	59	60
61	62	63	64	65	66	67	68	69	70
71	72	73	74	75	76	77	78	79	80
81	82	83	84	85	86	87	88	89	90
91	92	93	94	95	96	97	98	99	100

0	1	2	3	4	5	6	7	8	9
10	11	12	13	14	15	16	17	18	19
20	21	22	23	24	25	26	27	28	29
30	31	32	33	34	35	36	37	38	39
40	41	42	43	44	45	46	47	48	49
50	51	52	53	54	55	56	57	58	59
60	61	62	63	64	65	66	67	68	69
70	71	72	73	74	75	76	77	78	79
80	81	82	83	84	85	86	87	88	89
90	91	92	93	94	95	96	97	98	99

Yet, recent experience in year one and two classrooms shows a lack of emphasis on zero particularly with the display of 100 squares. The importance of representing zero was made by Merttens (1987) but still commercial representation excludes zero. Zero is important; why leave it out? Children at least need to see both representations of the 100 squares.

They also need to have number lines and number tracks featuring zero. For later work with multiplication or division we may select the number line which starts with one, but early exposure to zero is important. Number tracks as opposed to number lines tend to be used with younger children.

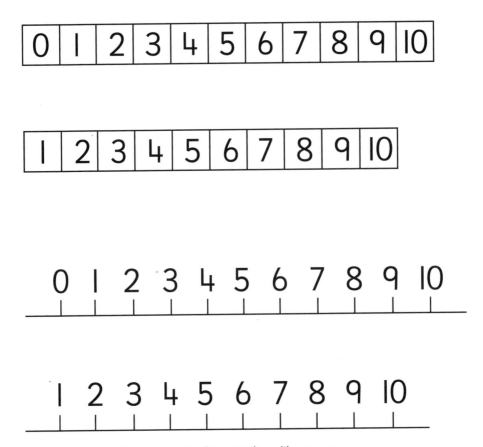

Figure 3.2 Number tracks and number lines starting with zero or one.

The 'tenness' of ten and place value

Failure to grasp the idea of place value is the route cause of computational difficulties later on (Merttens 1987, Merttens 2009). The application of place value is essential when working with larger numbers beyond 10 such as 22, where the 2 has a very different value depending on whether it is placed in the tens or unit position; or larger numbers such as 402, where there are four hundreds, no tens but the place is held, and two units, which relies on an appreciation of place value.

Understanding place value is rooted in earlier work, involving practical activities. Place value progresses through a series of learning stages, which need regular revisiting.

Activities involving grouping and exchange form the start of a sound understanding of place value. Young children need to work with a base lower than 10, for example base 5.

Egg boxes

The egg box activity is a great example of grouping. Children given one egg box with six spaces and eight hard boiled eggs, conclude that the eggs can be grouped into one box with two eggs spare. For older children the arrangement can be changed to two egg boxes and 14 eggs. The eggs are now grouped into two boxes of six with two spare eggs. Egg boxes of nine, 10 and 12 capacities can be used to develop grouping ideas.

This idea can be developed to include grouping and exchange through games.

Exchange games

The spider exchange game works well (Merttens 1987). Black play dough and pipe cleaners are used to make spider bodies and legs. A dice is thrown and the player collects that number of legs for their spider. When they have eight legs they exchange a spider for a web; the winner is the first to have four webs. A similar exchange game can be designed for smaller or larger numbers.

Button exchange game

The idea of grouping and exchanging can be further exploited in a button exchange, based on a board game suggested by Merttens (1987). The buttons are large, medium and small. Three small buttons can be exchanged for one medium-sized button: three medium-sized buttons can be exchanged for a large button. The children throw the dice, placing the corresponding number of buttons onto the right column of their board. When they have three or more buttons in the right hand column, those three may be exchanged for one of the next sized button. When they have three or more medium-sized buttons they can be exchanged for a large button. The winner is the first to get a large button. Children sense that the value of the left hand column is greater than that of the right. There is the realization that the small buttons build up to the value of the large button. The large button is worth three mediums; the medium is worth three smalls. So, a large button is worth or equivalent to nine small buttons. The game can be simplified to two columns, or increased to more.

Children cannot always see ten as equating with a unit. The perception that ten ones and one ten are the same is not apparent. Support is needed to allow children to see ten as a unit or a bundle made up of ten units. Unifix cubes combined to make a unit of ten placed alongside ten units visually communicate this.

Working with base ten, children make rods of ten unifix cubes and beside these place individual single cubes, building an understanding that one rod equals ten individual units. Moving into base 100 children can work with Dienes blocks, feeling how a block of 100 is equivalent to ten rods. Also using dots: blocks of 100 strips and ten individual strips reinforces this. These activities develop the groundwork for understanding place value. The child moves along 10, 20, 30, 40, 50, and 60, 70, 80, 90, 100. The concept of each block representing 10 is reinforced by asking the child to say how many strips were needed to arrive at 100. Ten strips can be used and each increase is by a ten only.

The abacus can be used to count in groups of 10, 20, 30, 40, 50, 60, 70, 80, 90 and 100, moving beads along in groups. The abacus can be used to count in tens. With a vertical abacus the beads are moved over the arch as a unit of ten each time, or across the frame with a horizontal model.

Combining the abacus and the dot strips reinforces the concept of ten units making a ten and how these tens relate decades to 100. The sense of ten being represented as an entity of one bundle may need tackling in diverse ways. It brings children to counting in tens, dividing by tens, and lays down the important track line of place value.

This work equips children to work with numbers like 124. They have a sense of bundling into tens, exchanging these for hundreds and having four over, as with the spare eggs. The idea of moving a unit of ten over in order to subtract and returning this later is then reasonable.

The place of ten is held in numbers such as 402 by the symbol 0, where there are four hundreds, zero tens and two units. The place of ten needs to be held by the zero. Children need to build this connection and when operating on this number need to employ the concept that the ten is equivalent to a bundle of ten. This concept of equivalence is needed for work with large numbers and can be arrived at through the above activities. The idea of grouping and exchanging transfers into understanding about money.

Place value squares encourage children to think where the number will be for colouring in. An example is to make a 7 × 7 square and colour every number with '4' in it. Asking children to find numbers 4, 14 and 44 in an interactive 100 square is exercising a search of place value. With these activities children search for the position the number takes in the square.

Working with eggs in boxes may be necessary even for older children in order to experience the sense of grouping which they need before understanding the exchange or equivalence demanded for more complex addition or subtraction operations which later learning brings. The place value system requires that we understand the principle of grouping into 10.

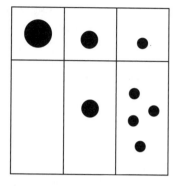

Button Exchange Game

H	T	U
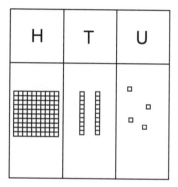

Structural Base Apparatus

£1	10p	1p

Figure 3.3 Button exchange, base ten materials, money, showing the principle of exchange (combining exchange ideas).

The subject of mathematics is hierarchical in nature. For every concept start from the bottom, bore down and move up to the level the child can reach. Knowing what comes before and after allows us to address misconceptions. If we layer the learning progression of place value we create the chance to fill gaps, consolidate previous learning and build confidence before moving on.

Writing numerals

Students find themselves working with children who are unable to write numerals correctly. A starting point is to establish if the child is ready to write. It is then wise to check the settings policy on writing. This may well state which representation of certain numerals are to be used.

It is essential to wait until children are ready before offering guidance. Too often children are expected to record numerically, but without knowing how, they repeatedly record incorrectly. Children seek out opportunity to record when they are ready.

Supporting numeral formation

The principle of story association can be used to support sequences of pencil movements required for numeral formation. The use of small story sketches can be applied to helping children record numerals correctly. The example below is about Shella the seahorse.

Shella the seahorse

Shella is turquoise blue, moves slowly, calmly through the waters of the sea. She is the size of the tip of your first finger. She can be drawn onto your finger or imagined. Shella whispers her movements like sounds in a seashell. Shella's dance movements make numbers. Shella always starts at the top for each dance. Her number dances are drawn in sand; waves wash them away, so she dances again and again.

Whatever story you decide on it needs to be simple, imaginative and consistent, so that it hooks into memory. This principle is in effect replicating an historical technique: 'for the Greeks, then, the infusion of energy (Zeus) into memory (Mnemosyne) produced both creativity and knowledge' (Buzan 1886:48).

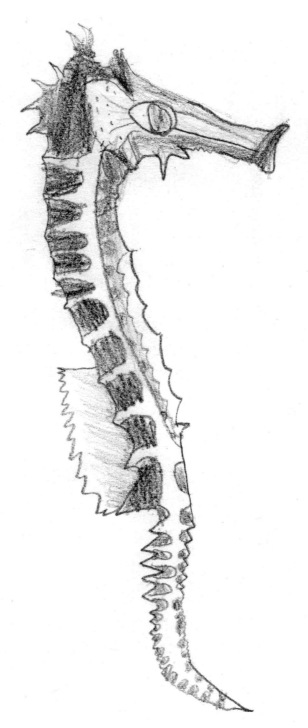

Figure 3.4 Shella the seahorse by Ben Lloyd aged seven years.

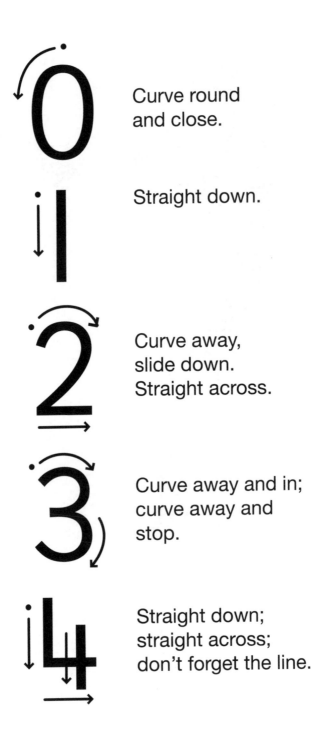

Curve round
and close.

Straight down.

Curve away,
slide down.
Straight across.

Curve away and in;
curve away and
stop.

Straight down;
straight across;
don't forget the line.

Figure 3.5 Words to support stroke motion or Shella's dance motion

 Short straight down; curve away; don't forget the hat.

 Glide down, curl inside.

 Straight across. Slant down.

 Curve round, curve away, and join.

 Curve round and close. Straight down.

Numeral formation key facts

The zero, eight and nine require an anticlockwise stroke. The associated words 'curve round' will be used to describe encircling or enclosing.

The two, three and five involve clockwise strokes. The associated words 'curve away' will be used to differentiate this motion as the child moves the pencil to a distance from the starting place.

2 3 5

The one, four, seven, part of nine and part of five require a straight stroke. 'Straight down' and 'straight across' are the associated words.

1 4 5 7 9

Note: it does depend on the version of nine used: 9 or 9

The numeral eight requires an anticlockwise and a clockwise stroke.

8

The three requires a clockwise stroke to the middle and again below.

3

The numeral six requires an unusual stroke anticlockwise that curls inwards.

The phrases 'don't forget the line' for four, 'the hat' for five and 'to join' for eight complete the stroke motions for these numerals.

4 5 8

Number of strokes for numerals

One stroke : 0, 1, 6, 8

Two strokes: 2, 3, 7, 9

Three strokes: 4, 5

Connection with letters

The following connections can be seen between numerals and letters in terms of sharing stroke motion: numeral formation is classified as a handwriting skill but is not always included in the range of descriptions; the numerals zero, one, four and eight share the same stroke motion as the following letters.

0 – O   1 – I
4 – L   8 – S

Starting the stroke motion

The starting point is always at the top. All numerals start at the top as do letters. The starting point can be marked with arrows or dots. Alternatively the starting and finishing points can both be indicated using green and red stickers with the associated traffic light connection: 'green means go', 'red means stop'.

It is better to wait until other skills are in place before expecting children to write numbers correctly. It is more relevant for children to work with practical applications of mathematics as Orton and Frobisher state,

> a possible solution to the learning of the numeration system is a delay in the introduction of written symbols, until it is apparent that children fully understand and can apply the system orally in many and varied contexts, and that when a written symbol or combination of symbols are introduced they are directly related to their oral counterparts in meaningful situations
>
> (1996: 70).

When fine motor skills are developed and motivation to form numerals is evident, then writing numbers can be addressed. Children who are posed with the challenge to write too early often form letters and numbers incorrectly, habits that are difficult to change.

Adam aged 5, with no inclination to write for most of the academic year, started to become interested towards the summer term. One day towards the end of July, he was called to the head teacher's office and had to write his name on a board for those who had misbehaved. As I stood behind him, he carefully wrote his Christian name and surname beautifully. There are moments which stay in one's memory and this was one of them. Pride in his writing won over disappointment in his behaviour.

Trainee and qualified practitioners need to intervene to support correct number formation. A child called Sky aged 4 in a reception class was repeatedly incorrectly forming the number '8'. This is the opportunity for the student to get some small white boards and work on this.

It is good to write the number '8' several times to demonstrate first. Attaching a description as to what to do, 'start at the top, curl round, curl back like a snake, join up', enabled Sky to form the '8' correctly. Modelling this intervention for the student gave her something to work from.

When children are ready there are some tips to help. Added to the story association suggested, a practical suggestion is to provide cards with green and red dot stickers, indicating where to start and where to stop each numeral. As with traffic lights green means 'go', red means 'stop'.

Learning to identify, recognize and write numerals can rightly be regarded an important part of early literacy development (Wright et al 2006: 24), creating a connection between literacy and numeracy. Again it is about making meaningful connections.

Counting accurately with one to one correspondence

One to one correspondence is central to accurate counting and can be encouraged through creating good habits. Errors in operations involving addition and subtraction are often due to inaccurate counting rather than applying adding or subtracting.

The importance of this principle is well documented. What seems to be needed is a step by step strategy to implement it in practice. The process described below has been tested and works. It is a combination of modelling, working together and allowing independence.

A first year Foundation Degree student organized a counting activity involving children rolling out their play dough and using raisins for counting. She supported these three year olds in counting accurately by touching each raisin. Her modelling of this way of counting will help children count accurately.

However, modelling accurate counting is not always enough. Miles, a three year old, was shown how to count in this way but when asked to count himself mismatched items and numbers arriving at 4 instead of 3. Children counting a set of objects inefficiently, tend to not touch each item as they count.

The practitioner needs to model but also reinforce through engaging the child in this action. The practitioner needs to model counting with one to one correspondence and then count parallel with the child using this technique. Finally the child needs to count independently either touching or removing items.

To create good counting habits with young children the following three steps will help.

Forming accurate counting habits:

1. Act as a role model by touching and saying each corresponding number.
Child listens. Adult counts.

2. Ask the child to touch each item and count with you, in parallel.
Child counts. Adult counts.

3. Allow the child to repeat and count by touching and saying numbers, checking they arrive at the number.
Child counts. Adult listens.

Repeat this sequence three times. Observe child count accurately at least three times.

Adjust the number to a lower one to establish the habit, if necessary.

Items can be removed, lined up, or touched as they are counted.

It is the second step of ensuring the child touches and counts with you that is vital. Counting accurately is essential for mathematical confidence and competence.

Encouraging children to touch each item they count helps make the connection between the number name sequence and the ordinal value of each number. As they touch the raisins and say 'one' there is the sense that this is the first button on the gingerbread man. Through counting experience children sense the difference between cardinal and ordinal. They are touching one item and saying 'five'. This is an expression of the difference between the order of the item in the set and the value of the items so far in the count.

Conclusion

Specific principles which need to underpin teaching mathematics summarized

Mathematical language

For most of us the words we use are the tracks our thinking runs on. Mathematical dictionaries are worth creating. Words can carry different meanings with multiple possibilities for some. The practitioner can test different word meanings until the mathematical meaning settles into place. Word banks can be created for tricky words. Rather than ask questions, another strategy is to provide information which the child questions.

Repetition at least three times

For adults assimilating new information, a good tip is to revisit material three times, on three consecutive days. Children are developing their working memory capacity and reinforcing previous learning, at least three times, helps with retrieval. Rapid responses build confidence as well as recall. A top tip is to start each lesson with a summary of the previous lesson, but with emphasis on the children providing the summary.

Mixed-ability groups

Children learn from one another. Adults can capitalize on this innate ability. Groups that self-select tend to be driven by motivation and desire. The adult can provide stimulating materials, step back making observations, intervene with relevant mathematical prompts and then step back again. The group self-selects as children are drawn in by interest. Children can achieve beyond an expectation, when given freedom to work with others.

Pictorial and photographic representation rather than worksheets

The expression of mathematical thinking needs to feature indoors and outdoors. Boards at child height allow this. Worksheets may well be needed as a survival strategy in mainstream classes. How many people could manage a group of 30 children from 8.50 am to 3.20 pm within the constraints of a primary school environment? It is no mean task. The reality is that worksheets may be necessary but don't always fulfil the aim of assessing learning. Blank paper, photographs and talk are evidence worth annotating.

Start at the very beginning

It is dangerous to make assumptions in life. Practitioners plug into the curriculum learning goal which is age- and stage-appropriate for the group. There may be gaps in a child's learning due to absences, poor teaching or broken concentration. The gaps can be filled by going back to the very start and travelling forward from there. The practitioner needs to go to the centre of the web and move out connecting previous learning. This is particularly relevant for concepts which are difficult to grasp and have an impact on future learning.

Playing with place value and knowing zero

Zero needs to be seen and heard in number lines and squares. Children need to have number lines and number tracks featuring zero. Understanding place value can be arrived at through practical activities. Grouping using egg boxes can be used to secure early ideas. Exchange games can develop this further. Base ten materials support learning about place value. The place value system requires that children understand principles of grouping and exchange.

Correct numeral formation

A starting point is to establish if the child is ready to write. Story sketches help children remember how to form numerals correctly. The wrapping of words describing writing motion, in a story, helps hook correct numeral formation into a child's memory. We can use a variety of media: whiteboards with marker pens; small white card with pens; sand, glue and other materials.

Counting accurately

Reliable counting is essential in order to avoid errors in addition operations. Following three steps and repeating these three times forms good counting habits.

1. Adult counts. Child watches.

2. Adult counts. Child counts.

3. Child counts. Adult watches.

Section 2

Connecting across curricula

'Is there any body there?' said the Traveller,
Knocking on the moonlit door;
And his horse in the silence champed the grasses
Of the forest's ferny floor:
And a bird flew up out of the turret,
Above the Traveller's head
And he smote upon the door again a second time:
'Is there anybody there?' he said.
    Walter de la Mare (1873–1956) *The Listeners*

The aims of this chapter are:

- To understand how early and later curricula connect
- To isolate certain strands which thread through both curricula
- To understand how pattern connects mathematics

Introduction

This chapter considers threads of teaching which we will pull through the eye of the curriculum needle from birth to eight years. We will thread through pattern, understanding number, number operations and problem solving. Other curriculum areas can be considered in the same way but require separate analysis. The learning goals are based on those of the Early Years Foundation Stage Curriculum Guidance (DfES 2008) and the Primary Framework for Mathematics (DfES 2006). The mathematical curriculum for primary schools will change from September 2011. For the purpose of this chapter the current curriculum is referred to and the same principle of looking forward to ensure continuity of progression can be applied whatever the curriculum. The Early Years Foundation Stage (DfES 2008) curriculum guidance is divided between 'Development Matters' and other sections 'Look, listen and note', 'Effective practice', and 'Planning and resourcing'.

At the time of writing, children in England encounter the Early Years Foundation Stage (DfES 2008) from birth to five, followed by the Primary Framework for literacy and mathematics (DfES 2006) from five to 11 years.

Wales employs a relatively new initiative for targeted areas, the Flying Start programme, from birth to three (Welsh Assembly Government 2008a); children then experience the Foundation Phase (Framework for Children's Learning for 3 to 7-year-olds in Wales 2008) (Welsh Assembly Government 2008b); followed by Mathematics in the National Curriculum for Wales which is applicable to children from seven to 16 years of age (Welsh Assembly Government 2008c).

Scottish children experience *Birth to Three: Supporting our youngest children* (Learning and Teaching Scotland 2005); followed by the *Curriculum for Excellence: Numeracy and mathematics: experiences and outcomes* (Learning and Teaching Scotland 2009), from three to 18 years of age, the completion of a child's secondary education.

A child's progressive curriculum experience in England, Scotland and Wales will look something along these lines:

English

0_____5_____11_____16

  Early Years Foundation Stage   Primary Framework   National Curriculum
                                                              Key stages 3 and 4

Welsh

0_____3_____7_____16

Flying Start Programme   Foundation Phase   National Curriculum for Wales

Scottish

0_____3_____18

  Birth to Three   Curriculum for excellence

How can curriculum experience be so different within Great Britain? Wales and Scotland have forged ahead with a play-based curriculum for children up to seven in Wales or a continuous curriculum in Scotland up to 18 years, more in line with European and Scandinavian practice. Are Wales and Scotland more attuned to research outcomes? Or are curricula driven by politics?

Thompson criticizes the lack of listening to the written word in England expressing the view that, 'even when research is available, those in positions of power often seem to remain unaware of its existence, or make deliberate attempts to disregard it' (2001: 77). Thompson (2001) refers to the Netherlands, where research determines developments as opposed to England, where research follows mandatory changes such as the National Numeracy Strategy. It is as if research in England exists separately from rather than sharing a relationship with practice. The final report from the Cambridge

Primary Review (2009) is advocating that the 'Early Years Foundation Stage should be renamed and extended to age six' and that 'the English insistence on the earliest possible start to formal schooling, against the grain of international evidence and practice, is educationally counterproductive' is dismissed by British Government with the response 'a school starting age of six would be completely counter-productive' (BBC News 2009).

Questions to reflect on:

How does learning progress through the curricula children experience from birth to eight?

How would you teach young children odd and even numbers?

Why is pattern so important in connecting mathematical strands?

We will consider pattern, understanding number and problem solving, looking closely at learning goals to track progression based on the curricula for children living in England. These will be examined for shortcomings which will be proposed as suggestions for practice.

Pattern

The first strand we will follow is pattern. Pattern is a binding ingredient which is highlighted in other chapters. The focus here will be on following patterns through learning goals from birth to eight years across England's curricula. Particular attention will be given to odd and even patterns of numbers. This is more complex than at first sight, yet essential for number work. This aspect of mathematics requires greater coverage than current guidance suggests, starting in the early years and continuing through a child's learning experience as Frobisher uncovers, 'although odd and even numbers are found in most curricula, seldom are the numbers explored to unearth their true richness' (1999: 33). This aspect of teaching mathematics will be examined in more detail.

Research indicates a need for children to learn pattern (Frobisher 1999; Pound 2008) in the very early years, yet this could easily be overlooked as guidance statements referring to pattern in the Early Years Foundation Stage (DfES 2008) are scattered through the document.

Pattern representation in the Early Years Foundation Stage (2008)

Like the crest of a peacock so is mathematics at the head of all knowledge.

Anonymous

Figure 4.1 Peacock showing pattern in nature.

Pattern is mentioned many times even if we have to search it out. However, there are but three mentions of pattern in the 'Development Matters' section of the Early Years Foundation Stage (DfES 2008): these and other mentions of pattern are collated below. It would be valuable to package pattern up and give it greater prominence in the Early Years Foundation Stage curriculum.

Pattern reference in the Early Years Foundation Stage Curriculum Guidance (DfES 2008)

'babies' and children's mathematics development occurs as they seek pattern' (DfES 2008: 63)

'encourage children to explore real-life problems, to make patterns' (DfES 2008: 63)

'provide a range of activities, some of which focus on mathematical learning and some of which enable mathematical learning to be drawn out, for example, exploring shape, size and pattern during block play' (DfES 2008: 64) 'move with babies to the rhythm patterns in songs and rhymes' (DfES 2008: 65)

'use a 100 square to show number patterns' (DfES 2008: 68)

'highlight patterns in daily activities and routines' (DfES 2008: 72)

'encourage children to create their own patterns in art, music and dance' (DfES 2008: 73)

'notice simple shapes and patterns in pictures' (DfES 2008: 73)

'talk about and help children to recognize patterns' (DfES 2008: 73)

'draw children's attention to the pattern of square / oblong / square which emerges as you fold or unfold a tablecloth or napkin' (DfES 2008: 73)

'collect pictures that illustrate the use of shapes and patterns from a variety of cultures for example Arabic designs' (DfES 2008: 73)

'show pictures that have symmetry or pattern and talk to children about them' (DfES 2008: 74)

'show awareness of symmetry' (DfES 2008: 74)

'make books ... about pattern' (DfES 2008: 74)

'provide materials and resources for children to observe and describe patterns in the indoor and outdoor environment and in daily routines, orally, in pictures or using objects' (DfES 2008: 74)

'use familiar objects and common shapes to create and recreate patterns and build models' (DfES 2008: 75)

The curriculum guidance also contains important reference to categorizing and sorting. When children are engaged in these essential activities they are looking for patterns and making decisions accordingly. The Scottish Curriculum for Excellence (2009) in 'Data and analysis' describes one outcome as 'match objects, and sort using my own and others' criteria, sharing my ideas with others', creating an opportunity to link sorting with pattern as the child articulates their criteria.

Categorizing and sorting references in the Early Years Foundation Stage (DfES 2008) and Primary National Strategy (DfES 2006)

'categorise objects according to their properties' (16–26 months calculating DfES 2008: 69)
'sort familiar objects to identify their similarities and differences' (Handling Data PNS 2006: 71; DfES 2008: 75)

The skills of sorting and categorizing relate further along the curriculum continuum to data handling in years one, two and three, where children are required 'to sort data and objects using more than one criterion' (DfES 2006: 76).

Children at a young age can be presented with sorting and categorizing challenges, for example cards of black and white cats. The sorting criteria can be made more complex by including pictures of black or white cats with or without tails, ears, whiskers and so on (Merttens 1987).

Children at a playgroup sorted a wide-ranging collection, including corks, frogs, rocking horses, stones, shells, up to 10 different items and then stored them in numbered boxes. This activity requires skills of sorting, counting and number recognition through simple well-thought-through provision, central to the early learning of mathematics, which we will explore in Chapter 5.

By the time the child has reached the age of five it is expected that they can, 'talk about, recognize and recreate simple pattern' (DfES 2008: 75). This final learning goal is arguably flawed as it places sole emphasis on recreating pattern rather than children creating their own patterns (Frobisher 1999).

This final learning goal does not encompass all of the other guidance points, and therefore full interpretation is dependent on the importance readers of the curriculum guidance place on other sections, that is, 'Look, listen and note', 'Effective practice', 'Planning and resourcing'.

Pattern and algebra are strong components of the Primary National Strategy as seen below.

Extracting pattern mention in the Primary National Strategy (DfES 2006) for children aged 5 to 8 years

Year one (children aged 5/6)

'describe simple patterns and relationships involving number or shapes: decide whether examples satisfy given conditions' (DfES 2006: 72)

'visualise and name common 2-D shapes and 3-D solids and describe their features; use them to make patterns, pictures and models' (DfES 2006: 73)

'use diagrams to sort objects into groups according to a given criterion; suggest a different criterion for grouping the same objects' (DfES 2006: 73)

Year two (children aged 6/7)

'describe patterns and relationships involving numbers or shapes, make predictions and test these with examples' (DfES 2006: 74) 'identify reflective symmetry in patterns and 2-D shapes and draw lines of symmetry in shapes' (DfES 2006: 75)

'describe and extend number sequences and recognize odd and even numbers' (DfES 2006: 74)

'use the symbols +, −, ×, ÷ and = to record and interpret number sentences involving all four operations; calculate the value of an unknown in a number sentence (e.g. □ ÷ 2 = 6, 30 − □ = 24)' (DfES 2006: 74)

'identify reflective symmetry in patterns and 2-D shapes and draw lines of symmetry in shapes' (DfES 2006: 75)

'use lists, tables and diagrams to sort objects; explain choices using appropriate language, including "not"' (DfES 2006: 75)

Year three (children aged 7/8)

'identify patterns and relationships involving numbers or shapes, and use these to solve problems' (DfES 2006: 76)

'use Venn diagrams or Carroll diagrams to sort data and objects using more than one criterion' (DfES 2006: 77)

Note: a Carroll diagram is named after Lewis Carroll. A Carroll diagram is used to sort objects and numbers based on certain properties. The diagram is presented as boxes where like items are recorded inside corresponding boxes, that is, prime numbers could be separated from non-prime numbers recording each set in boxes.

Note: a Venn diagram is presented as circles of which some of the enclosed area is separate and some overlaps with other circles. The intersecting space implies two sets share the items included here, that is, the item belongs to both sets as determined by the circle characteristics or stated properties.

Odd and even numbers

There is a certain mystery attached to odd and even number pattern and, 'there appears to be something special about odd and even numbers that fascinates children of all ages' (Frobisher 1999: 33) which we can exploit. There is a symmetry and asymmetry of even and odd numbers which children need to explore.

There is no specific mention of odd and even numbers until the year two curriculum. The Early Years Foundation Stage (DfES 2008: 66) suggests in 'Planning and resourcing' that we use 'a 100 square to show number patterns' which could include this feature. It would, however, be inappropriate to look at odd and even numbers on a 100 square unless children first have a sense of what makes a number odd or even. It is interesting that odd and even numbers are not mentioned in the English Year One curriculum aims; surely children aged five and six need practical exposure before being expected to relate this understanding to the more abstract representation of numbers on lines or squares. Individual number oddness and evenness needs to be realized before pattern is perceived in the arrangement of numbers to 10, 100 or beyond.

This is a curriculum omission and it would seem sensible to do this work in the early years, allowing children explicit experience of odd and even at each stage of mathematical learning. Frobisher recommends that odd and even number work continues throughout the primary years (1999).

The year two aim 'describe and extend number sequences and recognize odd and even numbers' (DfES 2006: 74), assumes children attach meaning to the context of recognizing odd and even numbers. Assumptions that number line and 100 square work achieve this understanding are misplaced. Unless children really understand what odd or even means how will they transfer this to the domain of larger numbers? Evidence suggests they do not (Frobisher 1999). Unless the mechanics of how to categorize a number as odd or even are secure, how will unfamiliar numbers be sorted? Common sense suggests they won't.

The complexity of odd and even

Frobisher (1999) refers to the definition by the famous Greek mathematician, Euclid:

> an even number is divisible into two equal parts
> an odd number is not divisible into two equal parts

This definition involves the partitioning of a natural number into two equal parts. However, there is also a different approach which we can use to set about experiencing odd and evenness. How else might we come to deciding whether a number is odd or even? We can group the number into pairs as suggested by Merttens (1987).

In the case of Numicon the odd or even feature is inbuilt into the plate, with even numbers making complete rectangles and odd numbers making incomplete ones.

There are therefore two ways to approach the odd and even characteristic of number: partitioning into two equal groups or grouping into twos. Frobisher states that 'much more quality time needs to be spent developing the idea of partitioning into two equal sets and the equivalent activity of dividing into sets of 2's in order that children are able to observe the patterns in odd and even numbers whatever the size of the numbers' (Frobisher 1999: 48).

Figure 4.2 Foundation Degree students seeing opportunities in everyday objects, e.g. washers for odd and even number work (the idea based on work of Merttens 1987; Numicon 2009).

These are two different ideas. A consistent approach is worth considering so children are not confused. We would need to sense when to communicate one or the other to achieve both.

Teaching odd and even numbers

A student on placement in a year one class implemented a planned activity based around odd and even numbers. A summary record of the session is set out below with my thoughts as observer. My subjective views are included in italics to show how the observation leads to intervention, changing the learning experience of the children and the student. Some years ago I would never dare to interfere with an activity, waiting until later to give feedback. Now, if I think children and/or students will benefit from immediate direction I intervene, as sensitively as possible. As an observer it is worth realizing the freedom this role gives you to see the situation strategically.

Observation of student odd and even activity

A year one class in a primary school

Student: Carley, second year Foundation Degree Early Childhood Studies

Children: Owen aged 6 years, Danya aged 6 years, Sophie aged 5 years

Learning goal: 'Recognise odd and even numbers' (DfES 2006: 74). This learning goal is in fact a year two learning goal (though it can be tailored for younger children)

Focus: odd and even numbers

Carley encourages the children to count to 10 starting with 0. She writes 'odd' and 'even' on a wipe board, drawing a line down the centre. She incorrectly writes '0' under 'odd' and '1' under 'even'.

She is probably nervous and therefore incorrectly writing zero in the column for odd numbers. She hopefully will spot this error before too long.

Realizing the mistake she wipes the numbers off and starts again. Under the 'odd' column are 1, 3, 5, 7, 9. Under the 'even' column is '0', '2', '4', '6', '8'. She states, 'any number which ends in one of these is odd' (pointing to 1, 3, 5, 7, 9) 'and even if it ends in these' (pointing to 0, 2, 4, 6, 8).

I would need to memorize each of these columns and what they contain. I can see ahead on the plan to the worksheet, where I will circle 19 as odd because it has a '9' at the end. This requires my memory. I wonder why these numbers are odd or even. The children need to experience this, otherwise they are relying on memory in a meaningless way. Perhaps this association is more of a useful tip for later on when they really understand oddness and evenness. They need practical materials to learn this first. I will not intervene yet. There is a box of Unifix cubes by her chair. Also another box with numbers.

Carley asks the children to look at the worksheets and decide if the numbers are even and circle accordingly. She holds up the board so they can check numbers on the worksheet against those on the board.

Would all children understand the written word 'odd' or 'even' (they will need to if they are interpreting this information)? It is good that zero is being included. Would the reason zero is even need explaining? It is neither odd nor even but readily takes the place of being even. Will I be able to explain to Carley why zero is even? Why has she decided not to include 10, especially as we counted from 0 to 10? The children need concrete materials to distinguish between odd and even. Don't intervene yet.

Carley moves the children on, 'odd numbers now. Super quick'.

Why 'super quick'? As a child I might need time to think. There is no rush. It's a turn of phrase, nothing to worry about. Am I being too fussy?

Carley notices she has written '3' in mirror image on the wipe board and corrects this. Then she picks up on Danya incorrectly circling 2, and 6 as odd numbers. She looks at the child's face and suggests she leaves it or crosses through.

Recording on the worksheet is now not working (for one of the three children at least). Intervene to steer the learning in a practical direction.

'Would you mind if I come and join in?' I ask Carley and the children. They invite me in. I ask if we can use the Unifix cubes and start to make paired representations of numbers. I start to do this but I find that this is difficult as it is tricky to keep the pieces as a unit. So I ask Carley if there is anything else we could use.

Carley goes off to look and I continue to represent numbers beyond 4. She comes back with Numicon. I line the plates 1 to 10 up in front of me.

I think that we cannot represent zero with this arrangement and that this would be an opening to discuss this but decide to concentrate on getting the children and Carley familiar with the structured pieces. I suggest that they can record the image of the plates on paper. Owen was not interested in this which is fair enough. The other children are however. I step back so that Carley can re-establish her role.

Danya and Sophie count the holes of each plate, ordering these both practically and on paper. There is silence as each child handles the pieces.

I then show Carley the pegs and boards suggesting she make odd and even number representations with the pegs and place corresponding plates on top. This idea is taken forward by all three children.

The children apply themselves in different ways. Owen stayed with the plates, deciding to place them on the peg board. Danya is keen on building towers of threes, then fives. Sophie settles on arranging pegs from 1 to 10 on her board with plates on top (see Figure 4.3).

When Carley asked which numbers were odd or even they could correctly answer this, sometimes pointing to the missing hole space of odd numbers. At one stage Sophie stands up and says while searching in the bag, 'I need nine'. She goes on to complete all number representations to ten.

Carley comments at the end when the children are gone, 'I wanted to use hands on activity rather than a work sheet'. Absolutely right. Follow your instinct. She had been discouraged and a later discussion revealed that Numicon is used only for children who need intervention. In this case it worked for each of these children.

We discussed how buttons or washers could be used to represent odd and even, though in this case the fixed frame worked well as a visual representation of odd and even through pairing.

An email the next day from Carley includes the comment, 'it was great to see how a resource such as Numicon can have such a positive impact on children's progress towards the learning goal. It is my aim to plan more activities working with this resource.'

Figure 4.3 Odd and even number work with Numicon.

In order to bridge learning from birth to eight years where children are expected to recognize odd and even numbers (DfES 2006), practical applications need to be experienced along the learning continuum. The observation above highlights that practical work is crucial to the acquisition of ideas such as odd and even number patterns (Merttens 1987).

Children must learn the odd and even characteristic of individual numbers and the collective odd and even pattern of numbers. Odd and even exist on two learning levels; inside the number and outside in relation to other numbers. The number 3 is odd itself and sits between 2 and 4 which are even. Practical work promotes deep thinking about and best understanding of this important number quality.

Pattern

An idea I had was to create a pattern learning continuum for children between birth and eight years of age. I set about scrutinizing the English, Welsh and Scottish curricula. The aim was to create an image which would show how children progress with learning pattern as they move through their education.

What I produced just did not work; this failed attempt prompted more exploration and insight. Firstly, conversations with other mathematics educators, raised the point that children might progress further with a strand of pattern set in a context which interests them. A child can understand a computer game offering complex pattern challenges and yet not grasp an 'easier' aspect of pattern; the context can determine the child's advancement with pattern.

Secondly, that pattern has many facets; this is revealed through reading *Pattern in the Teaching and Learning of Mathematics* edited by Orton (1999). In this book pattern is connected to bead work evoking spatial and colour organization; odd and even numbers; addition facts; linear and quadratic sequences; algebra; shape; randomness and data handling; problem solving and investigations; proof; the final chapter linking pattern in shape with pattern in number.

Both of these points make it difficult to plot a generic sequence of pattern progression. A child's journey towards mature pattern making is unique and unpredictable; pattern potentially encompasses so much mathematics and it's very complexity makes it difficult to capture on a timeline.

Curricula conflict

The combined analysis of each curriculum produced an inadequate outcome. Garrick, Threlfall and Orton comment that 'while much is known about developmental sequences in children's acquisition of literacy skills and in some aspects of mathematical learning, relatively limited attention has been given to pattern as a particular aspect of mathematical learning' (1999:2) confirming the fragility of such a search.

Not only is there weak representation with reference to pattern but the assumption about the sequence in which knowledge is developed in relation to pattern is flawed (Garrick, Threlfall and Orton 1999). The curriculum puts emphasis on children recognizing and copying the work of others before making patterns of their own. The 'recreation' of pattern does not necessarily precede 'creation' of children's own pattern; the expressions in curricula statements such as 'can copy and continue pattern' and 'can create own pattern', assume that one precedes the other. In conflict with the curricula guidance, Garrick, Threlfall and Orton (1999) state that for many children it is more important that they talk about their own pattern making activities before looking at those created by others.

Pattern perception

The way pattern is perceived and the ability to articulate this in a qualitative way is an important skill (Threlfall 1999) and different to that of copying, continuing or creating. Just because children can repeat pattern does not mean they have a deep understanding.

Assessment needs to consider the perception of pattern along with the ability to articulate that perception. It is not whether they can do this, but how well they can do this; 'competence is not a matter of whether a child can describe a pattern but how well' (Frobisher and Threlfall 1999). We also need to consider that understanding may be in advance of expression; children may lack the vocabulary to explain fully what they perceive.

A valuable suggestion is to pose the challenge of repeating a pattern created using different media i.e. peg pattern can be translated to bead threading which would help to develop the perception of the unit of repeat (Threfall 1999). The Scottish Curriculum refers to 'using a range of media experiences and outcomes', which invites the development of this idea.

We will now consider other aspects of mathematics connected to pattern. Again we will look at how learning is represented in both the early years and Primary National Strategy. If we track pattern through each stage of learning we see pattern progression along with connections to other areas of mathematical learning. Numbers, calculations, operations, shape, and problem solving are determined by pattern. In the Primary Framework for Numeracy (DfES 2006) the year 3 includes 'identify patterns and relationships involving numbers or shapes and use these to solve problems' connecting pattern to problem solving. It is as if pattern pins the rest of mathematics down.

Understanding number

We will consider counting with expectations of knowing and using number information. The order of numbers is itself an expression of the patterns 'one more than' or 'one less than' (Frobisher and Threlfall 1999). There is the pattern of number names and the relationship of number order to understand.

Children in their early years can learn to count reliably, which means they can apply one to one correspondence and arrive at an accurate number (see Chapter 3). This is a step on from being able to say the names of numbers in the correct order (see Chapter 6). Each item in the count needs a correctly ordered number name to land on it.

Conservation of number

In the Primary Framework Numeracy (DfES 2006) the year one curriculum describes how the idea of number conservation needs to be achieved up to 20. This can be considered for smaller numbers with younger children. Conserving number is remembering the count and realizing that how the items are arranged makes no difference. Whether the buttons are lined up neatly or scattered does not change the fact that there are 20 buttons.

Conservation of number can be experienced by having two lots of five arranged differently or one lot of five used in a different way. Counting five buttons then dropping them demonstrates this for younger children (Merttens 1987). Lining up one row of five and counting a sister group of five randomly arranged also shows this.

Number information

Early years brings recognition of numerals from 1 to 9; year one extends this to include 0 and goes to 20. In year one, children are to write the numerals 0–20. In year 2, this extends to two- and three-digit numbers and includes number words as well as figures.

The younger child needs to know enough about numbers to find one more or one less than any number from 1 to 10. Number bonds to 10 are a year one aim. The aim in year 2 is to teach children to understand relationships up to 100, and multiplication. Year 3 involves teaching children to read, write and order numbers to 1,000. They count on and back in single-digit steps or multiples of 10. They derive addition and subtraction facts for each number up to 20. They know number pairs up to 100. They learn multiplication and division facts for 2, 3, 4, 5, 6 and 10 times tables. They can spot multiples of 2, 5 or 10 up to 1,000.

Understanding number and using number information for children aged 0–8 based on Early Years Foundation Stage (DfES 2008) and Primary National Strategy (DfES 2006)

Counting

Early Years Foundation Stage (DfES 2008: 68)

'say and use number names in order in familiar contexts'

'count reliably up to ten everyday objects'

'recognise numerals 1 to 9'

'estimate how many objects they can see and check by counting them'

Year one Primary National Strategy (DfES 2006: 72)

'count reliably at least 20 objects, recognising that when rearranged the number of objects stays the same' 'estimate a number of objects that can be counted by checking'

'read and write numerals from 0 to 20, then beyond; use the knowledge of place value to position these numbers on a number track and number line'

Year two Primary National Strategy (DfES 2006: 74)

'count up to 100 by grouping them and counting in tens, fives or twos; explain what each digit in a two digit number represents, including numbers where 0 is a place holder'

'partition two digit numbers in different ways, including into multiples of 10 and 1'

'estimate a number of objects'

'round two digit numbers to the nearest 10'

Year three Primary National Strategy (DfES 2006: 76)

'read, write and order whole numbers to at least 1000'

'count on from and back to zero in single digit steps or multiples of 10'

'partition three-digit numbers into multiples of 100, 10 and 1 in different ways'

Number information/calculation

Early Years Foundation Strategy (DfES 2008: 71)

'find one more or one less than a number from 1 to 10'

Year one Primary Framework Numeracy (DfES 2006: 72)

'derive and recall all pairs of numbers with a total of 10 and addition facts for totals to at least 5'

'say the number that is one more or less than any given number, and 10 more or less for multiples of 10'

'count on or back in ones, twos, fives and tens and use this knowledge to derive the multiples of 2, 5 and 10 to the tenth multiple'

'recall the doubles of all numbers to at least 10'

Year two Primary Framework Numeracy (DfES 2006: 74)

'derive and recall all addition and subtraction facts for each number to at least 10, all pairs with totals to 20 and all pairs of multiples of 10 with totals up to 100'

'understand that halving is the inverse of doubling and derive and recall doubles of all numbers to 20, and the corresponding halves'

Year three Primary Framework Numeracy (DfES 2006: 76)

'derive and recall all addition and subtraction facts for each number to 20, sums and differences of multiples of 10 and number pairs that total 100'

'derive and recall multiplication facts for the 2, 3, 4, 5, 6 and 10 times-tables and the corresponding division facts; recognise multiples of 2, 5 or 10 up to 1000'

Children may not be ready to write numbers from 0 to 20 at the age of 6 or 7 as this will depend on their individual fine motor control (see Chapter 3). The curriculum focus up to the age of 6 or 7 need not include writing for those who are not ready. This good guidance is not always adhered to, resulting in premature poor numeral formation.

Counting progresses from 10 to 20, to 100 to 1,000, from the early years up to age 8. Children in a year 3 class may not all be competent counting to 100. Children who can count to 100 may not automatically progress to counting to 1,000. Those who speak another language may not have the same level of expertise in both languages.

It is important to note the later lack of focus on zero, yet the year two curriculum requirement to understand 0 as a place holder in a two-digit number. Within the Early Years Foundation Stage (2008) in the section 'Effective practice', the statement, 'emphasise the empty set and introduce the concept of nothing or zero' could be given greater priority by featuring in the 'Early Learning Goals' section, particularly as 'it is important that small children especially do not lose sight of the importance of zero' (Merttens 1987: 25). This emphasis should continue into year one in order that children aged 6 and 7 realize the significance of zero.

The requirement to 'derive and recall' as described in the Primary Framework Numeracy (DfES 2006), means number facts are stored in memory and are deeply understood in order that new connections can be made. A certain robust mental agility underpins these curriculum learning aims which can only be achieved through using practical materials. The emphasis on mental calculation is evident in the coverage of number operations.

Number operations

Addition, subtraction, multiplication and division operations are themselves based on number relationships and patterns. Children as young as two can see that three pigs each have four legs and can repeat this count of four, which is multiplication. Sharing is a form of division and is supported in the early years using purposeful reasons such as snack times.

Number operations in Early Years Foundation Stage (DfES 2008) and Primary Framework Numeracy (DfES 2006) for children aged 0–8 years

Number operation progression from 0 to 8

Early Years Foundation Stage (DfES 2008: 70–71)

'in practical activities and discussion, begin to use the vocabulary involved in adding and subtracting'

'begin to relate addition to combining two groups of objects and subtraction to "taking away"'

'share objects into equal groups and count how many in each group'

'count repeated groups of the same size'

Year one Primary Framework Numeracy (DfES 2006: 72)

'relate addition to counting on'

'recognise that addition can be done in any order'

'use practical and informal written methods'

'understand … subtraction as "take away" and find a "difference" by counting up'

'use the vocabulary related to addition and subtraction and symbols to describe and record addition and subtraction number sentences'

'solve practical problems that involve combining groups of 2, 5 or 10, or sharing into equal groups'

Year two Primary Framework Numeracy (DfES 2006: 74)

'understand subtraction is the inverse of addition and vice versa; use this to derive and record related addition and subtraction number sentences'

'represent repeated addition and arrays as multiplication, and sharing and repeated subtraction (grouping) as division'

'use practical and informal written methods and related vocabulary to support multiplication and division, including calculations with remainders'

'use the symbols $+$, $-$, $\div$ and $=$ to record and interpret number sentences involving all four operations'

'calculate the value of an unknown in a number sentence e.g. $\square \div 2 = 6$, $30 - \square = 24$'.

> **Year three Primary Framework Numeracy (DfES 2006: 76)**
>
> 'add or subtract mentally combinations of one-digit and two-digit numbers'
>
> 'develop and use written methods to record, support or explain addition and subtraction of two-digit and three-digit numbers'
>
> 'multiply one-digit and two-digit numbers by 10 or 100, and describe the effect'
>
> 'use practical and informal written methods to multiply and divide two-digit numbers (e.g. 13×3, $50 \div 4$)'
>
> 'round remainders up or down, depending on the context'
>
> 'understand that division is the inverse of multiplication and vice versa; use this to derive and record related multiplication and division number sentences'

There is a conflict in year one between 'informal written methods' which would imply pictures and the 'use of symbols' for number sentences. The expectation is that children as young as 5 or 6 express addition and subtraction mathematical operations in number sentences. The need for understanding before imposing pencil work should prevail.

Within the 'Effective Practice' section of the Early Years Foundation Strategy we find 'demonstrate methods of recording, using standard notation where appropriate' (DfES 2008: 69). This will depend on children's ability to fully understand the operation and to express this symbolically. Are we to interpret the word 'appropriate' as first, being secure with the operation and second, having the ability to attach abstract symbolism? 'Appropriate' needs careful consideration in relation to such young children.

The Early Years Foundation Stage (DfES 2008) advises that addition, subtraction, multiplication and division are experienced in a concrete way. Practical activities and stories should carry on into years one, two and three, ensuring continuous concrete coverage of these concepts.

The year three curriculum coverage bears direct relationship to earlier learning goals for children aged 40–60 months in the Early Years Foundation Stage (DfES 2008) guidance. There are differences in scaling up complexity and to express the idea in writing. This is exemplified in the aim of understanding 13×3 (a year 3 aim) which is rooted in counting 13 repeated groups of 3.

The division of 50 by 4 compares in principle to sharing objects into equal groups and counting how many in each. A larger number involving a remainder needs to be accommodated in year 3; practical principles still apply. For younger children 10 could be divided into five groups of two, or two groups of five, advancing to sharing 10 biscuits amongst four giving two and a half each. This projects to later challenges of sharing 50 amongst four giving 12 and a half each.

Years two and three seek an understanding of the interrelationships which exist between the operations. This understanding allows for mental manipulation of number facts.

It is interesting to note how each stage of a child's learning relates mathematical operations to problem solving in the Scottish Curriculum for Excellence (Learning and Teaching Scotland 2009) suggested outcome of 'I can use addition, subtraction, multiplication and division when solving problems, making best use of the mental strategies and written skills I have developed'.

Problem solving and problem posing

The curiosity of the youngest child drives continual connecting and problem solving. Young children are programmed to find out. It is an instinct at the core of their being.

The Early Years Foundation Stage (DfES 2008) perceptively suggests that young children pose problems for others to solve. This is evident in 'encourage children to make up their own story problems for other children to solve' or 'encourage children to extend problems', or again 'suppose there were three people to share the bricks between instead of two' ('Effective practice', DfES 2008: 69). This sophisticated level of problem work should be advocated for all ages.

Problem posing is considered in Chapter 9. Problems use patterns whether they are being solved or posed.

Early Years Foundation Stage and Primary Framework for mathematics curriculum guidance extracts for problem solving

Early Years Foundation Stage

'use developing mathematical ideas and methods to solve practical problems' (DfES 2008: 76)

'encourage children to make up their own story problems for other children to solve' (DfES 2008: 71)

'encourage children to extend problems; for example "suppose there were three people to share the bricks between instead of two"' (DfES 2008: 71)

'encourage estimation, for example, estimate how many sandwiches to make for the picnic' (DfES 2008: 67)

'estimate how many objects they can see and check by counting them' (DfES 2008: 68)

'categorise objects according to their properties' (DfES 2008: 69)

'use own methods to work through a problem' (DfES 2008: 70)

Year one Primary Framework Numeracy (DfES 2006: 72)

'describe ways of solving puzzles and problems, explaining choices and decisions orally or using pictures'

'solve practical problems that involve combining groups of 2, 5 or 10, or sharing into equal groups'

'estimate a number of objects that can be checked by counting'

Year two Primary Framework Numeracy (DfES 2006: 74)

'present solutions to puzzles and problems in an organized way; explain decisions, methods and results in pictorial, spoken or written form, using mathematical language and number sentences'

'identify and record the information or calculation needed to solve a puzzle or problem'

'carry out the steps or calculations and check the solution in the context of the problem'

'estimate a number of objects'

'use knowledge of number facts and operations to estimate and check answers to calculations'

Year three Primary Framework Numeracy (DfES 2006: 76)

'describe and explain methods, choices and solutions to puzzles and problems, orally and in writing, using pictures and diagrams'

'use knowledge of number operations and corresponding inverses, including doubling and halving, to estimate and check calculations'

Estimating and checking is encouraged for all children from birth to eight. The context of the problem can determine the appropriateness of the answer. The curriculum guidance places emphasis on applying these good habits to calculations. The Scottish Curriculum for Excellence sets an outcome for 'estimation and rounding' as 'I can share ideas with others to develop ways of estimating the answer to a calculation or problem, work out the actual answer, then check my solution by comparing it with the estimate.' Very small children can count, then check in parallel with an adult.

Orna aged two and a half, counting six milk bottles scuttled through the number names incorrectly ending with seven. The checking of the count slowed this down and encouraged her to try again. Sometimes providing the number in advance is helpful as there is the expectation that there will be six at the end. This skill of checking is discussed in more detail in the context of problem solving in Chapter 9. This habit crosses all areas of the mathematical curriculum and should become a life skill.

Conclusion

Pattern unites progression across all ages and stages of mathematics. Early pattern impresses upon all learning. Pattern is a thread, weaving in and out, over and under, straddling all of mathematics. Imagine mathematics as a patchwork quilt, with pattern on every square. We considered number, calculations, and problem solving but other areas such as 'shape space and measures', and 'handling data' are richly rooted in pattern.

All children at any stage of learning need practical, imaginative, creative teaching. The student teaching odd and even numbers illustrates this point. Teaching in a kinesthetic way allows for multi-sensory learning which travels across language divides. Mathematics can also be learnt with few words as the children in the 'odd and even' observation reveal, working through odd and even numbers to 10 using supporting apparatus.

Educators need to scaffold their teaching, starting at the core, working out towards the edge of the idea. There is a need to thread teaching carefully through the eye of young mathematical minds without allowing assumptions to weaken structure.

The children of Great Britain experience a different curriculum depending on where they are born. It is reassuring to note that, 'the overriding issues in the teaching and learning of arithmetic transcend national boundaries' (Yackel 2001: 31) which we must conclude is true too of national borders.

Early Years Foundation Stage Mathematics

The most beautiful experience we can have is the mysterious.

Albert Einstein (1954: 11)

The aims of this chapter are to look at:

- Early years practice as a craft
- Mathematical opportunities within early years curriculum
- Environment-led mathematical learning

Introduction

This chapter will promote early years practice as a creative craft, and the practitioner as a craftsman. The curriculum is a given, but what and how it is delivered is in our gift. Planned learning will be put in the context of projects which extend and develop over time. The practitioner's role involves modelling play; posing questions which achieve guided discovery.

We will emphasize teaching numerosity, subitizing, sorting and classifying, analysing, measuring, experiencing changes, estimating, shape and early topology; even 'tidying up' holds rich learning opportunities for children. The best way to teach mathematics is to think in a connectionist way (Askew et al 1997) and we will consider how mathematics connects to other curriculum areas, such as science.

Quality, well-resourced environments, indoors and outdoors, allow children and adults spontaneous learning and teaching opportunities. The manipulatives for mathematics include concrete, abstract and semi-abstract materials which contribute to children's experiences.

The craft of early years practice

We are always at the beginning. We never reach the end when working with small children. Craftsmanship is based on the 'desire to do a job well and for it's own sake' (Sennet 2008: 9). It is worth standing back and identifying the craft elements of early years teaching. The practice part of our craft warrants analysis in terms of our own experience, others' experience and research into the field. Through analysis we gain a heightened perception of our own practice and develop a better understanding of what we are about (Kiely 2009). Part of our craft is to monitor the quality of our work, ourselves; seeking to improve; setting new goals to achieve.

The way we interact with children, other professionals, parents and people of other nationalities demands skill; these interactions require struggle and perseverance. The skills of questioning, dissolving misconceptions, sensing children's self-esteem, adjusting interventions, are subtle.

Craftsmanship reflects the quality of what we do over time. The craft of teaching can be considered as cognitive activity, curriculum and policy creation, classroom orchestration, sociocultural interaction and as learning awareness (Kiely 2009). It is complex and requires practice. Sennet (2008) comments that people can and do improve in craftwork.

Planning progressive learning projects

Hangers and chains

The initial starting point uses coloured links of two different colours to make chains for the number 5. Children are encouraged to make as many combinations as possible and compare to check lengths.

A later session involves hanging the chains on wire hangers so the colour patterns are evident. The same activity is applied to other numbers 6, 7, 8.

> *A later session again involves number cards attached below the chains showing number bonds, that is, 3,2 for 5. The number cards are arranged to show increasing and decreasing relationships (0,5) (1,4) (2,3) (3,2) (4,1) (5,0) (0,5) (1,4) (2,3) (3,2) (4,1) (5,0).*
>
> *When children can verbalize the patterns and relationships involved, the chains are used vertically to represent 3 + 2 = 5, introducing the '+' and '=' signs.*
>
> *(Taken from Copley 2000)*

Copley (2000) describes children learning number bonds using coloured chains and hangers which are revisited and added to over months, allowing ideas and knowledge to develop over time; 'thoughtful teacher planning creates this development sequence and makes possible in-depth learning.' The context on which to hang the learning is constant, then revisited, with later learning layered on top and left to settle before more is drawn in.

In Reggio Emilia 'practitioners themselves work through a topic or focus prior to engaging the children in it, to ensure that they can predict the ways children might choose to experience the curriculum' (Moyles 2008: 37). Papatheodora (2006) makes the observations following a visit to Reggio Emilia that adults 'carefully plan and explore, in advance, the possible directions that proposed projects may take and the resources required', adding that this 'allows them to identify the best ways of facilitating children's exploration and investigations and it removes the potential danger and pitfalls of direct instruction.'

As Papatheodora notes 'by going through the process of careful planning, the adults know well what they expect the children to achieve; the children have to find this out for themselves' with the adult ready to intervene (2006).

Planning with resources

The same approach can be taken with resources. We can handle the resource, discuss the possibilities in advance rather than surmise. Why not bring resources into planning meetings and explore possibilities so the resource can be matched to curriculum learning? Move from the resource, collecting curriculum ideas as you go; a form of adult spider thinking. By starting from the inside and working out, potential learning is in our mind. On a small scale this applies to resources such as bricks and on a large scale to projects such as making hot air balloons.

> *Identify a simple resource*
>
> *Allow adults time to play and think of mathematical possibilities*
>
> *Connect the resource to intended learning, testing it for this purpose*

Crafting mathematics means taking themes and sensing when to add complexity to extend children's thinking. There is a real need for this, as 'spontaneous free play, while potentially rich in mathematics, is not sufficient to provide mathematical experiences for young children' (Anthony and Walshaw 2007; Gifford 2005); practitioners must take a proactive role.

Anthony and Walshaw state that 'the mathematical tasks with which learners engage determine not only what substance they learn, but how they come to think about, develop, use, and make sense of mathematics' (Anthony and Walshaw 2007); thus the tasks we create are the main providers of mathematical learning. It is the adult's knowledge and competency which drives the task; the underlying thinking makes the difference. The 'task' includes the resources available to learners.

Model

Adults working with babies and small children need to participate in dialogue and play. Moyles suggests that 'adults can learn much about children by engaging in a mutually respectful dialogue, rather than in asking endless questions' (2008: 36). Work with babies and young children requires that we describe what is happening, what we are doing, what could happen next. A 'running commentary' is to be maintained, a point explored in more depth in Chapter 6.

A speech therapist involved in training settings commented that practitioners need to talk more to young children. For some, this means overcoming a certain self-consciousness. Talking in monologue is more natural to children who are uninhibited; we need to go back to this. Talking in a descriptive way, articulating thoughts, takes practice; Moyles (2008) refers to it as 'self-talk'. The habit of describing what is going on, labelling actions and reactions, is essential to establishing the pattern of language. Language is important in expressing mathematical thinking. Language itself is mathematical; there are patterns and rhythms to words.

Students can find themselves unsure of how to work with babies. If they have not observed qualified staff engaging in 'self-talk' it is more difficult for them to do so. It is an essential skill to help children benefit from those around them.

> *Strategies for 'self-talk'*
>
> *Use precise descriptive words for what you see or hear in the immediate surrounds*
>
> *Describe what the child/adult is doing*
>
> *Repeat key words*

'Self-talk' includes songs, rhymes, poems, number names and descriptive observations of what is fixed or moving in the very young child's surrounds.

Questions to guide discovery

It is the interaction between adult and child that determines children's performance (Siraj-Blatchford and Sylva 2004) and research indicates that optimum learning takes place in settings where adult–child interactions involve sustained, shared thinking. How is this achieved? Gifford (2005) defines sustained shared thinking as two people focused on trying to understand each other. It requires energy and continual thinking by practitioners.

The aim of questioning is not to find out what children know, but how children think. Children will tell us readily, for example, what colours they know. Reading a book Orna aged two years seven months points and says the words 'green, red, blue and yellow' asking 'what's that?' pointing to the colour pink.

A skilful adult questions in a way which guides a child's discovery; the adult knows what is there to be explored. For the youngest child, adults can ask and respond themselves: 'What is going to happen if we take the lid off? Let's see what we will find inside. I see a ….'. For older children or those who have built up sufficient expressive vocabulary, questions such as, 'I wonder what?' can be presented to extend thinking. An effective approach in parallel play or shared play with construction materials is to ask: 'What do I need to do to make mine just like yours?'

The following questions and statements offer guidance on sustaining adult–child interactions:

> Scaffolding sustained shared mathematical thinking
>
> **Clarifying:** 'This is number 5. Can you find a number 5?'
>
> **Elaborating:** 'That is a good choice. It goes after 4 and before 6.'
>
> **Recognizing:** 'I can see how you have put each number in the correct order.'

Appreciating: 'What a great job you have done. We can see all the numbers from 1 to 10.'

Confirming: 'That is a good idea.'

Encouraging reflection by asking checking questions: 'Do we need more?'

Pretending not to know the answer: 'I'm not sure. Perhaps you will show me.'

Creating relevance by making links with the child's current knowledge: 'Press number two (calculator). You are two years old.'

Modelling curiosity: 'I need to find out how a spider starts a web. I will get a book.'

Inviting imaginative involvement: 'It looks like a silver snake.'

Inviting participation by offering choice: 'Where will I put this one?'

Inviting participation by offering challenge: 'Lets check how many blue sponges you used in the sponge train.'

(Adapted from Macmillan, 2002 cited in Anthony and Walshaw 2007)

Assessment

Assessing our own practice, the children's learning and our provision, informs planning and advances the wheels of practice.

Assessment of our practice

Assessment of our own craft is sustained by internal reflection. The habit of self-assessing in this way is developed initially by keeping reflective journals as part of training. This can be carried on by keeping a 'Day Book'; as described in Chapter 10.

External assessment is readily proffered by managers, Ofsted teams and other scrutinizing bodies who determine 'satisfactory', 'good', 'outstanding' or futuristically 'perfect' practice (Coffield and Edward 2008). The criteria used are interpreted by individuals, which brings an inevitable range of variables, but how can we sustain 'outstanding' or 'excellent' and what could 'perfect practice' mean?

A useful approach is to video yourself for dispassionate self-assessment. This method need not be shared and equips you with real insight into words you choose, questions you ask, the way you really are in practice. Transcribing some of it gives focus on particular aspects, offering specific aims on which to improve. What a powerful way to take ownership of your own professional development!

Assessing children

'The eye moves faster than the hand', Ben a boy of six tells me as he sketches a sea horse. So while observing and writing everything down, are we missing what is happening? Peter Elfer (2006) describes observations where the practitioner watches and remembers. We can and should be looking and absorbing the moment in the moment, as well as at other times recording accurately as best we can. There is room for both styles of observation in early years work.

Edgington (2009) introduced a lecture by alluding to confusion over whether 80 per cent or 50 per cent of evidence for the early years profile is sourced from child-initiated activity, leaving 20 per cent or 50 per cent evidenced from adult-led work. Featherstone and Featherstone describe 'confusion about the balance between child-initiated and adult directed activities', concluding that 50:50 is desirable (2008: 2). Lindon (2008) states how the Effective Provision of Pre-school Education (EPPE) research best practice had practitioners involved in half of the child-initiated work.

Whether it is 50 per cent or 80 per cent is neither here nor there, as 'truly child-initiated experiences or activities have to be genuinely chosen and organized by children' (Lindon 2008: 11), their choice being determined by what is there to choose from. The practicality of measuring percentages is untenable.

In England, learning diaries record rich clues about what children do on particular dates, providing evidence for the profile document which is completed at the end of the Foundation Stage. An inordinate amount of professional time can be devoted to these recordings and the question is, could some of this time be redirected to playing and thinking in a 'sustained shared way' with children? Evidence is necessary to record the learning experience, but its purpose is lost when it enters the frantic cutting and pasting of an assessment factory.

The benefit of planning in a project way is that children's knowledge can be recorded early and again later in the project, which is a measure of their learning. This offers the advantage of assessing how children progress along an avenue of learning over time.

Assessment can be made less onerous by using video recordings and digital photographs which lend themselves to sharing with parents, other professionals and Local Education Authority assessment moderators.

Assessing the environment

The myriad of early years care options (Craft 2002) along with the lack of real parental choice can result in a two-and-a-half-year-old child ending up in a private nursery for part of the week and a centre of excellence for the rest with absolutely polarized provision. The child tells the staff at the private setting about 'the yellow bikes at the other nursery', already aware of stark differences of choice on offer.

Moyles (2008) discusses resourcing the environment and states this is a key factor in ensuring children initiate their own activities. Edgington (2009) describes the need for a 'continuous' or as Moyles (2008) describes, a 'predictable arrangement of resources', for children to make choices or initiate play. The quality, presentation and accessibility of provision all determine the potential for child-initiated activities and this is variable from setting to setting.

The indoor and outdoor environments need to be reviewed in order that the learning opportunities are refreshed (Cole 2008). Over time new ideas lead to developing the way the environment is organized. Spaces are changed, new spaces created. Every setting has limitations, some of which are beyond change; the challenge is working around these. Assessment of permanent provision should consider visibility, variability and whether alternatives could be introduced.

Presentation of provision

Edgington (2009) considers presentation of provision. Rather than having equipment in boxes under the water tray for example, what if this were arranged on a shelf so it was all visible? Sometimes less is more.

One suggestion is to visit different settings and collect ideas about how these environments are arranged. Another idea is to use external environments which allow mathematical learning such as a forest, the zoo, museums, art galleries, train stations, beaches, all of which offer rich learning beyond the setting.

The early years curriculum and mathematics

Mathematical thinking opportunities already exist in the regular practice of early years. We will now focus on some key ideas which can be developed through this practice.

Numerosity or number sense

You really have to know numbers; what five means, regardless of how the fives are arranged, in order to function well in mathematics. Children need to build a clear pattern of what numbers mean and look like.

Numerosity is also about knowing that five dots are more than three dots. This number sense is established over time through practical work. Numerosity is beyond knowing number names or counting; it is sensing amounts and the relationship of one amount to another; five is five, five is more than three and less than seven. Activities such as sorting objects into different number quantities help establish a sense of number.

Subitizing or seeing immediately

Subitizing is recognizing numbers of things without counting (Gifford 2004). Clausen-May (2009) believes subitizing gets less attention than is required. Pound comments that 'although present in babies it is rarely acknowledged in early years settings and schools' (2008: 10). The automatic recognition of what an amount represents is a skill which should be encouraged in the early years.

We can help young children to subitize through seeing the number represented by dot dice, domino patterns, paired arrangements, or fingers, for example, subitizing differs from number recognition where the numeral gives the quantity name; it is seeing the quantity without needing the counting sequence. It is easier to subitize lower numbers.

Very young children can subitize. At the end of her lecture I asked Dr Tandi Clausen-May (2009), how she would do this in early years. She suggested asking children 'how many fingers am I showing?' (she held up five). 'Now, you hold up fingers and ask me, how many fingers?' (I held up four). Repeating such exchanges without the use of sequence helps children to subitize.

Orna aged two years seven months responded to this finger game, subitizing to three, confirming that 'two year olds can recognize up to three objects without counting' (Gifford 2005), but showing four fingers did not prompt the correct response. Repeating this game resulted in Orna subitizing to five a couple of months later. To extend thinking, gaps between fingers can be used, or two hands (still with low numbers) to change the spatial arrangement. This quickly becomes a game of my turn, your turn and the child deciding the number is empowering.

Dice games, dominoes, objects such as buttons can all be used to emphasize seeing numbers and developing number sense. With larger numbers children can start to see number pattern within number pattern, that is, 8 is made up of a 4-dot and 4-dot pattern, 'if children can visualize large numbers as made up of smaller numbers, and see six as two threes, they are developing a "part-whole" understanding of numbers, which can help them to learn number facts in a visual way' (Gifford 2005: 85). Thinking of numbers as made up of other numbers, that is, 5 is made of 2 and 3, can be seen in patterns and given greater focus in early years practice.

Patterns can be presented differently, that is, paired patterns, circular patterns, linear patterns can each represent 5. This work can be adapted to any number. The older child can subitize using multiple representations, thinking of their own ways of arranging loose items, expressing this in drawings (see Figure 5.1). Gifford states that 'subitizing in a variety of modes therefore has great potential to help children learn cardinal concepts and number facts, building on non-verbal strengths' (2005: 87).

Skittles and subitizing

A group of three and four year olds were given a set of six skittles and four balls. They were shown how to arrange the skittles with three at the back, two in the next row and one to complete the triangle.

When left to play, they set up small chairs to sit on while they waited their turn. The skittles were arranged in a triangle each time. Without counting the children could see how many were standing even though when the ball knocked some down, the pattern was left to chance. They were seeing the quantity six as well as the number remaining each time the ball removes skittles.

Figure 5.1 Different pattern representations for the number 6.

Figure 5.2 Playgroup child playing skittles.

Subitizing with a Slavonic abacus

A Slavonic abacus with 10s made of five red and five yellow beads arranged horizontally is a tool for more advanced subitizing. We can see the numbers through the pattern of light and dark beads, 10 is five dark with five light, 15 will be five dark, five light, five dark. The Association of Teachers of Mathematics (2009) gives clear explanations as to how the Slavonic abacus can be used to subitize and applies this to multiplication (see www.atm.org.uk/resources/slavonicabacus.html).

This abacus offers a visual representation of beads to 100 with colour sets of five making it easier to see this unit of count (see Figure 6.2 in Chapter 6).

The counting trap

We can develop these important skills of numerosity and subitizing to move children out of what Emmerson (2009) calls the 'counting trap'.

When playing a game with two dice, three of a group of four children aged six, needed to count each dot on each dice to find the number. The child who could subitize calculated the combined dice values with ease. Subitizing frees children from starting at the beginning, counting each dot. Pound (2008) notes how children who can subitize at an early stage, stop doing so, possibly as it is not actively encouraged. A greater emphasis needs to be placed on this aspect of early mathematics.

Sort, classify and analyze data

Reasoning is promoted through sorting and classifying (Copley 2000). Sorting means to arrange in sets according to size or quality or other standard; classifying means to arrange in classes (*Oxford English Dictionary*). Either skill can be made as simple or as complex as we wish and each is rich in mathematical thinking. The following activity was noted at a playgroup.

Sue Last's sorting activity with playgroup children

The children are given circular boxes with nesting bases. The lids are numbered zero to ten. There are objects including shells, pebble stones, shiny stones, rocking horses, buttons and a lizard.

The children start to separate and group the objects. The items are spread out and children pass objects to the individual who seems to be collecting that one. This happens in a natural way.

They start putting their collections into numbered boxes. Sue asks, 'how many have you got?' and Daisy assumes the role of matching numbered lids when children say the number they have.

Edward finds it difficult to count the amount of shiny stones. His box says 8 and he hurries to put them in. Sue intervenes suggesting that it is easier to count if they are all lined up. She encourages Edward to touch each stone as they all say the number name. The children count 10 shiny stones. Daisy solves the matter of finding the correct box for Edward's collection.

Daisy then holds up the smallest box saying, 'Zero, that means none'. She puts the lizard in the box labelled 'one'.

A small heavy collection is tipped out from a basket. Sue advises that they are not dropped. The children each reach and take some, excited by the weight and gold colour of the door handles. This collection is now across each of the six children, but not evenly.

Sue asks how many door handles she has in her collection. Sofia has four, Daisy has one, Rosa one, Hector three and Eddie one. After a lovely digression, 'that was some rainstorm last night', shaking of boxes to make storm noises, the children line up the door handles to be counted. Sue has 10 door handles in her collection which made us laugh as we thought it now must be difficult to close and open doors in her house!

In this sorting activity children are working with number names, numeral recognition, counting accurately, quantities, weight, size, problem solving, mathematical language and collaboratively using each other's knowledge, all of which feature in the Early Years Foundation Stage (DfES 2008) curriculum.

Sue intervened as she modelled how best to count Edward's shiny stones. This highlights to the children the idea that counting collections is not easy and the benefit of organizing objects first. Children are made aware of this strategy as it is explicitly demonstrated, confirming the view held by Copley that, 'one to one correspondence for the counting sequence is a skill that must be modeled and often directly taught' (2000: 56).

There was also a sense of seeing what happens rather than setting an agenda, allowing children's ideas to take shape. Sue Last is aware of where the activity can go, introducing more materials, such as the door handles, when the time is right.

Adult connecting to and extending opportunistic learning

Adult is conscious of the mathematical possibilities an object can lead to

The stimulating object is left out available

Child is allowed time to explore, use imagination, think mathematically

Adult senses what thinking is happening by stepping back and observing

Adult connects child's thinking to other possibilities

Figure 5.3 Playgroup children sorting and classifying.

This example of an open sorting activity is rich in mathematics. The activity can be used to place emphasis on problem solving or reasoning or numeracy to varying degrees (DfES 2008).

Stages children progress through with sorting and classifying

Copley (2000) explains the stages children go through in sorting and classifying.

1. A child separates objects from a collection which share a common attribute. They do not necessarily apply the rule consistently.
2. There is a consistency in sorting using one attribute. They classify things that have a certain attribute and things that do not. They may need support with 'has' and 'has not'.
3. The child sorts in more than one way. They may not be able to relate to another way which they have not thought of.
4. The child states the rule even when the grouping is done by someone else. They verbalize a rule, deciding on whether a new object is included or not.

The very young child can sort two coloured bricks into two piles. The older child can start using one feature, yellow or red bricks, then move on to two features, small yellow or large yellow bricks, then realize why other bricks are not included in the set.

Questions to extend thinking:

'How could we sort these another way?'

'Which pile will this object go into?'

'Why does this not belong in the set?'

Data analysis

Sorting and classifying relates closely to data analysis (Copley 2000). The outcome of sorting can be represented in a visual way, which is the analysis. A sorting activity with a question as a starting point leads to analysis. We can develop sorting to organizing and representing information. Data can be presented using the objects themselves, lined vertically or horizontally.

Copley (2000) comments that using concrete objects is an essential first step in representing data. When sorting stems from responses to likes or dislikes, pictures can be used to show individual choice. The question determines the complexity of the resulting data, for example, 'Is ice cream your favourite pudding?' demands yes or no, whereas 'what is your favourite pudding?' generates a wider range of responses to classify. The data allow us to talk about 'more' or 'which group has the most'.

When making bar charts small children realize that there must be consistency with unit size, 'one must use units of equal size to allow for accurate comparison' (Copley 2000: 157). Twenty with small-sized units could look smaller than 10 with large units. Possible misrepresentation is important for children to understand. Post-it notes are useful as they are of uniform size.

Asking children to explain the representation is a powerful way of crystallizing their learning; it moves their thinking towards allowing others to interpret what they mean. It is important to refer back to the initial reason behind the data. What was it we sorted or asked about?

Asking children to look at sets to determine sorting criteria, develops classifying skills. An object not yet classified can be presented with the question 'where should this go?'

This connects to science, for example, classifying minibeasts according to how many legs or spots they have. Sorting, classifying and analysing also makes children check, a valuable skill for problem solving.

Tidying up time

The daily act of tidying up is really resorting and reclassifying. It is worth allowing time for this as it involves so much mathematics.

Tidying up:

Sue Last's sorting activity

With minimal intervention playgroup children were set the task to tidy up the collection.

'Can you remember what I had in the basket?' Sue asks.

'Door handles', one child says.

'Lets put the white plates in a pile'.

'Boxes need to go inside each other, starting with the biggest'.

Stacking of boxes inside each other proved to be a challenge. They worked together to change the order of boxes when one would not fit, undoing the order to add in a box.

'Shells get sorted into the tub, but not the flat ones'.

'Pebbles go in the tub but not the glass ones'.

Finally, 'if its not a stone, pebble or door handle, it goes in here', says Sue holding a bag open.

Tidying up, resorting, reclassifying develops thinking, memory and understanding of language. The final instruction, is complex for a young child; the word 'not' is classification by elimination from other sets, that is, rocking horses, buttons, or lizards should go into the bag because they are not stones, pebbles or door handles.

It is valuable to observe children tidying up, to see the application of skills or note those who avoid the task. It is interesting to see the mathematical processes which will vary as does provision from setting to setting. Edgington (2009) defines a well-organized environment on the basis of the question:

'How well could a stranger to the setting tidy up?'

Questions to ask ourselves:

Could tidying up time be used more as a mathematical opportunity?

Could children be directed to tidying up different areas so the experience varies?

Could older children model the skills they use to younger children?

The EYFS Curriculum Guidance advises that we 'use "tidy up time" to promote logic and reasoning, about where things are kept' (DfES 2008: 69).

'Tidy up time' and tessellation

Tidying up bricks or blocks requires tessellation. Everything needs to fit neatly into the box or onto a shelf. Tessellating means placing things so there are no gaps, resembling mosaic tiling. Shelving systems for wooden blocks works well as each piece needs to tessellate into an allocated space.

Numicon or Cuisenaire rods are examples of structural apparatus offering tessellation. Numicon plates can fill the peg board (a problem-solving activity using number bonds); replacing the plates in the box results in tessellation. There are many other tessellation examples which can be used to assess and develop children's skills. The EYFS curriculum guidance advises that we 'use "tidy up time" to promote logic and reasoning about where things are kept' (DfES 2008: 69).

If we observe a child struggling with tidying up, we can demonstrate strategies which address the problem and observe the child achieving them; we have evidence of reasoning and problem solving resulting from intervention. We can seek out a different area of the setting requiring these skills, extending the child's thinking in a schematic way.

Measuring

Ben, a reception class boy aged 4 asked each day, 'Miss McGrath, can I measure?'.
Learning to measure encompasses length, area, volume, weight and time. Children start by realizing that objects have measurable properties (Copley 2000). They then compare measurements. They then realize there is a choice of methods to measure. A shoe could be used to measure the length of a room or a Unifix cube to determine the height of a runner bean. Children progress to using standard units of measurement such as meter rules.

Measuring requires language to express 'how long?' then 'shorter' or 'longer'. Fairy tales such as 'Goldilocks and the Three Bears' bring language such as small, medium, large to children's imagination. Many fairy tales contain mathematics, but we must train our minds to see it.

Connecting measurement to other areas of mathematics

Wrapping

Wrapping a package connects measuring to geometry and number. The piece of paper needs to be estimated against the surface area of the object to be wrapped. Then there is cutting of a required number of strips of tape, securing the paper as it is folded around the shape. Children as young as two enjoy wrapping, engaging with the complexity it brings. The early years environment needs to be a workshop with well-thought-through provision; sticking tapes of varying strengths, glue, paper, ribbon, string, boxes. There is a lovely Swedish story *Boo and Baa in a Party Mood* by Olof and Lena Landström, where two sheep inadvertently tape a stool to the present they wrap. They decide on a box and string to solve the wrapping problem.

Comparing

Start by comparing two objects before introducing more and sorting several by comparison. These can be ordered by the measurement criteria 'shortest' or 'longest'. Establishing which of two children has more can be achieved by lining one child's objects up against another's, using one to one correspondence as a comparison strategy.

Square tiles or carpet pieces can be used to compare area. Comparing applies to each aspect of measurement and 'comparison is the core activity and concept that starts children on the path to fully developed understanding and use of measurement' (Copley 2000).

Conservation and comparison

Conservation introduced in Chapter 3, relates to number, volume and mass and offers interesting adult-led activities which can be left for children to explore. Modelling requires clear questioning and, for the very young, comparing two representations. More sophisticated conservation is to see the first amount change and remember what it looked like originally. In this case, a set of objects is rearranged, spread out and the child compares this arrangement mentally to the previous closely ordered arrangement.

Blue balloons melting and other changes

Observing change is both mathematical and scientific. Unravelling what creates change integrates science and mathematics. In early years, the rate of change in children themselves is magical. Weight, height, capacity to remember, vocabulary grow exponentially. Children notice change around them, weather, seasons, routines. They read about caterpillars overeating, building cocoons and changing into butterflies (Carle 1970). Their world is fired with changes; they comment excitedly that the 'pavement is wet not dry'.

Cooking creates great change with mixing, heating, then cooling. Making jelly demonstrates change with liquid-made solid from moulds. A melting block of ice is a dramatic change which can be reversed. If we fill a balloon with water and blue food colouring, freeze it, then peel off the balloon, children are fascinated to observe it melt through the course of the day. This could be connected to *The Blue Balloon*, by Mick Inkpen.

Work with clay demonstrates change as it is shaped before being left to dry. The painting of a picture can bring unexpected change to a blank piece of paper. Spilling milk shows change as the liquid spreads out.

Estimation

Listening to estimates gives great insight into children's thinking.

> How long will the brick biscuits take to cook in the shoe box oven? Orna aged two years seven months, looks at her wrist, stating 'forty times, minutes'.

We can articulate estimations throughout the day, modelling this skill for children, checking if we are correct, close or way off. We can estimate across all areas of mathematics in early years. Wild estimates are valuable as they bring out children's fascination with large numbers. This opens horizons beyond curriculum-stipulated number ranges, establishing a sense of what lies beyond.

Shape, geometry and topology

> 'I am walking in a circle', Orna aged two years seven months walks around the kitchen.

There is a wonderful poem titled 'I am Running in a Circle' by Jack Prelutsky in *Poems for the Very Young* selected by Michael Rosen. It starts with the line 'I am running in a circle and my feet are getting sore', ending with a possible reference to experiences children have shopping and revolving doors.

This is an example of poetry cultivating language and concept of shape. Children need to experience shape language which intersects with everyday usage: 'side', 'corner', 'edge', 'face'. Children learn to apply different meanings, as words acquire multiple meanings.

Sorting shapes

Sorting and classifying shapes encourages recognition of properties, which is more important than remembering names (Merttens 1987). Children engaged with junk modelling handle three-dimensional shapes, deciding which boxes to use. In a natural way children describe shapes in relation to other experiences. The practitioner can prompt this with comments such as 'this shape looks like a ...'.

Spatial awareness

This skill comes from handling, building, experiencing construction components. Spatial sense contributes to three-dimensional thinking, seeing patterns, symmetries. Construction can be adult directed, left to child-initiated ideas, or ideally both. Children benefit from seeing adults model building, particularly in a specified context, that is, build a train track with eight pieces or a bridge using only so many Lego pieces.

Train tracks and early topology

Figure 5.4 Topology sketch drawn by Ben aged five and a half years on a rainy day in Cornwall.

Topology is about relationships between shape and space. Children have some under-standing of topology without being taught it. Train tracks are arrangements of shape and space to make circuits. A train track can be closed as circles, ovals or figures of eight, or open, as a stretch of track extending over an area. Very young children can experience closed and open spaces. Open spaces can be created with string on the floor where the loop is closed or open.

Children are highly motivated by trains; the youngest can make a train of sponges, moving to wooden trains with passengers, to designing configurations such as circles, ovals then figures of eight (see Chapter 9). Older children find further challenges in designing more complex configurations and representing these pictorially.

The benefit of work with train tracks is often missed. We can model how to piece together a circuit; we may need to learn this ourselves first. Train track work early on will develop spatial mathematical thinking (see Chapter 9).

Junctions of tracks and lines

A junction is where two or more track lines meet. Children can draw interesting line patterns. They can count the number of closed spaces and junctions; they can colour these (Figure 5.5, Merttens 1987). The mathematical challenge described by Merttens (1987) and Boaler (2009) centres on the fact that no pattern or design has been discovered which needs more than four colours so that no two adjacent spaces are the same colour. There is still the opportunity to make mathematical history if a pattern is created where adjacent spaces are of five different colours.

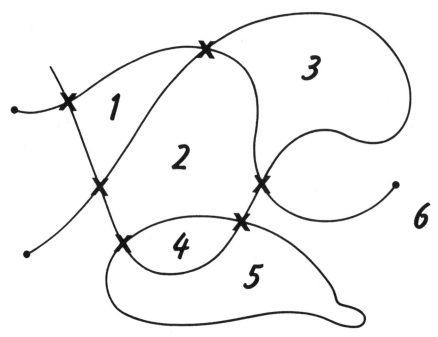

Figure 5.5 Squiggly patterns with closed spaces and junctions (Ruth Merttens 1987). Originally printed in Merttens, R. (1987) *Teaching Primary Mathematics*.

Lines of symmetry

A line of symmetry divides a shape into two parts which are mirror images of each other. Drawing half a picture and using a mirror to see the whole image helps to show this. Bridge making with construction materials employs symmetry. A mirror placed halfway along the bridge can be used to find the line of symmetry.

Shape pictures

The children can make their own shape pictures or play a game where they spin a dial with circles, triangles or squares, then roll a dice to determine how many of which shapes they can have and after so many goes, compose a picture.

To develop memory the adult can create a shape picture, the children look, the picture is covered, the children create the same picture, then check that their picture is the same (Copley 2000).

Shoe boxes

Shapes of two dimensions can be arranged imaginatively in shoe boxes to create underwater, space or city scenes. The boxes can then be double backed with velcro strips and attached to a display at child height.

The early years curriculum is full of scope for imaginative ideas which already hold mathematical experiences. Added to this is the greater emphasis on learning through play which allows the child to contribute fresh ideas, which often surprise us.

Mathematical provision in early years environments

We mentioned earlier the importance of how provision is presented in the environment. Visibility of materials available is influential in informing children's decisions. Variety of equipment allows for different lines of enquiry. Think how many different sieves there are; a different sieve a different experience. Watering cans with different nozzles develop different ways of thinking when taken outside to water the ground. The equipment needs to be accessible so that child-initiated ideas can be fulfilled without seeking adult assistance.

The outdoor environment offers a wealth of mathematical experiences, with even greater potential outdoors than inside. The outdoors also creates scope for games such as hopscotch, hide and seek, large-scale dominoes, snakes and ladders, skittles, hoops, quoits, bean bag throwing or tags and tails.

We have established important principles for the environment and will now consider more specific mathematical provision. Mathematics needs to be multi-sensory; manipulatives facilitate this.

The provision for mathematical materials can be broadly categorized as concrete or abstract. Concrete materials can be divided into two further groups of discrete and continuous. Abstract materials can be divided into semi-abstract or abstract.

We can therefore consider four broad categories for this provision: discrete, continuous, semi-abstract, and abstract. Our aim is to provide a balance across these categories.

Discrete materials include buttons, stones, compare bears or anything that represents a unit of count. These can be naturally occurring or commercially produced. Wooden bricks or blocks bring opportunities for building, tessellating, creating and solving problems.

Continuous materials include Cuisenaire rods, Numicon, or anything where the number represented is already combined to represent a ten, hundred or thousand. They lend themselves to learning place value, as discrete items can be exchanged for one block or continuous piece.

Semi-abstract materials include dice, dominoes, number lines, abacuses, bead bars, bead strings, where a count or amount can be abstracted from these representations. A 100 square also presents number in a semi-abstract way.

Abstract material would include an empty or partially empty number line. Research from the Netherlands extols the need for children to work with empty number lines (Rousham 1997).

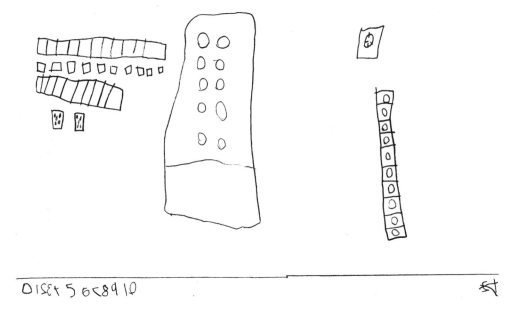

Figure 5.6 Child's drawing representing number with Dienes, Numicon, Unifix cubes, and a number line.

Provision has differing potential, which must be understood before using it for a specified purpose. We need to think which material best serves our intention for adult-led work and what to make available to children.

Arguably we need not become burdened with too many materials, as it is possible to teach the curriculum with what is available naturally. A twig can represent 10 twiglets or a number line can be sketched in sand. Stones or pebbles can be arranged in pairs, lines or dice patterns. We don't have to go far to see patterns in leaves, trees or clouds.

Stocking multiple mathematical materials reinforces a variety of experiences and engages children in mathematics simultaneously. This allows greater opportunity for one to one or small group work as children initiate their own play. Very young children can play with any of the manipulatives mentioned above. We do, however, need to be mindful of small pieces, so some will need to be adult directed.

Small children will make imaginative use of commercially produced items; Orna aged two laid out Numicon from one end of the room to the other calling it 'a silver snake'. Children can combine materials in ways we do not expect; one child placed buttons in the holes of the Numicon plates.

Imaginative collections of everyday objects, like the door handles which the playgroup children enjoyed, are themselves manipulatives which allow children essential experience and support the view that 'verbal explanations can be helpful to children, although teachers should never rely on language alone to convey maths concepts' (Copley 2000: 173). In fact mathematics can happen in silence as children play, internalizing their thinking.

Moyles advises that 'although child-initiated learning cannot be planned, it is vital that it is planned for' (2008: 47), which brings us to our responsibility to provide an instructive, predictable, flexible well-provided environment.

An environment-led curriculum

Out of a well-resourced, well-provided environment, falls the early years curriculum. Investing time in planning provision frees us from planning the curriculum. Establishing this connection removes the pressure of thinking of activity ideas when feeling least creative.

Conclusion

The early years educator constructs the curriculum. Children make their own choices and develop creative solutions and new connections (Cole 2008). Planning projects allows connections to other areas of the curriculum. Literacy and mathematics connect through patterns of stories, songs, poems or rhymes. Science and mathematics are inextricably linked.

Improved understanding of number and visualizing skills are central to early mathematics. Building numerosity is readily accessible through early years activities. Subitizing can be acquired using patterns to represent quantities. Heightened awareness of these features will alert us to possibilities in the provision we make.

Topology through train track work opens onto rich opportunity as children play with spatial skills. Tessellation through tidying up is a natural part of the routine, with mathematics happening intuitively.

Our job is to provide an environment in which all children can learn mathematics (Copley 2000). The curriculum can fall out of the environment rather than creating curriculum.

To develop a craft takes time, dedication and energy. Practitioners themselves can show inquisitive behaviour by asking, thinking aloud and speculating. In doing this they model the use of language and ways of thinking mathematically (Stevens 2008). While the manipulation of materials is essential, this alone does not create an active learning situation (Lafferty 2008). The adult, possessing knowledge and creative thinking combined with skilled questioning, is potentially the greatest resource available to the child.

Understanding number

To see a world in a grain of sand,
And a heaven in a wild flower:
Hold infinity in the palm of your hand,
And eternity in an hour.

'Auguries of Innocence', William Blake (1757–1827)

This chapter includes the following:

- Pattern and pre-algebraic concepts
- The complexity of number
- The connection between pattern, number and algebra

Introduction

This chapter will consider the importance of pattern in teaching and learning mathematics. Pre-algebraic concepts will be explored with suggestions as to how practitioners can provide them. Creativity in music, cooking, dance, nature and play provide opportunities to exploit pattern at home and in early years settings. Connections will be made between pattern, number and algebra.

> **Questions to reflect on:**
>
> What are pre-algebraic concepts?
>
> How does pattern relate to number?
>
> How does pattern relate to algebra?

In Chapter 4 we examined both the Early Years Foundation Stage (DfES 2008) and the Primary National Strategy (DfES 2006) for reference to pattern and algebra. We concluded that pattern is evident in both curricula. Pattern is a critical strand of mathematics and yet 'pattern is an aspect of the mathematics curriculum which is frequently underrepresented in the early years' (Pound 2008: 41).

Pre-algebraic concepts

Pattern is not easy to define; symmetry and repetition come to mind. Pattern tends to be the search for order and regularity. If we consider the youngest child, the newborn searches for clues. Babies start with recognizing the faces of adults and children they meet. They connect a voice to a person and a voice print is made. Very early on they identify voices and map out their immediate surroundings. Pictures, shadows and people become familiar. Children are driven to make sense of their immediate world. Mathematics helps them do this.

Let us consider what pre-algebraic concepts are and how practitioners can optimize opportunities for the youngest child. To experience, feel and sense pattern is the starting point for young children. Older children make pattern happen in play as a natural outcome of their early experience.

The pattern of the day is universal. The way every city wakes up is similar and yet different across the world. The first light, the first boat out to sea, the milk float delivering before the rush hour traffic, the intensity of workers walking and driving, this pattern repeats again later at the close of business. The routine of the day is both universal and individual; within the large pattern we create our own personal picture.

A group of Foundation Degree students looking at story books for mathematical opportunities chose *Oliver's Wood* by Sue Hendra which is about an owl waking up at night. The owl and his animal friends play all night and when the daylight comes, sleep. One day Oliver decides to stay up and see a very different world. Oliver feels lonely as he doesn't fit in. He tells the nocturnal animals that he has seen the sun, but somehow this unusual sighting isn't enough. He is happier to slip back into his familiar pattern of night and day. A simple story, marking out the sequence night, day and night to the child.

The pattern of the week often brings different daily routines for Saturday and Sunday. A book titled *Today is Monday* by Eric Carle associates a different animal, a different food with each day of the week. The sequence builds up, day by day and children exercise short-term working memory skills, moving forward with days of the week and the food item. The book is based on the words below. In the book each new day recalls the preceding days and the associated food.

Today is Monday
Today is Monday
Monday string beans
All you hungry children
Come and eat it up.

Today is Tuesday
Today is Tuesday
Tuesday spaghetti,
All you hungry children
Come and eat it up.

Today is Wednesday
Today is Wednesday
Wednesday soup
All you hungry children
Come and eat it up.

Today is Thursday
Today is Thursday
Thursday, roast beef
All you hungry children
Come and eat it up.

Today is Friday
Today is Friday
Friday, fresh fish
All you hungry children
Come and eat it up.

Today is Saturday
Today is Saturday
Saturday, Chicken
All you hungry children
Come and eat it up.

Today is Sunday
Today is Sunday
Sunday, ice cream
All you hungry children
Come and eat it up.

Or Sunday can list all the preceding days and associated foods:

Today is Sunday, today is Sunday
Sunday, ice cream
Saturday, chicken
Friday, fresh fish
Thursday, roast beef

Wednesday, soup
Tuesday, spaghetti
Monday, string beans
All you hungry children
Come and eat it up.

The pattern of the year is marked with birthdays, bonuses, celebrations, ceremonies, holidays, monsoons and so on. There is a certain rhythm to the day, week and year which we step in and out of. There is a comfort in this regularity.

Life itself is a pattern. Pattern is evident in all we do. We are born, live and die. Realizing the extent to which pattern is part of our lives illuminates much of mathematics. Pattern is so simple and so intricate it is difficult to define. Life is in this detail. The adult expressing this to the small child helps piece together the meaning of their world. The uninhibited expression of that which is automatic or obvious presents difficulties to some adults but is of immense value to the child. Describing what is happening is a habit worth forming. Descriptive monologue or commentary helps define pattern.

Talking to babies and copying a baby's first sounds establishes a pattern of communication. When working with babies, adults need to employ this external monologue. As adults we feel the need for a dialogue but it is the ability to immerse oneself in the commentary that babies need. This is a powerful way of laying down language exchange. The repetition of number songs helps children know the pattern and order of number names. Children filter out the words they hear frequently and store them in a vocabulary bank.

Creativity

When we hear and appreciate a piece of music we are experiencing an arrangement of sounds. When we take a baby in our arms and move around to music we feel the rhythm together. When we step into the rhythm and punctuate the sounds with steps we translate the music into dance. Both of us experience the pattern and rhythm of the piece. We do not have to be musical to interpret the music in our own way.

As children walk they experience and create a pattern of movement. When they run this pattern increases in speed with arms, legs and knees coordinated to move faster. As an audience at a concert we clap. Consider the sense of pattern created by clapping and how sometimes there is a sense of clapping with hands, heart and soul. Clapping can focus all the emotions of the human spirit. The beat of a clap can be long, slow, deliberate or short, rapid and congratulatory. Encouraging children to clap or stamp to a beat in a piece of music engages them in pattern making.

Reading stories is a great opportunity to teach sequence. A similar sequence supports most stories: beginning, middle and end. The pages turn in a certain numerical order. Children as young as two realize it is 'the end' as the last page is turned. For older children the sequence can be expressed as a story or rhyme mountain.

The book *PEEPO!* by Janet and Allan Ahlberg is old fashioned, not necessarily representing current everyday life, yet there is a magical rhythm to the words which captures the imagination of babies and adults. The book can be read over and over again as each time there is something new to notice in the words and illustrations.

Here's a little baby
One, two, three
Stands in his cot
What does he see?

Here's a little baby
One, two, three
Sits in his high chair
What does he see?

Here's a little baby
One, two, three
Sits in his pushchair
What does he see?

The story continues with words describing the baby sitting on the grass, his sister's lap, in the bath, and then on his way to bed. The routine of the day is expressed through lovely rhythmic words.

The book expresses the routine of a day through the eyes of a baby. The rhythm of the language carries us along. An alternative approach is to sing the words. This is a different experience to having words read. The adult need not worry about what tune to use, it's a question of going with the first one that comes into your mind; babies respond particularly well to this. The pattern of words expressed through song offers a different experience for the child.

As part of the day small routines are repeated, for example making a cup of tea. There is opportunity to describe each step of this process; we go through the following sequence:

Making a cup of tea.

Put water in kettle. Turn kettle on. Wait for kettle to boil. Take mug from cupboard. Take tea bag from box. Place tea bag in mug. Add milk (if you like milk in first). Pour hot water into mug. Squeeze tea bag with spoon. Remove tea bag. Put tea bag in bin.

There are 11 steps in this example. The sequence can be changed but there is a definite order to the process. Describing the steps is defining pattern on two levels: language and process.

Pattern is about recognizing similarities and differences. The provision of sorting and classifying activities as described in Chapter 5 helps children do this on a practical level. Children realize that things belong or do not belong to particular sets. One activity is to ask the child to identify the odd one out in a group or picture of objects. By identifying the odd one out, the child is defining a description of the set. By explaining why the chosen item is the odd one out, they verbalize the set criteria. Depending on the range of objects provided children may isolate the odd one out differently. The activity can be advanced by specifying categories and having items which meet different criteria. Say one set is for yellow objects and the other for wood, a yellow wooden brick will pose a challenge, intersecting both sets. This work can be extended to matching equivalent sets. This concept of equivalence is important for one to one correspondence, also calculations, which we will consider later.

The search for similarity and difference can be established through the medium of poetry. Poetry is interesting as it may or may not follow a regular pattern. There is scope to let children experience irregular pattern through poetry. With familiar songs and rhymes the adult can take a regular rhyme and distort it: 'Humpty Dumpty had a great **crash**'.

Young children take great pleasure in correcting mistakes and fixing the pattern. Inserting irregularities in this way reinforces the alliteration of rhyming words. It is experimenting with pattern of language. For children aged four and upwards, there is great opportunity to find and make regular and irregular pattern in poetry. Poetry gives children freedom to create their own pattern.

The Hill was Steep

The hill was steep,
So steep I could not climb it.
I tried and I tried
But I could not do it.
So I came down for a rest.
I think going down is best.

(Raj Tanday, age 8)

The Moon

The moon out
There.
The sun out
There.
The world out
There.
The whole galaxy out
There
and me stuck in my bedroom.

(Ki Ellwood-Friery, age 8)

Taken from *Poems for the Very Young* selected by Michael Rosen, illustrated by Bob Graham.

At home the child can experience pattern in cooking. In Chapter 3 we looked at the relevance of cooking to mathematics. Following on from this we can consider making fairy cakes and how sequence or pattern can be followed by a child as young as two years. In general terms the sequential steps of the process can be summarized as weighing out the ingredients, mixing and folding in flour, spooning the mixture out into baking cases, baking, waiting for the cakes to cool, decorating with icing, waiting for icing to solidify, eating; a sequence of at least nine stages. So within recipes there is mathematical potential in terms of measuring and in the pattern or sequence of the process.

Nature

Nature offers a rich source of pattern. We only need to look at the threads of a spider's web, or the legs of a zebra to see wide ranges of pattern. Yet nature will never offer total symmetry, which is worth exploring with children. No two halves of an apple are exactly the same. A patterned animal skin will not be symmetrically perfect. In seeking regularity we need to be aware of this, so children are given the correct impression.

Play

In play children engage in pattern. They may well recreate part or all of an everyday life routine. In a shoe shop they are measuring, deciding on suitable footwear, and selling the selected pair. In imaginative play children mimic the pattern of life. If building, they are carefully constructing an arrangement of bricks and blocks. Building a tower with bricks is a perfect example of pattern in construction, or the bricks can be used to build a flat raft for animals, which is a practical application of tessellation.

Painting

Children create their own patterns when painting. In art they can search and observe the patterns made by others. An effective activity with children aged four and five is to offer a picture by another artist with the corresponding colours and to suggest children create their own interpretation. This sharpens their eye to the detail of another's work. Gifford supports this view with the comment 'copying a design requires closer attention to shape and positions than creating one from the imagination' (2005: 127).

This level of detail can then be applied to the skill of completing jigsaws and puzzles. The pattern has been cut up and the child is looking for clues in corners, colours and images. The recreation of the original picture is a challenge. When the last piece is placed there is satisfaction in achieving an exact replication of the original picture pattern.

Jigsaws

Jigsaws provide differentiation through the complexity of the image and the number of pieces. They offer recreation of pattern for an individual, or larger floor jigsaws offer peer collaboration. Jigsaws require spatial awareness, concentration and determination to complete the picture.

A second year Foundation Degree student Nina, used a rhyming number puzzle with her peers to demonstrate how she would teach numbers to nursery children. She identified a learning goal from the curriculum and imaginatively used the jigsaw to teach numbers. She was creative in how she used the jigsaw holding back a 'secret pile' of numeral pieces.

Jigsaw Sequence

One whale swims in the sea,
Two elephants come to tea,
Three giraffes reach for the sky,
Four hippos eat some pie,
Five horses read a book,
Six tigers learn to cook,
Seven penguins wake up late,
Eight monkeys love to skate,
Nine crocodiles go for a roam,
Ten lady birds fly away home.

Pattern contributes to the learning process children engage with. With very young children it is enough to experience its existence and its appeal (Frobisher et al 1999), which the adult can help by having an awareness of how steeped in pattern ordinary life is. Early pattern work such as looking for differences in objects, feeling rhythms in music, recreating images, moving to music, hearing words, all contribute to pre-algebraic thinking. Later on we will see how these pre-algebraic concepts relate to number and algebra. First we will consider number in more detail.

The complexity of number

In earlier chapters we considered the value of securing the pattern of number names, through repetition of stories, songs, rhymes and counting. We will now examine the complexity of number and counting. Children progress through different stages to count and calculate with competence. It is important that we understand the levels of progression so we can scaffold children's knowledge. Numbers create a more complex structure than we may realize.

Stages children progress through in learning number

The first natural step is articulation of the forward number sequence to a given number. This is naming numerals in the correct sequence. Memory skills are used to recall and provide 'one, two, three, four, five, six, seven, eight, nine, and ten'. This can be arrived at by saying, singing, repeating this sequence of words over and over. Counting everyday objects such as potatoes, cans of beans, cups, plates, pegs, chairs, and tables builds this familiarity with number names along with a sense of the counting process. Stories showing counting to five include *The Very Hungry Caterpillar* by Eric Carle. Taking every opportunity to sing, talk, and read number lays down this track of information in the child's mind. Once familiar with the story, children can work in an interactive way creating the story on a board. This serves to reinforce the numbers with, 'one apple, two pears, three plums, four strawberries and five oranges'.

Figure 6.1 Child using a storyboard (mathematical thinking using a story).

When the sequence of words is secure children can provide the number word after a given number. The adults say the number names to a number, for example 'one, two, three, four' and pause. The child provides 'five'. The adult can strengthen this skill through repetition in the form of a game: 'I have forgotten my numbers and need your help'. Starting with low numbers, for example 'one, two,' builds confidence and establishes the game quickly.

The next natural step is counting and attributing a number name to an item in the count. This requires that the child applies *one to one correspondence*. This we achieve through repeated counting. The way to ensure this is achieved is outlined as a three-step strategy in Chapter 3.

A teddy bears' tea party with cups, saucers, plates, spoons and cakes gives a natural opportunity for repeated and layered one to one correspondence, so that each child has a teddy bear, each bear a saucer, a cup, a spoon, a plate and a cake. We will return to one to one correspondence for larger numbers later.

Identifying and recognizing number are two different demands. If we consider identification as working with single numerals the child is providing the name for that numeral. Children move to numeral identification as they become aware of numbers and what they look like.

> *Number identification is asking for an individual number to be named.*
>
> *Number recognition is asking for the selection of a number from a collection of numerals.*

Children start to see numbers represented in print. The process of number identification is gradual. It is not realistic to set about teaching recognition of more than one numeral at any one time. Even then, time to connect this information about what '4' looks like to other contexts is required. The child out and about starts to look at house numbers and, with repeated looking at these, starts to forge numeral identification links with numbers seen in different places.

What number is this? Children may find numbers such as '12' difficult to identify and call it 'twenty one'. Sorting this information is gradual and comes with a greater understanding of place value (see Chapter 3). The process is helped by providing a number-rich environment; children notice features of numbers in their environment.

For number recognition the child is selecting a number from several numbers, a more complex process. The adult can provide numbers on playing cards and the child can recognize particular numbers from a hand. The numbers on a washing line or in a row or in a 100 square are offered and the child removes the number which the adult is asking them to recognize. Differentiation is achieved by presenting 4, 14, or 44 as the challenge to the child.

Numeral recognition is advancing number identification. Children select a nominated number from a collection. The adult says a number name and the child has to select the numeral matching the number named from among others. A simple activity is to shuffle number cards and ask children to pick out a named number. The rule of the game can be established quickly using low numbers such as number cards 1, 2, 3, 4 and asking for number 3 to be picked out.

A paired game is particularly effective for identification and recognition of number. Each child has a number line and a set of individual number cards. The two sets of number cards are placed face down between the children. Children take turns lifting a number card and place it on their number line if the space is available. If they have the number they replace the card and it is the other child's turn. There is the opportunity to memorize where the number has been placed, which is a valuable skill in itself. If the number cards go beyond six, each child needs two dice. The card needs to be thick so the number cannot be seen. The game can be played with pairs of children, introducing turn taking and collaboration within the pair of children and between competing pairs.

Simple number card recognition game

Two number boards with numbers 1 to 12 (arranged horizontally or vertically or in rows of four across and four down)

Two sets of numbers 1, 2, 3, 4, 5, 6, 7, 8, 9, 10, 11, 12 (on thick card)

Four dice

Children work in pairs each pair sharing a number board. They each have a dice which they take turns to throw. They pick up a number and turn it over. If it matches the dice throw they place it on the board. When they need numbers greater than 6 they need to roll both dice.

Backward number word sequence and number word before

Backward number word sequence demands a firm knowledge of the sequence of number names and short-term memory. Counting backwards places greater demands on recall (Chinn 2004). There are songs and rhymes which focus on counting down from, or backwards. Examples of 'counting down' from a number include:

'Ten green bottles'
'Five little ducks went swimming one day'
'Five little buns in a bakers shop'
'Five little speckled frogs'

Children who have secure knowledge of backward number sequence can be posed the question to provide a number word before a given number word. Questions such as: 'What number comes before five?' 'What number comes before eight?' A prompt answer indicates recall and ability on the child's part. Songs which count backwards support this skill. Mental challenges such as 'say the number just before 7' can be made more challenging by asking children to count back from a number and stop at another chosen number.

Travelling down the number line can present problems when moving to lower decades and it is worth investing time in questions like 'say the number just before 30' or 'count back from 31 and stop at 28'. For this example, two memory markers need to be employed and a sound understanding of number sequence is required. Exercising the memory in this way brings a greater rate of responsiveness to operations such as subtraction.

A suggestion here is to work with mental and physical number lines. The physical number lines can extend from 0 to 5, 0 to 10, 0 to 20, 0 to 30, 0 to 100. The orientation of the number lines can be vertical and horizontal. Number lines can extend in both directions to include positive and negative numbers. A powerful application of number lines is to use those created by children themselves. The use of blank number lines (Rowland et al 2009) is a powerful way to execute mental calculations.

The next stage will be to use knowledge number name sequences and numeral recognition. These two strands of learning working together enable a child to sequence written numerals. The practitioner provides number cards in a random order and the child arranges them correctly. The child demonstrates a number of levels of understanding if the response is definite and without hesitation. They understand value of number names and identify numerals and know how to combine this information.

The child within each stage takes an individual journey. The emergent counter cannot yet coordinate the word sequence with the objects to be counted (Wright, Martland and Stafford 2006). One to one correspondence and knowing number names in sequence will bring the child closer to matching object, number name and meaning of number name.

Children move from having to see items counted to being able to recall a number of items not visible. The next step is storing the value of a covered set and counting on to include other items. At some stage children realize the benefit of starting from the larger amount and counting on. For some this strategy may need to be pointed out. It is always sensible to add a small number to a large number. The first step here is deciding which is the larger number. Applying this to number line work, the child places their finger on the large number, and counts on the value of the small number, arriving at the answer. Children who can count on from a set value to arrive at an addition sum are in command of the previous layers of learning about number and counting. This technique takes time and may need pointing out.

Alex, a child in a year one class who could readily identify the six dots on the face of a dice, still counted each individual dot when asked to add the total of two dice. Counting on from six was not happening even though he had a sense of six. A dice with six and another with two still required a total count from one. Managing to use stored information was another stage in his development. He needed direction on how to do this. This tactic needs to be made explicit with sensitive adult demonstration. The adult can judge if the child is ready for this connection to be made.

> ### The process of counting is complex and when we ask children to count and record we are asking for:
>
> *The ability to count accurately with one to one correspondence*
>
> *The ability to understand that this final number represents the sum of the set*
>
> *The ability to remember the numerical symbol for this number name*
>
> *The ability to record this symbol accurately*
>
> *The ability to repeat this in different contexts, some with no obvious meaning*

Difficulties children may have with number and counting need to be understood in order to help overcome them. We can benefit our teaching by understanding what leads to misunderstandings. Children's 'arithmetical difficulties are highly susceptible to intervention' (Wright, Martland and Stafford 2006: 3). Understanding the complexity of counting puts us in a better position to intervene. We now look at specific examples of how we can support counting larger numbers.

Counting larger numbers

Children may find it difficult to count into new decades without omitting numbers, for example, '19, 20' and '29, 30' and '39, 40'. Children may keep the pattern of sound going but utter incorrect sequences. There is an analogy with reciting the 26 letters of the alphabet. Sections may become secure even though they remain meaningless beyond the rhythm of the tune and the order of words. Somehow, learning the alphabet song lays down a track which later learning can run on. The same principle applies for counting larger numbers. The track line can be disjointed but chanting numbers as a group can help secure this information. Stopping at numbers like 5 and 10, allows children for whom certain number names are insecure to catch up.

Counting with accuracy is central to working with number and number operations; it lifts a group's confidence. For some children chanting as part of a group offers a comfort and is less threatening, as they can join in with the section they are most familiar with. For children with English as a second language this provides an opportunity to learn counting words.

Providing a range of abacuses with different bead orientations gives a different counting experience. Some beads are presented vertically as in the photograph and others horizontally (see Figure 6.2). Working with both widens the children's experience. Presenting abacus beads and number lines with vertical and horizontal representations makes a connection that the same number can be arrived at, regardless of presentation. The number is conserved either way. I asked a year one child to tell me what the difference between the two abacuses was and he told me that mine (the vertical one) was dusty!

Figure 6.2 Slavonic and vertical abacuses.

Counting larger numbers with individual children, pairs or large groups can be achieved using an abacus. The pattern of numbers extending beyond 10 can be reinforced using a vertical bead abacus with a 'catch me out game'. Here the adult moves the beads over the arch to drop down the other side; children can only say the number of the bead as it falls. The speed is changed to try and catch the children out. If the children say the number name before the bead is over the arch, they are caught out. Slowing down for numbers which complete a decade such as 'twenty' reinforces them. Over time, this activity allows children to become familiar with the word 'thirty' replacing a natural tendency to say 'twenty ten'.

The abacus for this game is demonstrating *one to one correspondence* and sequencing larger number names. Children can experiment and reinforce this learning using mini versions of the abacus. Without intending to, a reception class in Swindon advanced to counting to 100 using the 'catch me out' game. They became so enthusiastic with this simple game that their interest drove counting on beyond the curriculum guidance for their age and stage. The same game can be used with small groups or pairs of children.

Nominal, ordinal and cardinal aspects of number

Understanding the different role numbers can take helps realize nominal, ordinal and cardinal aspects of number (Haylock and Cockburn 2008). It is important practitioners are aware of the different emphasis each term has and which property of numbers it refers to. This presents another complexity of number which children arrive at through a gradual learning experience, both in early years settings and at home.

Nominal

The number 9 bus is an example of *nominal* use of number as it is labelling the route this bus takes. It is a marker determining a different destination from other buses. Nominal numbers are evident in the environment around us. The child in the pushchair notices house numbers, telephone numbers and registration numbers. The Early Years Foundation Stage suggests in 'planning and resourcing' that practitioners 'create a "number rich" environment in the home play area' and 'introduce number labels to use outdoors for car number plates, house and bus numbers' (DfES 2008: 64). If we consider labelling as using the nominal aspect of number, it helps secure this feature.

Ordinal

Ordinal means the order a number takes in a collection. Here the number is one of a group and takes a certain position. It is the number's relationship to others.

The Early Years Foundation Stage (DfES 2008: 65) suggests practitioners 'look, listen and note' for evidence of 'accuracy in the use of ordinals (first, second, third and so on)'. The corresponding 'development matters' indicates 'use ordinal numbers in different contexts' (DfES 2008: 66).

Cardinal

Cardinal is the 'count amount' or the number of items in the collection. It is the last number said in the sequence used to count the items. In fact the last ordinal number is the cardinal number of items counted. The child counts three compare bears, three is the cardinal application of number. The Early Years Foundation Stage (DfES 2008: 64) offers guidance that children aged 22–36 months have 'some understanding of 1 and 2, especially when the number is important for them'. Initially we could think of relating this to age, but this is a difficult concept for children to grasp and relates to measure. How old you are in years holds significance, demanding a deep understanding of time. Candles on a cake help children grasp the concept of age. The candles mark a passing year. Using shoes, slippers, wellingtons, hats, coats and buttons is more tangible in understanding the cardinal aspect of number.

So part of the complexity of number lies in understanding the different role the number can take. It requires the child to understand the symbol, the word name, the count amount in a collection, where the number is in relation to others, that a number

9 bus is a label and not really using the number for anything else. Children are interpreting on two levels: the situation and the number in that context. The child is stepping across tracks depending on which route the number train is taking.

Haylock and Cockburn (2008) make the point that it is important not to emphasize the cardinal aspect of number at the expense of its ordinal role. Children creating their own number line exercise understanding of ordinal and cardinal as they order the numbers, arriving at a final cardinal value.

This has particular relevance for *zero*. The cardinal aspect of zero is that it means nothing. In its role as an ordinal number it separates the positive and negative numbers. It holds value when related to temperature, as zero degrees means coldness (Haylock and Cockburn 2008).

Children who understand zero and the ordinal aspect of numbers will be able to relate to negative numbers. The number line is extending to the other side of zero. Children may notice real applications of negative numbers in car parks or shopping centres. There is the same pattern of numbers above and below zero (Haylock and Cockburn 2008).

The complexity of number is further advanced through the application of number operations such as addition and subtraction. We will look more closely at number operation in Chapters 7 and 8. The consideration for the adult is that there is more to number than we might think. The process of counting is complex and relies on several concepts coming together. With experience and time children realize that the pattern of number names is always the same. Children sense that the number name is associated with an item and this one to one correspondence makes for accurate counting. Children connect the last ordinal number with the cardinal number of the items. They realize that how objects are arranged makes no difference to the total number of the count. Children move through these milestones of mathematical learning with practical activities and play practice.

Connecting pattern, number and algebra

Through achieving deep understanding of pattern, children are more able to undo a pattern and engage in algebraic thinking. Undoing a pattern is a way of really understanding its construction. We will now explore the relationship between number, pattern and algebra. First we will look at pattern in numbers and how to help children with this. Then we will connect pattern to shape, number and algebra.

Looking for pattern in numbers

The aim of this section is to show how early pattern forms the bedrock for later algebra. Pre-algebraic work bridges the cognitive gap between number and algebra (Frobisher et al 1999). These authors comment that 'relationships and the establishment and recording of general statements about numbers have their foundations in pattern' (Frobisher et al 1999: 240).

The pre-algebraic work of play, story, rhyme, music and painting equips children to order, structure, search for regularity, realize repetitions, spot symmetry, which is what pattern is about. This brings us to algebra and the point that 'the ultimate summing up of where pattern leads is algebra' (Frobisher et al 1999: 247).

The child is naturally investigative and driven to explore. The practitioner can ensure that 'the search for pattern and structure is made easier by planning activities involving sorting into categories, rearranging in particular orders, predicting new elements of a list and encouraging children to extend a pattern' (Frobisher et al 1999: 246).

The early familiarity with pattern of number names leads on to more complex pattern of number. Counting forwards and backwards is establishing the additive and subtractive pattern and sequence of number, say up to 20.

Forwards 1, 2, 3, 4, 5, 6, 7, 8, 9, 10, 11, 12, 13, 14, 15, 16, 17, 18, 19, 20.
Backwards 20, 19, 18, 17, 16, 15, 14, 13, 12, 11, 10, 9, 8, 7, 6, 5, 4, 3, 2, 1.
Counting in twos follows the pattern of even numbers,
2, 4, 6, 8, 10, 12, 14, 16, 18, 20,
or indeed counting in twos follows the pattern of odd numbers,
1, 3, 5, 7, 9, 11, 13, 15, 17, 19.

To help with odd and even numbers children need to see the coupling of numbers. If all the units can be coupled, it is an even number; if they are not coupled, we have an odd number. This can be presented visually using loose parts like washers or buttons, people on a bus, arranged in pairs. Using fixed arrangements such as Numicon expresses this idea clearly (see Chapter 4).

This becomes more problematic when large numbers are to be categorized as odd or even. When walking down a street as adults we divide the house number we are looking for by 2 and determine if it will be on the left or right hand side of the street. This strategy depends on knowing division by two outcomes. If it can be divided by 2 it will be on the left. If not it will be on the right. The left and right hand side will go up in twos so we need to look out for the number we are after, with knowledge of odd and even number sequences.

Counting in tens corresponds to another pattern within larger numbers to say 100.
10, 20, 30, 40, 50, 60, 70, 80, 90, 100.

Exploring all possible ways of making 10 is itself a pattern of number combinations. Children notice the increasing and decreasing number names and the reverse pattern after the pivotal 5 + 5 is reached. The number bond work can be achieved using Unifix cubes of two different colours. Children build towers 10 cubes high, showing all combinations of 10, with two colours. To support this activity it is useful to isolate two colours, say red and blue and ensure there are sufficient cubes, say 55 of either colour, 110 cubes altogether. A completed set will provide a model for children to work with.

$$0 + 10 = 10$$

$$1 + 9 = 10$$

$$2 + 8 = 10$$

$$3 + 7 = 10$$

$$4 + 6 = 10$$

$$\mathbf{5 + 5 = 10}$$

$$6 + 4 = 10$$

$$7 + 3 = 10$$

$$8 + 2 = 10$$

$$9 + 1 = 10$$

$$10 + 0 = 10$$

10 9 8 7 6 **5** 4 3 2 1 0

0 1 2 3 4 **5** 6 7 8 9 10

Number bonds establish patterns of addition and subtraction. A large ladybird and mini versions can be used to work with all the possible number bonds to five or 10.

Number bond work for older children can look at larger numbers like 18, with three additions to make the 18. This can be related to magic squares. Making magic squares is fixing this addition firmly for children. All the rows and columns in the magic square below add up to 18. The diagonals add up to 18. The number 18 is the magic number.

Table 6.1 A magic square.

9	2	7
4	6	8
5	10	3

The number square provides a good opportunity for older children to see a pattern across decades to 100. The pattern depends on which representation of the 100 square is chosen, as discussed in Chapter 3. The number track can be extended beyond 10 to show this pattern in a linear orientation. A mixture of fixed and removable numbers adds variety to how working with these numbers can be achieved.

Children need to be presented with practical opportunities to see, hear and feel these number patterns. The presentation of numbers in squares can be extended to mini-table squares and spiral tables (Merttens 1987). The child is exercising searching and mapping of number skills.

Table 6.2 Tables square alongside a number spiral (Merttens 1987). Originally printed in Merttens, R. (1987) *Teaching Primary Mathematics*.

1	2	3	4	5	6
2	4	6	8	10	12
3	6	9	12	15	18
4	8	12	16	20	24
5	10	15	20	25	30
6	12	18	24	30	36

20	21	22	23	24	25
19	6	7	8	9	26
18	5	0	1	10	27
17	4	3	2	11	28
37 16	15	14	13	12	29
36	35	34	33	32	31	30

Prime numbers are numbers with themselves and one as factors. The marking of these off on the 100 square shows how prime numbers do not create a regular pattern. This irregularity is an insight into the surprise springing from prime numbers. The irregularity of primes is worth experiencing. Poetry and prime numbers open up the possibility of displacing harmonious pattern.

We will now move away from looking at pattern in number squares, considering instead numbers, shapes and the patterns they make. The tessellation of shapes such as triangles to make a square is found in early pattern work. The same idea connects to later work with number into algebra which will be explored. This will highlight the value of pre-algebraic concepts for later learning.

Let us start by looking at numbers and arrangements that make triangles, squares, and cubes.

Triangular numbers

The sum of consecutive counting numbers starting at 1 is a triangle number.

1   1 + 2 = 3   1 + 2 + 3 = 6   1 + 2 + 3 + 4 = 10   1 + 2 + 3 + 4 + 5 = 15

This can be expressed as a numerical pattern

1 = 1 •

3 = 1 + 2

6 = 1 + 2 + 3

10 = 1 + 2 + 3 + 4

15 = 1 + 2 + 3 + 4 + 5

Figure 6.3 Triangular numbers.

1 = 1
3 = 1 + 2
6 = 1 + 2 + 3
10 = 1 + 2 + 3 + 4
15 = 1 + 2 + 3 + 4 + 5

Two of the *same* triangle numbers can be put together to make a rectangle. For example, triangle number 3 added to triangle number 3 makes a rectangle number 6 (Orton and Frobisher 1996).

$$3 + 3 = 6$$

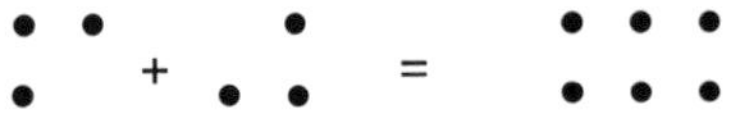

Figure 6.4 Two triangles make a rectangle.

6 = 3 + 3

Square numbers

Square numbers are those which can be represented as a square array. They are whole numbers multiplied by themselves.

$1 \times 1 = 1$

$2 \times 2 = 4$

$3 \times 3 = 9$

$4 \times 4 = 16$

$5 \times 5 = 25$

$6 \times 6 = 36$

This can be expressed as a numerical pattern.

$$1 = 1 \times 1$$

$$4 = 2 \times 2$$

$$9 = 3 \times 3$$

$$16 = 4 \times 4$$

$$25 = 5 \times 5$$

$$36 = 6 \times 6$$

Figure 6.5 Square numbers.

$1 = 1 \times 1$
$4 = 2 \times 2$
$9 = 3 \times 3$
$16 = 4 \times 4$
$25 = 5 \times 5$
$36 = 6 \times 6$

Each number can be made into a square number by multiplying it by itself or squaring itself. We looked at the square numbers, 1, 4, 9, 16, 25 …

They are made by (1 × 1) (2 × 2) (3 × 3) (4 × 4) (5 × 5). The resulting number is the number in the number sequence squared. This can be represented as $t = n^2$. This allows for prediction of any square number. Prediction is the power of algebra.

Another way of constructing square numbers is to add *consecutive* triangle numbers, starting at 1. The sum of two consecutive triangle numbers is a square number.
Triangle numbers 1, 3, 6, 10 …
Adding 1 + 3 makes a square number 4
Adding 3 + 6 makes a square number 9
Adding 6 + 10 makes a square number 16

Cube numbers

Early concepts of working with six squares can show how a cube can be made. However, a cube number is not connected to square numbers in this way. Whereas before we have put two triangle shapes together to make a square and can do this with triangular numbers to make square numbers, we need to deviate from this for cubes. In practical tessellation terms, six squares can be put together to make a cube. The pattern for cube numbers does not relate to six; instead the relationship is more with the number of corners, say eight for a cube made by putting six faces together. James in a year one class, making his model needed eight ball bearings but six plastic square faces to make his first cube.

A cube number is arrived at by multiplying a whole number by itself and by itself again.

1, 8, 27, 64, 125, 216
The number pattern is:
1 = 1 × 1 × 1
8 = 2 × 2 × 2
27 = 3 × 3 × 3
64 = 4 × 4 × 4
125 = 5 × 5 × 5
216 = 6 × 6 × 6

The shape and pattern work which children encounter in early stages projects forward to later concepts. We can see the connection between shape and number which could escape our attention. It highlights how there is a pattern to the sequence of numbers but also 'numbers can be described by the patterns they make e.g. even, odd, square, cube, triangular numbers' (Suggate, Davis and Goulding 2006: 54). Another pattern to note is that the sum of two odd numbers is always even.

Pattern takes a central role for number, operations and algebra. The essence of algebra is that it allows for generalization. In order to arrive at algebra we need to spot pattern and generalize the sequence. This leads to predictions and from this a formula can be settled on. This formula allows for generalization on a larger or global scale. An example of this is evident in the following taken from Haylock (2006).

What's my rule game? (Or guess my pattern.)

If you give me 3 the answer is 7. If you give me 4 the answer is 9. If you give me 5 the answer is 11. From an initial investigation a pattern is established. The rule being that the number is doubled and then one is added.

If presented as $y = 2x + 1$ the rule is that y has twice the value of x plus one. If x is 6, then y will be twice 6 which is 12, plus one, which is 13. Applying this rule, if x is one value then y will always be twice the value of x plus one and we can predict any answer.

If children can express the pattern they can make one statement which is true more generally (Haylock 2006). Realizing the generalization allows us to predict or determine for possibilities. This again is the power behind algebra.

Pattern, problem solving and algebra

An example of early problem solving is to disrupt the sequence of number names. Orna aged 2 years having a cuddle was offered 'one, ten' and corrected this to 'one, two', repeating this correction up to seven. Leaving a gap or using an incorrect number is prompting very young children to solve problems. This can then extend to hanging numbered items on a washing line which are then rearranged out of order, providing a number recognition problem for children to solve. This does depend on number recognition and counting skills being secure. Understanding number bonds can be used for problem activities by finding out how many are needed to make 10. This allows for later addition- and subtraction-related problems.

More advanced problem solving depends on equations. Equations show the inter-relationship between numbers. An equation is a mathematical statement. An algebraic equation tends to have a variable or unknown, for example, $6 + x = 13$. A good learning experience is to ask children to convert an equation into a problem scenario. For this example the scenario could be: a family of six went on holiday; they met up with friends for lunch; a table was booked for 13. How many friends joined them? The unknown can be confirmed by subtracting 6 from 13 leaving 7. This shows the link between problem solving and algebra. The application of algebraic equations is using a 'compact and efficient set of tools for solving problems' (Suggate, Davis and Goulding 2006: 127). This problem is pinned down with a mathematical equation $13 = 6 + \boxed{}$. A deep understanding is revealed if children can translate the operation with the unknown into a story. We will come to this in Chapter 9.

Conclusion

Returning to the questions posed at the start, it is hoped that there is a sense of what pre-algebraic concepts might be. Pattern is difficult to define. Practitioners need an awareness of the extent to which pattern is already part of our lives. The skill when working with very young children is to articulate daily experiences as fluidly as one can. Pre-algebraic concepts are present in music, story, dance, movement and daily life. Express these and we are teaching pattern of language and processes.

The next question was, how does pattern relate to number? The complexity of number was explored so that the teaching can be tailored to where a child is at and practitioners see the connections to later learning. Learning to count is a challenge and demanding on several levels. It is worth noting that, 'when children in the early years of primary school learn to count on and count back in steps of 1, 2, 3 and so on, they are creating the basis for study of pattern and sequences' (Frobisher 1999: 247). The laying of number sequences is achieved through repeated songs, rhymes and stories. Children move on to associating a value to these number names. Good counting habits give children the satisfaction of arriving at accuracy. Early emphasis on one to one correspondence achieves this.

The final question was, how does pattern relate to algebra? This chapter has shown how important early number, pattern and shape work contributes to algebraic thinking. We have touched on the way bigger numbers can be predicted by encoding a pattern. We have seen how numbers can relate to shapes such as triangles, squares and cubes.

If we put teaching pattern first, as if it were the engine of the train, then other aspects of mathematics follow like carriages behind. It is interesting to note that algebra is a consequence of pattern and yet pattern is central to early mathematical learning. Algebra allows us to step into infinity and bring it back down to manageable smallness. We are giving children an understanding of infinity in the palm of their hands when we teach number. Our aim is to express pattern to children and to spark an enthusiasm and love for it. Pattern is, after all, life and life a pattern of different experiences.

Section 3

Understanding number operations: addition and subtraction

7

'When I use a word,' Humpty Dumpty said, in a rather scornful tone, 'it means just what I choose it to mean – neither more or less.'

'The question is,' said Alice, 'whether you can make words mean so many different things.'

'The question is,' said Humpty Dumpty, 'which is to be master – that's all.'

Through the Looking Glass, Lewis Carroll (1832–1898)

The aims of this chapter are:

- To explore the different meanings behind addition and subtraction
- To find strategies for mental calculations
- To highlight subtleties of language prompting mathematical operations

Introduction

Children are more aware of differences in meaning than adults for whom there is less need. As adults we sense more readily what is required and arrive at the answer. This automatic ease can mean 'the teacher simply cannot see what could be complex about something so familiar to them' (Rowland et al 2009: 118). Children respond more carefully in order to determine what to do. We need to be conscious of the different meanings within calculations. We need awareness of how words prompt different meanings. We need to communicate strategies for mental calculations.

> **Questions to reflect on:**
>
> Can you determine four different meanings behind addition?
>
> Can you describe five different meanings for subtraction?
>
> Why would you use the word 'subtract' rather than 'take away'?

This chapter is about realizing the complexities which children face as learners and the delicacy of communicating mathematics.

We will consider practical strategies to teach mental calculations. The Qualifications and Curriculum Authority (QCA 1999a) guidelines recommend that children learn written methods after they fully understand mental strategies and that children are in year 4 before formal methods are introduced. Children should be recording horizontally and there is an overemphasis on working with vertical sums too early (Haylock and Cockburn 2008).

As educators, our meaning needs to be consistent with our language. Children need to sense the integrated meanings of concepts so they can respond to any language prompts or situations underlying the words (Brown 2003; Frobisher 1999). It's not what we know but how we think. It's about seeing relationships; building a store of facts on which more can be scaffolded; thinking connectively.

To explore the different meanings behind addition and subtraction

We will start with an account of a mathematics lesson in a reception class, then unravel four possible meanings behind the addition operation. This will bring us to explore the subtraction operation, then strategies for mental and written addition and subtraction calculations.

Addition

Observing in a class of 30 children aged four and five, a simple idea using fruit which was later eaten at snack time worked well; this activity could be extended for older children, which we will consider.

Oranges and bananas

Whole class 'burst' with the objective:

'select two groups of objects to make a given total of objects'

Early Years Foundation Stage Curriculum Guidance: Problem Solving, Reasoning and Numeracy, Calculating (DfES 2008: 71)

Key questions:

Is there a different way we could give eight pieces of fruit?

How many different ways?

Taking the register, Suzanne (class teacher) recorded what children would have for lunch.

Some children were to have packed lunches, others chose beef pie or vegetable lasagne.

There were '19' packed lunches on the register. Suzanne asked Daisy how she would write '19', pointing out it was important the digits were recorded in the right order. Two boys went to check how many lunch boxes were stacked up outside. We could hear them count loudly, arriving at '19'. This system of checking made perfect sense.

Then there was a short focus on hot meals. Five beef pies and six vegetable lasagnes were represented by a horizontal number sentence $5 + 6 = 11$. Children were asked to do the calculation and explain how they arrived at 11. Lilly used her fingers splitting 6 into 5 and 1, $5 + (5) + (1) = 11$. Another child kept 5 in his head, counting on using six fingers.

Then as a group they opened and closed fists, counting in tens to a hundred. James announced he could count to 100, proceeding to count in ones. He counted accurately from 0 to 39, and then jumped from there to pick up from 89 to 100. His counting was praised and it was pointed out to James that he had skipped from 39 to 89.

Suzanne then presented the problem-solving situation to the children. She asked for their help and described how a customer wants eight pieces of fruit from the fruit stall outside in the role-play area. The parameters were a fixed sum of 8, with two types of fruit, oranges and bananas. The children moved into a large circle to work through possibilities.

Volunteers decided on the selection of fruit. The first child chose one banana and two oranges. Counting from one they realized they needed more fruit to arrive at eight, adding six more bananas.

Suzanne asked, 'Can you do eight pieces a different way?'

Two boys were chosen, Marlon and Joey. This pair started off well and then went off task, misbehaving. They were asked whether they made good working partners. With prompting they arrived at five bananas and three oranges. Marlon checked the total, counting from the start. He was praised for checking.

Lilly decided on four oranges and four bananas. She arranged the four bananas in a repeating arc with the oranges tucked under. She was asked, 'how would you write this as a number sentence?' She hesitated and was prompted, 'remember when we were using symbols. Can you make links with your learning from yesterday?' She described using her fingers how she could express the $4 + 4 = 8$.

The children then worked in pairs using wipe boards to record the different ways they could give their customers eight pieces of fruit. One boy close to me asked his partner, 'how much fruit do you want?' then 'how does an "8" go?' He then asked, 'how many apples do you want?' His partner replied, '5'. He wrote 8 + 5 and then wiped it away (possibly because it was too difficult to calculate). He replaced it with 1 + 7 using his fingers saying, 'you need another number'. 'How much bananas?' 'How does a nine go?' He writes 'p', commenting, 'looks like a "p"'.

From the corner of my eye I noticed a small group looking at the fruit arranged in a circle. The circular representation created a refreshing impression on the mind. The number 8 was represented as a circular pattern of oranges and bananas.

The children were then invited to share their work with the rest of the group, placing wipe boards on a visualiser.

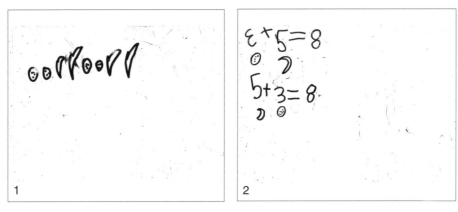

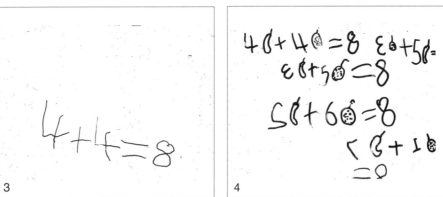

Figure 7.1 Children's representations showing the story of eight oranges and bananas, samples 1 to 4.

Sample 1: Amy
A repeating pattern of two oranges, two bananas, two oranges, two bananas.

Sample 2: Ella
3 + 5 = 8
5 + 3 = 8

This piece demonstrates a connection to the commutative property of addition. The order for addition does not matter. This is a very useful law when calculating with larger numbers. An effective strategy will be to start with the larger number.

Suzanne comments: 'They have been spiders making links in their learning'.

Sample 3: Fay
4 + 4 = 8

She uses symbols learnt and states, '4 add 4 make 8'.

Sample 4: Lilly and Erin
4 + 4 = 8
3 + 5 = 8
2 + 6 = 8
7 + 1 = 8

This sample shows an understanding of number relationships or bonds making 8.

When looking at this example, a child on the carpet says, 'they all equal 8, because we discovered it'.

This short burst of mathematics used pockets of mathematical opportunity. The adult was thinking in a connective way, creating contexts, which meant something to the children. The differentiation happened naturally through questioning. Children were made aware of how they were thinking, 'like spiders'. They were working with real fruit. This activity was simple and effective.

For some children recording number sentences is not appropriate, particularly when they are unfamiliar with how to form numerals. They could be encouraged to record the fruit pictorially as in sample 1, where the pieces of fruit were drawn without numerals.

A development of this activity for, say a year one class, could be to systematically go through the different ways of making 8. This could be presented to older children along with the challenge to investigate the outcome if we have two or more fruit types.

The starting point would be to confirm that there are nine number bonds relating to 8.
$8 + 0 = 8$, $7 + 1 = 8$, $6 + 2 = 8$, $5 + 3 = 8$, $4 + 4 = 8$, $3 + 5 = 8$, $2 + 6 = 8$, $1 + 7 = 8$, $0 + 8 = 8$

With oranges and bananas the possibilities are:
8 oranges + 0 bananas = 8
7 oranges + 1 banana = 8
6 oranges + 2 bananas = 8
5 oranges + 3 bananas = 8
4 oranges + 4 bananas = 8
3 oranges + 5 bananas = 8
2 oranges + 6 bananas = 8
1 orange + 7 bananas = 8
0 oranges + 8 bananas = 8

There are nine ways of offering a customer oranges and bananas amounting to 8. The systematic recording of possibilities teases out this pattern. Older children or children ready for a greater challenge could see what happens if the customer were given oranges, bananas and kiwis, that is, three fruit types.

Meanings behind addition

Frobisher (1999) outlines four possibilities for addition meanings. These are determined by different words and situations. We will continue the theme of fruit to illustrate the differences.

Combining or (part-part-whole)

Here we ask children to combine the cardinal value of two sets to make a new set; this means the child needs to hold in their memory the value of each subset. Two parts are combined to make a whole. It is important that we remember the amount of each set so that when they are combined we are experiencing addition. These numbers need to be recorded either mentally or physically so that the original position is not lost or left to memory.

Idea: select three hoops with fruit such as bananas in one and oranges in another.

Physically combine these into a third hoop. Record by placing number cards by the subsets and final set.

Questions: how many fruit are there altogether?

Key word: 'altogether'

Augmenting

The original amount of fruit, say three bananas is increased by two to arrive at a new amount.

An action is applied to a given, which results in an increase. Using one fruit type, a customer buying five bananas returns to the market stall as they realize they need to buy more.

Question: a customer bought five bananas and returns to the stall to buy three more. How many has he now?

Key word: 'now'

Comparing

We have a fixed amount, say five oranges. We compare combinations that make this amount.

So 1 + 4 compares to 5 and 3 + 2 compares to 5. The meaning is comparing to find equivalences. Structural apparatus such as Cuisenaire rods will do this where one piece is a fixed length and smaller pieces are put alongside to match it. This relates to possible number complements or bonds of the given number.

It could be adapted to show the comparison of eight bananas in a row along with the possibility of creating another row to make an equivalent amount for another customer who wants the same amount.

Question: if we had eight bananas in a row, how could we make another row have the same number of bananas?

Key words: 'has the same number as', 'equivalent to'

Changing position down

In this case we are relating the meaning behind addition to a number line or ordinal position. So, if we are adding two places or positions to someone who is third in the queue, they become fifth in the queue.

Question: a customer is waiting in the market stall queue and starts to fiddle in their purse for money. He is not ready to pay so moves down two places. What is his new position in the queue?

Key words: 'moves down', 'new position'

The oranges and bananas were used with the reception class 'short burst' for the combining meaning of addition. Children had to consider different ways of combining bananas and oranges to arrive at 8. Depending on the language we select, we prompt one of four possible addition meanings.

There are subtle differences within addition depending on the scenario along with the selection of words. When planning lessons or activities it is good to isolate the key words to heighten our awareness (see ladybird activity plan later). It is worth noting the advice to use 'the same as' or 'balances' rather than 'makes' as recommended by QCA (1999a). The word 'makes' is only appropriate if the calculation needs to be done.

Subtraction

Subtraction is the inverse of addition, but that is not all. As an operation it is not as flexible as addition, as we cannot necessarily change the order without changing the possible outcomes. Children need to realize that 8 – 3 does not equal 3 – 8. Order does matter for subtraction.

A number line or a hundred square can demonstrate subtraction. We do, however, need to consider the appropriateness of our choice of resource, as will be discussed below. Again the choice of language, such as 'take away' or 'difference', leads us to different subtraction meanings.

Research suggests that we need to be aware of two aspects of teaching subtraction:

1. Comparing sets to find out whether one has more is not related to subtraction meaning as much as it possibly could be (Frobisher et al 1999). If one set of bears has more there is an opportunity to talk about the other having less. How many bears would need to be removed to make both sets equal? The deceptiveness of 'more' needs to be explored in both directions at an early stage. With young children we can make this point explicit by exposing two ways of looking at a situation. As well as checking how many more bricks are required to make one tower as tall as the other, we can check to see how many would need to be removed from the tall tower, that is, how many more bricks were used to build the taller tower.
2. There is an overemphasis on 'take away', according to Haylock and Cockburn (2008) and a need to focus on other meanings to achieve the full scope of subtraction. Rowland et al (2009) point out that the curriculum emphasis is 'take away' at Reception stage and 'comparison' in year 1. Rowland et al (2009) suggest the more neutral use of 'subtraction'.

Meanings behind subtraction

Rowland et al (2009) consider it sufficient to look at two structures for subtraction, but for the purpose of completion and consistency we will continue with the work of Frobisher (1999) who outlines five possible subtraction meanings. It is, however, useful to think broadly before looking at more subtle variations.

To demonstrate two broad structures of subtraction, consider first the scenario of 20 marbles; when eight are removed to leave 12, we would need 20 marbles. To demonstrate an alternative subtraction where one person has 20 marbles, another has 12 and we need to find how many more the person with 20 has, we would need 32 marbles in order to set out a row of 20 and below this a row of 12. Therefore there is a need to think through our intended meaning so that we have adequate resources. The second meaning is matching one to one between sets and counting unmatched items.

Rowland et al (2009) outline these two categories referring to the first as 'partition' and the second as 'comparison'. We will use different terms in order that we can consider 'partition' more as a strategy, though arguably 'partition' is both a meaning and a strategy. A more specific analysis using the work of Frobisher (1999) gives us the following:

Splitting a quantity (whole-part-whole)

An initial amount is split into two. Relating it to the fruit theme it could be presented as:

Question: a market stall has eight pieces of fruit. Five are bananas. How many are oranges?

Key words: 'how many are'

Reducing a quantity

Rowland et al (2009) refer to this as the, 'change structure'. The original set is changed through the action of taking away. A quantity is reduced by an amount. There is a need to establish the amount left. An initial state is followed by a transformation, resulting in a final state. Some are partitioned off (Haylock 2006; Rowland et al 2009). Think of it as the dynamics of change.

Question: a market stall has eight bananas. A customer buys five. How many bananas are left?

Key word: 'left'

Comparing a quantity

This is termed by Rowland et al (2009) as a 'compare structure'. This meaning presents word problems, often misleading children to add. The word 'more' is where the deception lies; the answer is in the numerical difference between the two sets.

Perhaps a greater focus on this feature of subtraction will help unblock this obstacle. The clue here is that we need to consider both amounts at the same time.

There is no dynamic of change, so a static state of comparison is required (Rowland et al 2009). This structure has difference associated with it, though Rowland (2006) points out to avoid confusion the word 'comparison' is more appropriate.

Question: Joey has five bananas. Marlon has three. How many more bananas has Joey?

Key words: 'many more'

A useful way to expose this feature of subtraction is to work with bricks, making towers as described earlier.

Question: how many more blocks does the tallest tower have which need to be removed to make the two towers the same height?

Key words: 'same', 'more'

Question: how many more blocks need to be placed on top of the shorter tower to make it equal to the other?

Changing a position up

The best way to think of this meaning is to look at a number line and consider moving from position 5 to position 3. The action means we are subtracting 2 from 5. Relating to our theme, the question would be:

Question: a customer in the market stall queue moves up from being fifth in the queue to being third. How many places have they moved?

Key words: 'moves up'

There is a twist here. When in a queue you are better if placed at a corresponding lower number, that is, second in the queue is better than fourth. This will also apply to league tables for football or schools! This idea needs to be understood for these problems.

Inverse of addition

This meaning of subtraction is evident when we know the total, say eight pieces of fruit. We know the number of bananas is five and can therefore deduce by subtraction the number of oranges to be three. This could be presented as a number sentence $5 + \boxed{} = 8$.

Question: a customer has bought eight pieces of fruit. In one bag there are bananas and in the other, oranges. He remembers that there are five bananas. How many oranges did he buy?

Key words: 'how many'

This last subtraction meaning shows the intimacy between addition and subtraction. This realization of the interrelationship of addition and subtraction opens up real under-standing. It will be arrived at through repetition of transactions taking place over time. This requires a deep sense of mathematics, language, and schematic experience.

Table 7.1 Key words and questions for addition and subtraction.

Operation structure	Key words	Key questions
Addition		
Combining	'altogether'	A market stall has five bananas and three oranges. How many fruits are there are altogether?
Augmenting	'more', 'now'	A customer buys five bananas and returns to the stall to buy three more. How many has he now?
Changing position down	'moves down', 'new position'	A customer is third in the market stall queue and starts to fiddle in his purse for money. He is not ready to pay so moves down two places. What is his new position in the queue? Note: imagine position 3 on a number line. Then move further along to position 5 i.e. $(3 + 2 = 5)$.
Comparing	'same as'	Marlon has five pieces of fruit in one bag. He has the same number of fruit as Joey. Joey has two in one bag. How many has Joey in his other bag?

Subtraction		
Splitting a quantity	'are'	A market stall has eight pieces of fruit. Five are bananas. How many are oranges?
Reducing a quantity	'left', 'remain', 'take away'	A market stall has eight bananas. A customer buys five. How many bananas are left?
		A marketer has eight bananas. He removes three. How many bananas remain on his stall?
		The marketer has eight bananas. He takes away five. How many does he have to sell?
Comparing a quantity (difference meaning of subtraction) **Note: this is open to interpretation and highlights the intersection or overlap between addition and subtraction**	'more' (direct comparison)	Joey has five bananas. Marlon has three. How many more bananas does Joey have than his friend?
	'more' (reducing down to make equal: starting with larger)	There are two towers. The tallest has eight bricks; the other has five bricks. How many more blocks does the tallest tower have which would need to be removed to make the two towers the same height?
	'more' (increasing to make equal: starting with smaller)	How many more blocks need to be placed on top of the shortest tower to make it equal to the other? Note: this is comparing to see how many to add to the smallest tower to make them equal (Frobisher et al 1999)
Changing a position up	'moves up'	A customer in the market stall moves up from being fifth in the queue to being third. How many places have they moved? Imagine a number line with the customer in position 5. They move to position 3 closer to the stall i.e. $(5 - 2 = 3)$
Inverse of addition	'has', 'there are', 'how many'	A customer has bought eight pieces of fruit. In one bag there are the bananas and in the other the oranges. He remembers that there are five bananas. How many oranges did he buy?

The language of addition and subtraction

The purpose of Table 7.1 is to isolate language associated with addition and subtraction. The question to ask is how convinced are you that my categories are correct or indeed appropriate?

There are several complications, which we can tangle ourselves up in as I did; let's get into a tangle or two. When presented with word problems we start with the words and create an image or 'internal representation' of the text (De Corte and Verschaffel 1991). A different semantic structure can express the same operation. De Corte and Verschaffel (1991:119) state that 'word problems that are solvable using the same arithmetic operation can be described in terms of different networks of concepts and relationships underlying the problem'. Let's look at some examples provided by De Corte and Verschaffel (1991):

Addition

$3 + 5 = 8$

Joe has three marbles; Tom has five marbles; how many marbles do they have altogether?

Joe has three marbles; Tom has five more marbles than Joe; how many marbles does Tom have?

Subtraction

$8 - 5 = 3$

Joe had eight marbles; then he gave five marbles to Tom; how many marbles does Joe have now?

Joe has eight marbles; he has five more marbles than Tom; how many marbles does Tom have?

We can see from the examples above that a difference in expression with words leads to the same operation. For the reader who would like to look at these complexities further De Corte and Verschaffel (1991) provide a table with 14 categories of simple addition and subtraction word problems illustrating semantic subtleties.

In attempting to categorize language and questions associated with operations of addition or subtraction, another point raises its head; another tangle to get into. Not only can the addition or subtraction be disguised in different semantics, the words can lead to visualizing the problem as either addition or subtraction.

If we look at Table 7.1 and the categorization of subtraction:

'Comparing a quantity'

Joey has five bananas. Marlon has three. How many more bananas does Joey have than his friend? Could we add on from three until we arrive at five? ($3 + 1 + 1 = 5$ so he has two more) as opposed to seeing the subtraction ($5 - 3 = 2$).

'Inverse of addition'

Taking the inverse of addition as another example: 'A customer has bought eight pieces of fruit. In one bag there are the bananas and in the other oranges. He remembers that there are five bananas. How many oranges did he buy?'

Could it be seen as 5 + 3 = 8 rather than the suggested 8 − 5 = 3?

Taking other examples can you see possibilities for both addition or subtraction depending on the visual image that springs to mind? Reducing down to make one tower equal to the other; could this be seen as adding on from a small tower? This is suggested by the inclusion of the reference to blocks being placed on top of a tower to make it equal. Frobisher et al (1999) acknowledge a crossover between operations when comparing quantities or looking at difference.

There is crossover between the operations of addition and subtraction. It depends on how we interpret words; how we see the action. Some descriptions in the table allow for either operation to be applied. Perhaps we need to see one operation with two arms; addition and subtraction.

In summary

The one operation can be disguised in different semantic expressions; the expression can employ more than one operation. The descriptions are open to interpretation. There is potential crossover which needs to be accepted, even explored. The chosen operation is determined by word images in our mind.

A way of connecting across the semantic intention of words, images created and solutions chosen, is to encourage children to draw their interpretation. De Corte and Verschaffel (1991: 127) advocate that 'the principle of explicitly teaching multiple forms of graphic representation deserves further study'.

So to answer the question, categorizing language associated with addition and subtraction is not to be taken too rigidly. The advantage of categorization is that it separates out possibilities; the disadvantage is that there are semantic flaws. As long as we allow children to step over divides without narrowing their wide view of many different meanings, we can use categories to see it as they may.

Separating addition from subtraction, or multiplication from division, is not necessarily the correct approach, as Anghileri (1991: 95) comments; 'although they are introduced as distinct operations, their separation in the early stages of learning may inhibit children's understanding of addition and subtraction and between multiplication and division, and the fact that much of the language for each pair is shared'.

Number bond relationships

At some stage with the market stall the emphasis could be placed on how the fruit is bagged up. The bananas are in one bag, the oranges in another, the customer leaves one bag on the bus on the way home; the number 8 is a fixture in the story, so the number can be determined through knowledge of number bonds to 8 in both addition and subtraction directions. This number bond relationship is central to mental calculations.

Addition and subtraction
number bonds interrelating

$$8 - 0 = 8$$
$$8 + 0 = 8$$

$$8 - 1 = 7$$
$$7 + 1 = 8$$

$$8 - 2 = 6$$
$$6 + 2 = 8$$

$$8 - 3 = 5$$
$$5 + 3 = 8$$

$$8 - 4 = 4$$
$$4 + 4 = 8$$

$$8 - 5 = 3$$
$$3 + 5 = 8$$

$$8 - 6 = 2$$
$$2 + 6 = 8$$

$$8 - 7 = 1$$
$$1 + 7 = 8$$

Important that children learn
these through experience.

We looked at using fruit to create meaningful expressions of the addition operation. We will now look at using a simple narrative story about a ladybird in a rainstorm to tell children in a participative way about subtraction. The activity is set out as an activity plan and is evaluated to give you an example of planning and evaluating. The lesson plan can be adapted to suit your needs. A blank copy of the plan is included in the Appendix.

Table 7.2 Ladybird in a rainstorm subtraction activity plan.

Learning objectives/Goals (Identify Early Learning Goals, National Curriculum) 'Understand subtraction as "take away"' Primary National Strategy (DfES 2006: 94)	**KEY WORDS** Take away

Topic/Theme
Calculating/subtraction

Children involved
(Number of children, age, gender)
Twenty eight Year one children aged 6/7 years. Ratio 40:60 boys to girls.

Resources
Primary National Strategy; Primary Framework for Literacy and Mathematics (DfES 2006).
Large giant-size ladybird with set of large spots. Small mini ladybirds with sets of 10 spots.
Magnetic boards with examples of subtraction number sentences with numerals, subtraction
(–) and equals (=) symbols.

Health and safety considerations
Ensure children are sitting comfortably and safely for whole class teaching. Ensure the mini
ladybirds are laminated and smooth to avoid finger cuts. Ensure doors are firmly closed and
there are no distractions or draughts.

Session/Activity

Introduction
This ladybird is lying on a leaf in a rain forest. It is the rainy season and the rain is getting
heavier. Can you make the rain noise using the palm of one hand and the first finger of your
other hand? Let me hear the rain softly, softly and then harder getting louder and louder.
Children participate by making the rain sound using a greater number of fingers each time.

Now, this giant ladybird needs your help. She is losing her spots in the heavy rain. She needs
to know how many spots she has on her body to recognize herself. Will you help her by
counting the spots? The children count the number of spots she starts with. Let's check how
many spots she has to start with 1, 2, 3, 4, 5, 6, 7, 8, 9, 10. So this ladybird has ten spots on
her body.

Content
(What will you do? What will the children do? What questions will you ask?)

As the rain falls one of her spots falls away sliding off her body. Let's check how many spots
the ladybird has now 1, 2, 3, 4, 5, 6, 7, 8, 9. So ten take away one is nine. The ladybird
returns to her leaf, sleeps while the spot which fell off is replaced on her body. She then sets
about searching for food in the forest. Will you help her again if she loses another spot?

Again the rain comes, softly, softly then louder and louder, harder and harder ... Oh that is
heavy rain ... oh so now two spots are washed away ... Now she needs your help ... as she
needs to know how many spots she has on her body so that she can recognize herself. Let's
check ... 1, 2, 3, 4, 5, 6, 7, 8. So ten take away two is eight. She returns to her leaf and sleeps
while we replace the spots on her body. Repeat this to arrive at ten take away ten is zero. The
ladybird then has no spots left on her body.

Conclusion (How will you finish the activity and reinforce the learning goals?)
The ladybird started off her day with ten spots and found that she looked different after each rainstorm. Ten spots take away one is nine. Ten spots take away two is eight. Let's just make a note of this e.g. $10 - 1 = 9$; $10 - 2 = 8$; $10 - 3 = 7$; $10 - 4 = 6$; $10 - 5 = 5$; $10 - 6 = 4$; $10 - 7 = 3$; $10 - 8 = 2$; $10 - 9 = 1$; $10 - 10 = 0$.

If appropriate relate this verbalizing to the number sentences. It may be more appropriate to do this on subsequent sessions or with the children for whom the concepts of number recognition and subtraction are secure.

Now you are going to meet other ladybirds and they will need your help. Some have five spots on their bodies, some have ten spots, and some need a note made of what happens to them, like keeping a diary. Let's go and help them and then we will come back and tell each other what we found.

Present children with the appropriate paired work task. Only use the recording in the form of number sentence with the children for whom the concepts of number recognition and subtraction are secure. The main aim is practical working with subtraction of spots so that children understand subtraction as 'take away'.

Differentiation
● How will you support children for whom this concept is new?

The children will work with a mini ladybird and a set of five spots and focus on the repetition of the story and the appropriate use of language.

● How will you extend for children who are more familiar with the concept of subtraction?

The children with secure knowledge of counting, number recognition and subtraction will create number sentences on magnetic boards to complement their practical experience.

Children will be encouraged to draw pictures to represent their thinking.

Assessment. How will you assess the children's learning?
Assessment will be evident through questioning children directly as they manipulate the spots on their individual ladybirds. It is important to assess appropriate use of language.

Children will be assessed through the expression they make in their drawings. Some assessment will be gathered in a spontaneous way. A true assessment would be planned for with one to one directed questioning at a subsequent date.

Detailed analysis and evaluation
What went well? Why? Were the learning objectives/goals achieved or did you work towards them? What would you do differently if you carried out the activity again?
How could you extend the activity to increase learning?

Overview
The children were fully engaged from the outset and were captivated by the story element and the way the ladybird needed their help. All children participated and enjoyed making the rain sound. There was a wide range of abilities in the group and this lesson allowed for all levels to be involved.

The main session could be adapted to work with number bonds to 5 i.e. $5 - 1 = 4$; $5 - 2 = 3$; $5 - 3 = 2$; $5 - 4 = 1$; $5 - 5 = 0$. The children who are ready to work with number bonds to 10 can then do so with the mini ladybirds.

A small point to note is to avoid winged ladybirds as this could indicate addition. Though the same story can be adapted for addition using ladybirds with defined wings for the purpose of achieving the learning objective of understanding subtraction this ladybird's wings are tightly closed.

The group work afterwards was practical and children enjoyed working with their own individual ladybird which they were to keep and bring home to work on with their parents or carers. This served to extend learning from the setting to home.

Delicacy in delivery
As practitioners we need to be sure how we are approaching the goal. We could start at 10 and remove a single spot each time i.e. $10 - 1 = 9$: $9 - 1 = 8$; $8 - 1 = 7$; $7 - 1 = 6$; $6 - 1 = 5$; $5 - 1 = 4$; $4 - 1 = 3$; $3 - 1 = 2$; $2 - 1 = 1$; $1 - 1 = 0$ where the number removed is always one and the number subtracted from decreases.

In the example followed we replace the washed off spots each time, so that we are always returning to 10 and we are subtracting an increasing number each time. The subtraction pattern then becomes $10 - 1 = 9$; $10 - 2 = 8$; $10 - 3 = 7$; $10 - 4 = 6$; $10 - 5 = 5$; $10 - 6 = 4$; $10 - 7 = 3$; $10 - 8 = 2$; $10 - 9 = 1$; $10 - 10 = 0$.

The second option is more cumbersome to express as between rainstorms the spots need replacing. However it does provide an opportunity to work with number bonds to ten. We need to decide on the story version as there is a delicate difference depending on which line we follow.

Subtraction structure
This subtraction structure is described by Frobisher et al (1999) as 'reducing a quantity'. It was necessary to decide if it was always subtraction from 10 in which case it is important to keep on this track with the subtracted spots visible. The question to consider before we start is whether we are reducing the same quantity repeatedly or a different quantity each time by the same amount.

Either way we are subtracting but counting up from one each time to establish the number of spots. It is important to put greater emphasis on the subtraction part of the story.

On reflection more encouragement could be given to encourage children to draw their findings as recommended by Hughes (1986). This could be achieved with all children who have adequate fine motor skills to control a pencil. Multi-sensory teaching was achieved as children were looking, listening to the mathematical language and carrying out number operations practically with miniature models of ladybirds.

Consistency of language
It is important to remain consistent with the use of language and 'take away' was the only subtraction word used. It was tempting to use 'minus' or 'subtract'. It is best to stay with 'take away' for this session particularly as a quarter of the group are learning English as a second language.

Pattern of subtraction

In order to reinforce this objective it will be necessary to repeat this many times to ensure learning is secure. The rhythm of the pattern of number bonds; *Ten take away one is nine. Ten take away two is eight. Ten take away three is seven. Ten take away four is six. Ten take away five is five; Ten take away six is four; Ten take away seven is three; Ten take away eight is two; Ten take away nine is one; Ten take away ten is zero,* needs to become meaningful and automatic for all in the group.

Zero

Zero is unable to change numbers when added or subtracted. It is worth pointing out how zero has this preserving power.

Strategies for mental addition and subtraction calculations

The main strategy required for mental calculations is to find the most efficient route. It is about economy of thought. It is playing with numbers to make them manageable. It is knowing how to order, partition or adjust numbers. If a number is increased to make it more user friendly, we need to balance that change, reducing the answer by this same amount.

The QCA (1999a) recommendation is that children have learned number facts such that they can be recalled instantly. They are then taught mental strategies, which allow them to draw from these stored facts to work out unfamiliar facts. This is connecting the familiar to the unfamiliar using manipulation. Mental calculations need to be taught explicitly.

Manipulations need to be compared to see which are more efficient. Informal recordings will aid memory; these can be in the form of pictures. To approximate and to return to check are to be encouraged as they prompt a strategic viewpoint and complete the cycle.

The answer can be presented as a horizontal number sentence but formal written methods should be introduced from year 4 (QCA 1999b) with full application by year 6.

There are three key questions to apply to this area of work.

How did you work out that answer?

Has anyone got another way?

Which way is easier and why do you think so?

Number relationships through counting forwards and backwards

To fully employ good strategies requires familiarity with number relationships both within the number 'interrelationships' and beyond, in the way the number relates to other 'outer relationships'. Another way of describing this is number bonds within the number and bonds the number can form with other numbers. For example, numbers bond to make a number, say 4 (3 + 1) and then how 4 relates to 6 (4 + 6) to make 10, and the way that number relates to others onwards to 100 (4 + 96).

> Idea: consider the number 4. Move forward in ones from 4 first on a number line.
>
> Move forward in tens on the number line from 4.
>
> Idea: consider number 44. Move forward in ones from 44 on a number line.
>
> Move forward in tens on the number line from 44.

For subtraction the movement can be back in ones or back in tens.

> Idea: consider the number 44. Move back in ones from this number noting the numbers you meet. Move back in tens from 44 along a number line.

Counting forwards and backwards can be extended to counting in twos, tens and hundreds (QCA 1999a).

> Idea: an empty number line is a powerful aid to visualizing numbers. Challenging children to place a number, say 26, on a number line and asking for other numbers to be placed alongside it crystallizes this knowledge. Landmark numbers can be provided offering differentiation.

Patterns of similar calculations

Work with the hundred square opens up the realization that 5 + 6 = 11 has a similar pattern to 15 + 6 = 21. The positions of 11 and 21 illustrate the inherent increase of 10 which is subsumed in 15. The pattern can be extrapolated to 25 + 6 = 31. The relative positions of 11, 21, and 31 can be physically experienced on the 100 square. This realization of pattern in operations will help store facts for recall.

Adding and subtracting near multiples of ten

This strategy is useful for adding numbers close to a multiple of 10. Adding numbers that end in 1, 2, 8 or 9. The number to be added is rounded to a multiple of 10 plus a small number or a multiple of 10 minus a small number. This is an intricate manipulation. Adding 9 is facilitated by adding 10 and then subtracting 1. Subtracting 18 is arrived at by subtracting 20 and adding 2 (QCA 1999a).

Through classroom teaching analysis, Rowland et al (2009) describe very clearly the pitfalls of using a hundred square to do this if prior understanding on a number line is not secure.

QCA (1999a: 31) gives the example 36 + 28; so really we would say 36 + 30 − 2. Applying to a hundred square:

1. We would find 36.
2. Go down three rows to add 30 landing on 66.
3. Go back along that row 2 places to subtract the additional 2 as we really only wanted to add 28, not 30.
4. Connect this action to the original 36 + 28 = 64.

31 32 33 34 35 36 37 38 39 40
41 42 43 44 45 46 47 48 49 50
51 52 53 54 55 56 57 58 59 60
61 62 63 64 65 66 67 68 69 70

This is a complex set of manoeuvres demanding a layering of language, concepts, and memory, so not necessarily a clear starting point.

Applying the strategy to a number line,

1. We would find 36.
2. Move forwards 30 landing on 66.
3. Move back two spaces.
4. Connect to original 36 + 28 = 64.

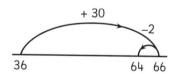

There are the same numbers of steps but less directionality or language confusion. Rowland et al (2009) give a great transcript of a classroom lesson employing the hundred square illustrating the confusion evoked in the children.

If we take the example, add 9 to a single-digit number by adding 10 and subtracting 1, to do this manipulation children need to understand the number bond between 9 and 1.

They would need to sense the inverse connection of addition and subtraction. There is also the need to be in a position of power where one can make changes, returning to reverse these.

Rowland et al (2009) recommend, when demonstrating addition of 9, that on a number line individual steps forward to 10 are taken and then one step is taken back. They advocate that with the number line, 'the connection with rounding and compensation is more visible than in the hundred square where this is hidden by the layout'

(2009: 63). The hundred square would be used at a later stage when number line competence has been mastered.

A strategy for mental addition or subtraction when we have to add or subtract 9 or 19 or 29 or 39 or 49 or 59 or 69 or 79 or 89 or 99 would be to round these numbers up by 1, making 10, 20, 30, 40, 50, 60, 70, 80, 90 and 100. We do need to remember to readjust to balance the books.

A strategy for mental addition or subtraction with 11, 21, 31, 41, 51, 61, 71, 81, 91, 101 would be to round these numbers down working with 10, 20, 30, 40, 50, 60, 70, 80, 90 and 100. Again it is essential to adjust the answer and this is where errors creep in. Pen and paper may assist with these mental calculations.

Rounding up and down is a mental strategy, which requires understanding about number relationships along with memory of actions taken. The calculation 9 + 7 can be changed to 10 + 7 − 1, arriving at 16, but easily incorrectly represented by forgetting to subtract the 1.

With each of these calculations it is important that the rounding up or down is understood rather than latched onto as a rule. We need to think which number representation will best achieve this. On a number line we move forwards and backwards. On a hundred square we move up or down and forwards and backwards. Also the hundred square can offer differing layout of number depending on whether 0 is included (see Chapter 3).

> Add or subtract 9, 19, 11 or 21 by rounding and compensating.
>
> With 9, 19 round up 1.
>
> With 11, 21 round down 1.

Using known doubles to work out near doubles

If we know that 5 and 5 equals 10, we can extend this to addition of 5 and 7 by thinking 5 and 5 and 2. We need to partition 7 into 5 and 2. So if we don't know that 5 and 7 is 12 we can derive this fact from double 5 is 10 and add 2 is 12. We are manipulating what we know to find what we need to know.

Example: 13 + 14 is double 13 add 1 or double 14 subtract 1.

> Idea: give unfamiliar double facts, for example, 17 + 17 = 34 and ask for near doubles (QCA 1999a).
>
> Idea: make a double chain. Choose a number less than 10. Continue to double (QCA 1999a).

Use halving as the inverse of doubling

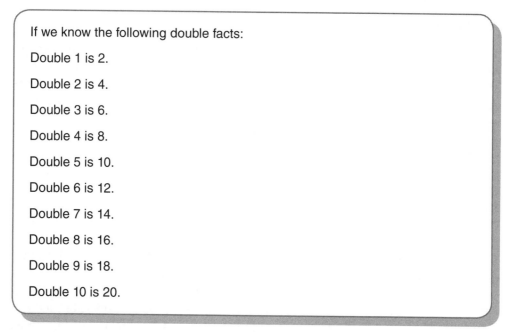

If we know the following double facts:

Double 1 is 2.

Double 2 is 4.

Double 3 is 6.

Double 4 is 8.

Double 5 is 10.

Double 6 is 12.

Double 7 is 14.

Double 8 is 16.

Double 9 is 18.

Double 10 is 20.

Then we can readily deduce that:

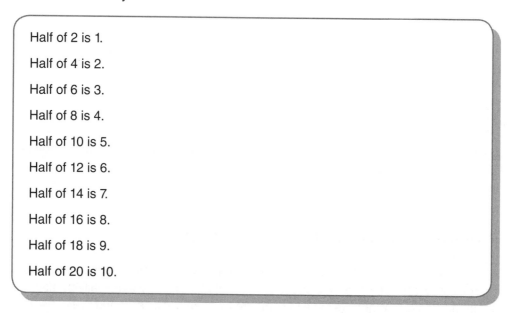

Half of 2 is 1.

Half of 4 is 2.

Half of 6 is 3.

Half of 8 is 4.

Half of 10 is 5.

Half of 12 is 6.

Half of 14 is 7.

Half of 16 is 8.

Half of 18 is 9.

Half of 20 is 10.

As part of our manipulations we may like to double a number to make it more useable.

There may be instances when working with 14 is better than seven. Or nine is more manipulable than 18.

Partitioning

Partitioning to isolate 5

Younger children use their fingers to support counting, advancing this use to calculating. The fact that there are five fingers in each hand makes this number a great anchor. This leads on to natural partitioning of numbers into five and whatever makes up the rest of a number. A powerful strategy is to partition into five and some more when adding 6, 7, 8 or 9 then recombine all the parts when calculating.

Six partitions into 5 and 1
Seven partitions into 5 and 2
Eight partitions into 5 and 3
Nine partitions into 5 and 4
Ten partitions into 5 and 5

So applying the partitioning principle, 6 + 2 could be thought of as 5 + 1 added to 2 using one hand and then fingers from the next hand to arrive at 8.

Partitioning is applying knowledge of number bonds. Partitioning is splitting a number into manageable parts: it is unbonding a number. It could be going beyond two parts to more, for example, 5 can be partitioned to 2 + 1 + 1 + 1, that is, into four parts. This pattern of possible bonds within a number can be used to introduce the idea of repeated subtraction.

The visual representation of,

3 + 3 + 3 + 3 = 12
or
4 + 4 + 4 = 12

starts to lay the idea of taking away a 3 or a 4 repeatedly from 12, to leave nothing. This could also be related to the number line and jumping down in these amounts from 12 to 0.

Partitioning as a mental comparison image

For mental calculations partitioning is particularly key. It unlocks addition; it unlocks subtraction. When we have to subtract 4 from 6, that is, 6 − 4 we mentally partition off 4 from 6 to leave 2. When we have to compare two numbers, say 8 and 6, we mentally partition 8 into 6 and 2, concluding that 8 is two more than 6, or 6 is two less than 8.

Partitioning according to place value

First tens and units

Partitioning relates to place value when working with larger numbers; say for the number 17, children arrange a stack of 10 and then seven individual cubes. To solve the problem $17 = 14 + \square$, they would partition off 14 and count 3 (Liebeck 1984). When comparing two towers, again the partitioning idea is valuable. One tower is 17 bricks high, another 14 bricks. So one tower is three bricks taller, as we compare heights, or conversely the other tower three bricks shorter. Tower building serves to separate the 17 into 14 and 3.

Progressing to hundreds, tens and units

For larger numbers such as 757, the number can be partitioned into 700 + 50 + 7, making it easier to work with the components. This is separating the number according to place value; seven hundreds, five tens and seven units. It is worth noting that for certain calculations it might work better to separate out differently, say 700 + 57, referred to by Chinn (2004) as a creative split rather than a place value split. Liebeck (1984) makes the valid point that children need to know that 320 can be represented as 300 + 20 but is 32 × 10 or 32 tens or 32 sets of 10.

Partitioning means numbers are seen as whole rather than single digits (QCA 1999a), which is essential prerequisite knowledge for later written calculations when this sense is lost.

Example: 30 + 47

These numbers can be added using mental calculation by partitioning 47 into 40 + 7 and then adding 30 + 40 + 7.

Example: 23 + 45

Here we can apply two partitions. 23 is 20 + 3. 45 is 40 + 5. We then add each component part. We can change the order of working with the numbers to:

40 + 20 + 5 + 3 arriving at 68.

Example: 68 − 32

Here we partition 68 into 60 + 8. We partition 32 into 30 and 2.

We need to be careful here with order and use 60 + 8 − 30 − 2 which can be dealt with as 60 − 30 + 8 − 2 arriving at 36.

Example: 85 – 37

We will look at two ways of working this out.

By adding on from 37 we have to see what we add before we get to 85.

37 and 3 makes 40 (added 3).

40 and 40 makes 80 (added 40).

80 and 5 makes 85 (added 5).

We added a total of (48).

Here 48 is in effect partitioned into 40 + 5 + 3 though the order is different.

Or another way we can count back from 85 by the equivalent of 37 in component form

37 = 30 + 5 + 2

Count back by 30 means we are at 55.

Count back by 5 means we are at 50.

Count back by 2 means we are at 48.

Note: examples taken from QCA (1999a).

The need to know box for teaching addition and subtraction mental calculations

Order and reordering

The order does not matter for addition. This is handy when working with large numbers as we can start with the largest. Holding the larger number in your head and counting on liberates us from counting everything. The order does matter for subtraction.

Number bonds connects to partitioning

Number bonds are important. How many ways can six be partitioned? Looking for quick ways to calculate means knowing number bonds for numbers to 10. This can then be projected to numbers to 100. Numbers can be partitioned into more than two components, $5 = 3 + 2$, $5 = 4 + 1$, $5 = 1 + 4$, $5 = 2 + 1 + 1 + 1$ (Liebeck 1984).

Place value connects to partitioning

The principle of exchange is a powerful tool.

Ten ones for one ten. One ten for ten ones.

Ten tens for one hundred. One hundred for ten tens.

Partitioning numbers into hundreds tens and units utilizes this idea.

This means separating a number such as 324 into $300 + 20 + 4$. This is partitioning according to place value. Numbers can be separated out in other ways.

Relationships between numbers and possible multiples of ten

The use of number lines then hundred squares to count forwards and backwards in ones and tens, establishes number relationships beyond the number itself. Adding or subtracting numbers closely related to multiples of 10 can be arrived at through understanding the relationship of the number to a multiple of 10. Instead of adding 18 we add 20 but know that 18 is 2 less than 20, so make the adjustment accordingly.

We have unfolded different meanings behind the operations of addition and subtraction. Then we have explored strategies needed for mental calculations using these operations. The complexity of teaching and resulting understanding cannot be underestimated. The differences within each operation are delicate, determined by choice of words, through carefully chosen questions.

The strategies stem from partitioning numbers into their component parts along with relating these to numbers to one hundred and beyond, 'partitioning is a major organizational strategic principle' (QCA 1999a: 30). The importance of teaching internal number relationships along with those beyond the number is fundamental.

Conclusion

An aim of this chapter was to highlight the importance of language associated with addition and subtraction. With this in mind, Table 7.1 draws together key words, along with questions for each addition and subtraction structure we considered. We challenged the appropriateness of such categorisation. We need to be sensitive to subtleties of language prompting mathematical operations.

We can't afford to presuppose what children know. What is heard from the carpet chorus will not necessarily be spoken by individual children. We could assume that children will see the complexities within mathematical operations more clearly than we do. We need to think connectively like the children in the reception class with the fruit. We need to work with four meanings for addition along with five for subtraction. This will integrate operations into children's thinking.

Strategies for mental calculations seem to progress from strong number bonding. We could think of this as thinking in a schematic way as we assist children in assimilation of new meanings. Our choice of words will need to be connected to our intended meaning; we may need to clarify our line of thought so as to avoid confusing ourselves or children.

Understanding number operations: multiplication and division

'Then you should say what you mean,' the March Hare went on.

'I do,' Alice hastily replied; 'at least I mean what I say, that's the same thing, you know.'

'Not the same thing a bit!' said the Hatter. 'Why, you might just as well say that "I see what I eat" is the same thing as "I eat what I see!"'

Alice in Wonderland, Lewis Carroll (1832–1898)

The aims of this chapter are:

- To explore the different meanings behind multiplication and division
- To find strategies for mental multiplication and division calculations
- To highlight subtleties of language prompting multiplication and division

Introduction

This chapter will focus on the teaching of multiplication and division to children from birth to eight years. The multiple meanings behind multiplication and division will be unveiled; this will highlight the subtleties of language and the variation of expression which can be used to teach these operations. Use of practical resources and stories will be considered. We will consider mental strategies children need to manage these operations.

> **Questions to reflect on:**
>
> How could you use buttons and boxes to show multiplication?
>
> Why is place value important for multiplication?
>
> What pattern can you hear or see in multiplication times tables?

Multiplication

> *One, Two ... Where's the Shoe?* by Richard Rosenstein
>
> Mr and Mrs Shoemaker have 10 children who line their shoes up outside the house when they go inside to bed. Each evening there are 10 pairs of shoes arranged in twos. The shoes are counted to check all are safely inside. One evening there are only nine pairs of children's shoes. The shoe count is checked in a number of languages: Spanish, Italian, German and French, providing opportunity to repeatedly count. An older child solves the worrying puzzle by showing the adults a little boy who has gone to sleep with his shoes on. This is a lovely twist to the custom of leaving shoes in porches showing who is home.

The idea of the total shoe count requiring division by two to determine the number of children is a natural progression from this.

Pairs of shoes can be used to repeat additions of two, which is a form of multiplication. If there are 10 sets of shoes with two in each, there are 20 shoes, that is, $10 \times 2 = 20$ (10 times two) or $2 \times 10 = 20$ (two multiplied by 10). Counting in twos can be used to arrive at 20. Counting in twos expresses multiplication as repeated addition. This is a very visual way of working with multiplication and can be connected to the daily register. A class of 30 children will create $30 \times 2 = 60$ (30 times two) or $2 \times 30 = 60$ (two multiplied by 30). The set is the shoes; the variable is the number of children.

This can form the theme for imaginative play in a shoe shop. There is great opportunity to include numbers, measuring, sorting money. Including slippers, wellingtons, sandals and flip flops, broadens the theme to consider different materials.

Multiplication involves numbers of identical sets; there is a sense of pattern to this operation. One interpretation of multiplication is grouping objects into sets and counting how many sets there are. Another is repeatedly adding the same-sized set. There are other meanings which we consider below.

The three laws of commutativity, associativity and distributivity apply to multiplication. The skills of doubling, halving, inversing and recognizing multiples, serve as strategies to execute multiplication and division calculations. The array model of multiplication will be explored as a way to build the concept and as a strategy to multiply. First we need to be aware of the meanings behind multiplication.

Meanings behind multiplication

A distinguishing feature of multiplication which sets it apart from addition is that it involves equivalent sets of the same item (Frobisher 1999). Addition can be different items in different quantities. Multiplication requires a schematic shift in thinking. If we take the example of three cars, we multiply four by three to arrive at the number of wheels. We are not adding the number of cars but we are repeatedly adding the number of wheels by the number of cars. The emphasis is placed on the number of cars rather than the number of wheels. Whereas before emphasis was placed on counting accurately with one to one correspondence, now for multiplication there is a correspondence between the number of sets and the number of times the feature, say wheels, is multiplied.

Multiplication is complex, requiring practical application in order to arrive at meaningful understanding. With multiplication, the two numbers refer to different things. One number is cars and the other is wheels on cars, but it is not cars and cars. However, this defining boundary blurs when using multiplication to find area, where both numbers being multiplied refer to length (Haylock and Cockburn 2008). Children assimilate a new schema when multiplying and again when using multiplication to calculate area.

The difficulty children have with contextualizing multiplication is revealed in work by Haylock and Cockburn (2008), where children are asked to make a story for a multiplication sentence. A clear mental image appears to be missing. Requesting children to create a multiplication story is a good way of checking if understanding is really secure.

Six meanings for multiplication

Frobisher et al (1999) outline six meanings behind multiplication. These meanings of multiplication are important to consider as they are driven by different language.

Equal grouping/collections

Children first realize multiplication, as Anghileri expresses, 'when they make groups with equal numbers of objects and recognize the possibility of counting the groups rather than counting individual items' (1997: 41). It is the moment when children see pairs of shoes, rather than individual shoes, as a way of counting to arrive at the total number.

Anghileri (1997) makes the suggestion that children could make a pattern stick using five colours with three of *each* colour. The making of towers of repeating units uses pattern and grouping. The word *each* communicates the unit of repeat. The use of coloured bricks, buttons or beads allows this expression of multiplication.

A brief snippet from a playgroup session exemplifies equal grouping.

> The playgroup was going to a farm. Children were shown three pigs and asked: what was the same about each pig? Interestingly they could identify what was different about the pigs more readily. Two pigs were pink and the third was black with a white stripe. They looked at the three pigs for some time and one child suggested 'four'. This suggestion was applied to counting 12 legs.

This equal grouping of four legs with a repeat of three pigs is essentially 4×3 = 12 (four multiplied by three). This question represents an intersection between looking for 'the same', 'difference' and 'count repeated groups of the same size' as referred to in the Early Years Foundation Stage Curriculum Guidance (DfES 2008: 68).

Objects which occur naturally in sets include sets of two: shoes, gloves, bicycle wheels; sets of three: tricycle wheels; sets of four: table legs, car wheels, animal legs; sets of five: fingers on one hand; sets of six: eggs in boxes, legs of insects; sets of seven: days in a week; sets of eight: spiders' legs; sets of nine: shirt buttons; sets of 10: fingers on both hands (Liebeck 1984). The correspondence is one to two, one to three, one to four, one to five, one to six, one to seven, one to eight, one to nine, one to ten, accommodating alteration in the grouping.

Equal grouping is essentially repeatedly adding. The pattern would be disrupted if the unit of repeat became different, that is, a truck with eight wheels was introduced. The one to four correspondence of cars is broken by the one to eight of the truck, disrupting the regular repeat pattern precious to multiplication.

Buttons and boxes

True understanding requires that the child sees the number of items in the group and the number of groups. The skill of grouping a collection in different ways is important for further multiplication work. A set of buttons and boxes can be used for this. A different number of boxes can be used, allowing for grouping of buttons using different factors.

Activities involving breaking the collection up and storing it in boxes or other ways, lays down this model of multiplication. Where there are remainders these need to be facilitated. Like truths of other sorts, children need to be exposed to remainders early on. Remainders are a reality of life and 'it is important that remainders or left overs form part of division since in "real life" things rarely share out equally' (Merttens 1987: 61).

Question: there are three pigs. Each pig has four legs. How many legs are there altogether?
Or
Question: there are three boxes. Each box has four buttons. How many buttons are there altogether?
Key words: 'each', 'altogether'

Number track

This representation ties multiplication to number pattern in tracks or lines. The size of every jump on the number track is constant. The number of jumps needs to be totaled. It is similar to the cars being lined up. The size of the jump is four; the number of cars being equal to the number of jumps. This is counting in multiples along the number line. This model places importance on counting on, which is a precursor to learning multiplication (Frobisher 1999). Here multiplication is taking a number of steps, all the same size, along the number line.

Number line 1 to 16

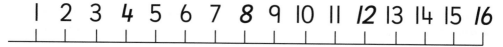

Figure 8.1 Number line 1–16.

The number of jumps is equal to the number of cars above, that is, four jumps of four. Note the need to land on and jump from the same number, that is, four or multiples of four. There is a need to keep a tally of the jumps.

The expression of the commutative nature of multiplication using the number line is made very visual by showing different combinations of multiplication on number lines. Three steps of nine or nine steps of three, multiplying to 27 can be illustrated using two number lines one below the other.

Number line 1 to 27

3 jumps of 9

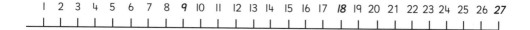

9 jumps of 3

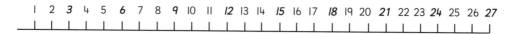

Figure 8.2 Number lines 1–27.

Work with 3 × 9 = 27 and 9 × 3 = 27
Three jumps of 9 or 9 jumps of 3
Three steps of 9 or 9 steps of 3.

Question: how many jumps along the number line to 27, if each is a jump of 3?
Key words: 'jumps of', 'steps of'

Rectangular pattern

This interpretation of multiplication, as described by Frobisher et al (1999), relies on arranging items in rectangles. Buttons can be arranged in rows and columns with the total being the number of rows multiplied by the number of columns. The collection is now arranged as a complete set. The buttons are not separated into boxes for this model of multiplication. It is the arrangement of rows and columns that changes. The pattern of rows and columns reveals the many multiplication possibilities for a given number.

Haylock and Cockburn (2008) identify how the rectangular array also makes the commutative property transparent. A collection of 12 buttons can be arranged as three rows by four columns or four rows by three columns.

The making of all possible rectangles searches out factors. An association with windows and window panes is useful and connects this to the environment, that is, '3 rows of 4 windows' or '4 rows of 3 windows'. This work leads to later work finding areas of rectangles using multiplication (Haylock and Cockburn 2008). Buttons can be arranged in different rows and columns, that is, three rows by four columns of buttons or four rows by three columns of buttons.

Question: how many buttons are there if there are four rows by three columns?
Key words: 'rows of', 'rows by columns'

Cross-product

The cross-product model connects multiplication to a problem-solving scenario. What are all the possible ways of combining two sets of objects? This lends itself to systematic recording, a positive strategy for solving problems.

Jam sandwich

Raspberry and strawberry jam options. Two bread types brown or white.

Possible jam sandwich combinations:

Raspberry jam — brown bread

Raspberry jam — white bread

Strawberry jam — brown bread

Strawberry jam — white bread

There are four jam and bread sandwich combinations.

Question: how many combinations of two jams and two breads can be made as sandwiches?

Key word: 'combinations'

Scale factor or the scaling structure

This is scaling up based on an amount and then another amount 'so many times as many'. As described by Haylock and Cockburn (2008) a quantity is scaled by a factor. The language gives the clue and indicates scaling up that many times or repeatedly adding that many times, for example, one child has three marbles. His friend has three times as many. We need to imagine the three set out three times, giving nine for the friend. Familiarity with the language 'times as many' triggers the appropriate mental action. There is a relationship between the two sets of the same item.

The act of doubling is using a scale factor of two (Haylock and Cockburn 2008). It is worth noting that this mode of multiplication can make a number smaller if the scale factor is less than one. This dispels the myth that multiplication always enlarges. What happens if we multiply 10 by 0.2? We get 2, which is five times smaller than 10.

Question: if Orna has four buttons and Macey has three times as many as Orna, how many does Macey have?

Key words: 'so many times as many', 'so many times bigger', 'as long as', 'as much as', 'as heavy as'

Cost

This is application of multiplication in a similar way to repeated addition and is common to shopping type situations. If one item costs so much, then we can find the price of any number of items using multiplication.

Question: a button costs 3p. How much will four buttons cost?
Key word: 'costs'

Multiplication is the operation; language drives different meanings. We need to step across each of the meanings, building up familiarity with what is required by the words. Words which are unfamiliar put children off the scent, as they try to make sense of what to do. It is advisable to conquer one model of multiplication before moving to another.

Language of multiplication

When analysing material to write about the language of multiplication I found myself in a knot. I was reassured when someone more specialized in the area confirmed that yes, it is tricky. I had to read and reread material on the subject to sort the confusion out in my mind. It raised the issue that this could go unnoticed and tangle others up.

My confusion is in untangling the expression 'three times four' which refers to a set of four elements taken three times, whereas 'three multiplied by four' refers to a set of three elements taken four times (Anghileri 1991). These two phrases create different images (see below). In order to arrive at the same image (three sets of four buttons) we would need to have 'three times four' (3×4) and 'four multiplied by three' (4×3). Depending on whether we are using 'times' or 'multiplication' we need to change the order of the numerals to convey the same image.

If we consider the story of three cars each with four wheels, the story can be told as 'four multiplied by three' (4×3) or 'three times four' (3×4). We need to swap the notation over depending on the words chosen; in changing the language we have to reverse the digits.

The commutative law of multiplication allows for either presentation. However, it is worth noting the complexity behind the scenes, which potentially allows for a deeper understanding.

The visual images of:

three lots of four

three sets of four

is represented mathematically by   (4 × 3) which is read as 'four multiplied by three'

but can be described as   (3 × 4) read as 'three times four'

four lots of three

four sets of three

is represented mathematically by   (3 × 4) which is read as 'three multiplied by four'

but can be described as   (4 × 3) read as 'four times three'

Anghileri (1991) notes that 'three times four' may appear to children to be an easier construction to understand than 'four multiplied by three'. This together with the prevalence of the use of the word 'times' by adults results in widespread use of the word by children (Anghileri 1991). The suggestion to modify the word 'multiplied' to 'multiply' does create a more active sense: 'three multiply four' or 'three multiply by four'. I find this expression presents a clearer image as I have three and I set it out four times, but by doing this we are introducing yet another expression!

In summary:

- The visualization of the process is important: that we create the correct mental image as prompted by the words. The image can also prompt words; both words and images reinforce each other.
- The awareness that language can create a difference and that children may favour expressions different to our own preference.
- The use of the words 'times' and 'multiplied by' require that we reverse the order of the digits in the algebraic expression if they are both applied to one mathematical picture.

It is difficult to use consistent expressions when we are less aware of variation in meaning. Observation of practitioners teaching mathematics reveals how different words used casually to emphasize the same point can confuse the issue. As adults we transgress more readily; children need to hear one expression many times before an alternative can be assimilated. We now consider these delicate language differences for division.

Division

A story describing division in the context of sharing

The Doorbell Rang by Pat Hutchins

'No one makes cookies like Grandma,' said Ma as the doorbell rang.

Ma makes 12 cookies and gives them to Victoria and Sam; six cookies each.

The doorbell rings and is opened to two children. Twelve cookies shared between four children gives three cookies each. The doorbell rings and is opened to two more children. Twelve cookies shared between six children gives two cookies each. The doorbell rings and is opened to six children. Twelve cookies shared between 12 children gives one cookie each. The doorbell rings. Ma suggests the children eat the cookies before it is opened. Sam overrides this and the door is opened to Grandma with a tray of cookies.

The doorbell rings again.

The story stops there but can be taken further as Grandma has a tray of what looks like 58 cookies. This, along with the 12 they have, makes 70 biscuits to be shared between 12 children. Seventy divided by 12 will present a challenge, but if the mother and Grandma are included it would work evenly as it would be 70 divided by 14 giving five cookies each.

This is an example of a simple story which can be used to explain an idea to children at various stages of mathematical thinking. The final page can be used as a starting place for a more complex calculation.

Relating division to the story above allows the idea of remainders to be introduced alongside fractions. Imagine there are 13 biscuits to share between two children, giving six and a half each.

Chinn states that 'division is often perceived as an almost mystical process' (2004: 167). The mystical association with the division operation means many children find this operation harder to perform than multiplication (Liebeck 1984).

Ironically, preschool children arrive at school with 'a wide collection of strategies for solving division problems' (Frobisher 1999: 217). It is a question of capturing this informal knowledge through practical application to meaningful tasks.

Meanings behind division

Frobisher et al (1999) advance on the two ways described by Merttens (1987), offering five meanings for division. From these five ways we will extract associated language.

This is particularly relevant as Haylock and Cockburn (2008) advise against an over-emphasis on 'sharing'. This we can address by providing all five division experiences for children. As with multiplication, each expression of division is driven by different words. The devil is in the detail and the detail is devilish for division.

Sharing

The idea of sharing appeals to very young children and their sense of justice. At the age of two Orna was presented with the challenge of sharing a chocolate bunny among three others and herself. Apart from being given four bowls and the broken egg, she was very much left to her own devices. She did manage to share out the chocolate, even though three of the four bowls had the smallest pieces possible. Perhaps there is a limit to 'equal' when you are two.

What is useful about *The Doorbell Rang* is that the number of cookies stays the same but the number of people increases, so the number of sets into which the cookies need to be divided changes. The calculation becomes less favourable with a sense of loss each time the door bell rings. The moral dilemma of whether to eat the biscuits rather than risk further reduction in the number of cookies with the next ring of the door is correctly decided upon and rewarded with the generous tray, more than enough for everyone, brought by Grandma.

Question: twelve buttons are shared equally between four children. How many buttons will each child have?
Key words: 'sharing equally between'

Grouping or equal grouping

The principle here is, 'how many times a given quantity can be made from a collection of objects' (Frobisher 1999: 220). This mirrors multiplication, where we boxed the collection of buttons into mini collections. Now we are concerned with how many times this can be done, that is, how many divisions can be made? As highlighted above we need to consider remainders. Twelve buttons can be grouped into three sets of four, but 13 buttons would leave one button unboxed.

Question: how many boxes of four buttons can be made from 12 buttons?
Or group 12 buttons into sets of four.
Key words: 'how many', 'into sets of', 'into groups of'

Repeated subtraction

This expression of division is exposed using the number line; it mirrors the repeated addition feature of multiplication. Division with small numbers can be managed in this way. How many times can 2 be taken away from 8? (Frobisher et al 1999). The associated language is 'taken away'; it is relying on the ability to count back. We can apply this to number line work, starting at a number and counting how many times another number can be removed, counting down in steps of that number. This is an essential strategy for mental and written division calculations (Haylock and Cockburn 2008). It is worth looking at the forwards and backwards jumps simultaneously, using one number line beneath the other.

Question: how many times can 4 be taken away from 12, until there is nothing left?
Key words: 'taken away'

It is interesting to note that, 'evidence of children's informal strategies indicates that they are very aware of the role that counting back and repeated subtraction can play when answering division word problems, but this does not appear to be developed by teachers into a conscious awareness where all children are able to deliberately select counting back or repeated subtraction as strategies' (Frobisher et al 1999: 224).

Ratio

This is the inverse of the scaling structure of multiplication (Haylock and Cockburn 2008). The intricate language of 'how many times' is different to 'how much' as described by Frobisher (1999). This expression of division is common to problems such as: one person is so many years old; another is so many years old; how many times older is the first than the second? It is arrived at through repeated subtraction or grouping the first person's age amount by the youngest person's age. The interpretation of 'times' is essential in order to avoid the mistake of subtracting one person's age from the other. The question is not how *much* older, but *how many* times older. We are looking for the number of times the unit repeats. Relating it to the tower of bricks, how many times taller is one compared to another?

Question: how many times bigger than three is 12?
Or
Question: Macey is 12 years old. Orna is three years old. How many times older is Macey than Orna?
Key words: 'many times'

Inverse of multiplication

If we know multiplication we can deduce the division combination. Understanding this interrelationship allows for a reduction in the number of table facts to be remembered. The inverse relationship needs to be arrived at gradually, like realizing naturally the relationship of subtraction to addition. Relating the work the playgroup children did with the farm animals, they could be presented with the challenge, 'if there were 12 legs how many pigs would there be?'

Question: what multiplied by four gives 12?
Or
Question: how many threes give 12?
Key words: 'What multiplied', 'gives'

The language of division

Children arrive at nursery with experience of division in the context of sharing. Yet the journey children make with division will take them on to more complex interpretations. If they remain fixated on sharing as the only context, they may not see division differently. Sharing is not the only way to divide; grouping or repeated subtraction is another division activity.

Children will need to experience the range of language associated with division; words evoke images of various actions. Visual images are determined by words written or spoken; take for example 12 shared by three is four, whereas 12 divided into threes creates four collections of three. One image leads to the number of objects in the collection given to each person; the other is the number of groups, which can be arranged. Anghileri (1995) makes the observation that '12 divided by three' is passive and '12 divide by three' is active and that as with multiplication, children favour the active operation of the word.

twelve shared into threes

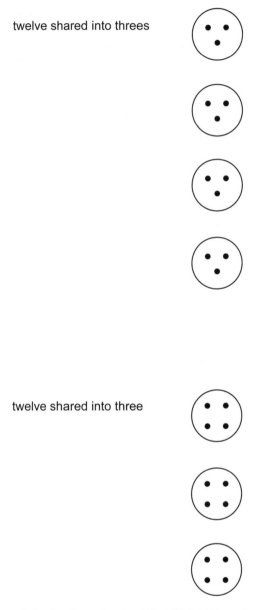

twelve shared into three

Figure 8.3 The language of division (see also Anghileri (1997) '12 apples divided into threes' or '12 apples divided into three').

A further subtlety is
12 divided into threes is grouping or repeated subtraction of threes
12 divided into three is sharing into three portions

The correct interpretation of the ÷ symbol is 12 divided by three (Anghileri 1991).

Children need to be able to take a strategic view and apply the strategy that best fits the situation. As practitioners we need to realize these subtleties so that we can broaden children's experiences of the language and meanings associated with formal mathematical expressions (Anghileri 1995). The words 'divide by', 'divided by', 'shared into three', 'shared into threes', 'grouped into' will need to be exposed, rather than restricted, in order that division is delved into.

Points to note

Interpretation of sharing varies. Share with or share between (one way excludes the person executing the operation). With 'twelve shared equally between three' (Haylock and Cockburn 2008), young children tend to be included in the share. Older children might exclude themselves from the share.

Strategies for mental multiplication and division calculations

The strategies outlined below are based on guidance provided by QCA (1999a). These combine to satisfy solving calculations without formal recording. QCA (1999a) guidelines advise that some children cannot retain what is needed in their heads for mental calculations and so propose that informal recordings be encouraged. They suggest that mental calculations be explained and recorded as number sentences. Horizontal expression of the calculation is deemed suitable for this age. The advantage of mental work over written is that numbers are seen as representation of quantities rather than mere digits (QCA 1999a). As far as possible, mental work should be used as a priority over written calculations.

Economy of thought through three laws

There are three laws which, like levers, help manoeuvre mental calculations. Multiplication obeys whereas division disobeys these laws. However, division is the inverse of multiplication, which is itself a lever to pull on.

Commutative

Changing the order of numbers to multiply can make calculations easier to envisage. Applying commutativity to buttons and boxes the child needs to see that 12 buttons can be arranged as four buttons in each of three boxes or three buttons in each of four boxes, that is, $3 \times 4 = 4 \times 3$. Providing two sets of 12 buttons along with four and three boxes presents practical application of this idea.

Associative

Any order can be followed for multiplication, that is, a × (b × c) = (a × b) × c. Where three things need to be multiplied the order does not matter. We can rearrange as we wish.

Distributive

Multiplication is distributive over addition and subtraction. This is useful when we decide to partition a number up and then need to work with individual parts. We will see this law when we look at the area model for multiplication, where larger numbers are broken up and multiplied by the corresponding broken factors and these are added. We will see this applied in the area model strategy next.

Area model

This strategy splits the numbers to be multiplied into manageable parts. The manageable parts are multiplied and the areas added. The application of the area model uses partitioning, distribution of multiplication over addition, and place value.

We talked earlier about arranging a collection of, say buttons into rows and columns forming different-shaped rectangles. For larger numbers the area model uses this principle along with partitioning numbers.

Taking the example of 27 × 14, we could break 27 into 20 and 7. The number 14 can be broken into 10 and 4. We could multiply 20 by 10, 7 by 10, 20 by 4, 7 by 4 and then add the products 200 and 70 and 80 and 28 to give 378 in a more manageable way.

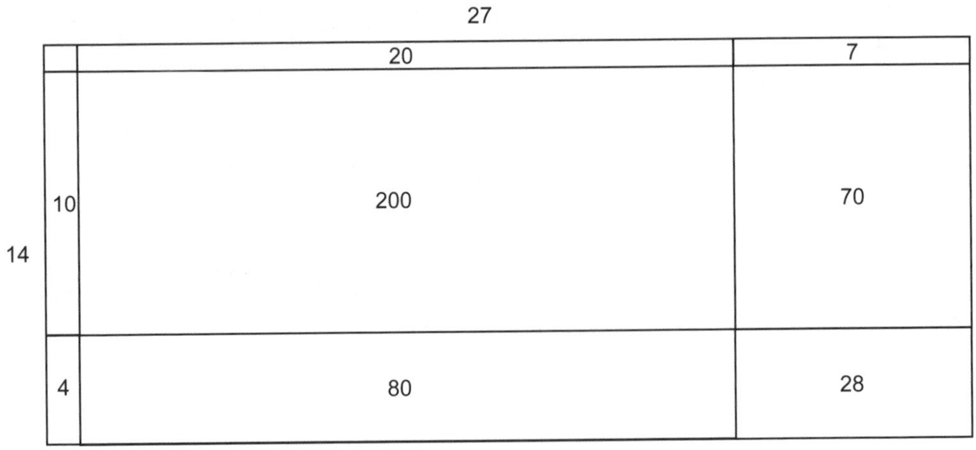

$$200 + 70 + 80 + 28 = 378$$

Figure 8.4 Area model.

Chinn (2004) favours this strategy, also advocated by QCA, which states 'the area model is a useful one, especially to show how a number can be partitioned into tens' (QCA 1999a: 45).

Facts

The facts are collated in the 10 × 10 multiplication tables. Children can use strategies with core facts to work on the unknown, 'research shows that committing some number facts to memory helps children develop strategies, and that the use of strategies to figure out answers helps them commit further facts to memory' (QCA 1999a). Children need some facts to work from.

Tables and counting in multiples

Table pattern is both auditory and visual, which helps children memorize these facts. Listen to the rhythm of the two times tables:

2 × 0 = 0	2 × 1 = 2	2 × 2 = 4
2 × 3 = 6	2 × 4 = 8	2 × 5 = 10
2 × 6 = 12	2 × 7 = 14	2 × 8 = 16
2 × 9 = 18	2 × 10 = 20	

This series of table facts can be arrived also by counting in twos, that is, 2, 4, 6, 8, 10, 12, 14, 16, 18, 20. Similarly the five times tables have a certain rhythm:

5 × 0 = 0	5 × 1 = 5	5 × 2 = 10
5 × 3 = 15	5 × 4 = 20	5 × 5 = 25
5 × 6 = 30	5 × 7 = 35	5 × 8 = 40
5 × 9 = 45	5 × 10 = 50	

The pattern of five times tables can be arrived at by counting in fives, that is, 0, 5, 10, 15, 20, 25, 30, 35, 40, 45, 50.

The same is true of the tens pattern 0, 10, 20, 30, 40, 50, 60, 70, 80, 90, 100. Curriculum guidance up to year two includes these table facts for twos, fives and tens. The expectation for year 3 is that children count in threes and fives with the corresponding division facts.

So counting in multiples runs parallel to times tables. The children can be arranged in a circle and pass the count on or count as a group, clapping to mark the rhythm. If children can count in these sequences they are on their way to working out related facts. The use of fingers to keep a tally of the count can be encouraged, moving into sensing multiplication, as it is not the fingers being counted but the numbers of sets of twos, fives or tens. This is laying down the thought line that it is the pigs that need to be counted rather than the legs.

Doubling again has a rhythmic appeal. Double two is four, double three is six and so on; the ability to double is a fundamental tool for multiplication (QCA 1999a: 50). Halving is both division by two as well as being the inverse of the doubling action. Halving two gives one, four gives two, six gives three.

The number chain game

If a number is even, halve it

If a number is odd, add one and halve it

This game brings you from the edge of the web into the centre, to number one. All the chosen numbers connect into the centre after going on a journey of reduction. If each number is circled, the end result looks like an arrangement of planets. The chains themselves also build up to what look like planet patterns. Either planet patterns or spider webs are appealing to young children.

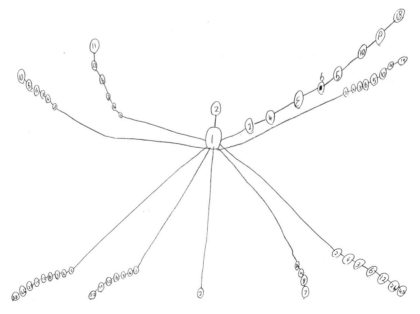

Figure 8.5 Child's drawing of a number chain like a 'spider's web'.

Facts from facts

When some facts are secure they can be used to derive other facts. This requires a certain command of techniques such as partitioning, doubling or halving a number. We need confidence that we can manipulate what is known in order to find what is unknown. We need to explore, test and return to the original question.

Examples using facts and manipulations to arrive at new facts

If children can count in multiples of two, that is, 2, 4, 6, 8, 10, 12 they can then use fingers to calculate 2×6. They hold up six fingers and use each finger to mark the multiple, counting 2, 4, 6, 8, 10, 12. The use of fingers is bridging between counting in twos and using this information to multiply 2 by 6.

Fact to find 7×8

If you know 7×7 is 49 then hold this fact and add 7 giving 56,

or

if you know 5×8 is 40 you could add the value of 2×8 which is 16, giving 56,

or

if you know 8×8 is 64 then we have overshot by 8 so we can subtract this leaving 56,

or

count in multiples of 7 carrying on eight times keeping tally with fingers, 7, 14, 21, 28, 35, 42, 49, 56.

Manipulate table facts to make new table facts

Nine times tables can be arrived at by stepping down one multiple from the 10 times tables. The 6×9 can be arrived at by looking at 6×10 which is 60 and then take away a 6 (we want nine sets of six not 10), giving 54.

Compensation

This strategy is referred to in Chapter 7. It is adjusting numbers to make them more manageable and remembering to readjust or compensate for changes made. In the case of multiplication we might overmultiply but then need to modify accordingly, as with the last example above.

Complements

The principle of complements (Haylock and Cockburn 2008) draws on patterns in numbers and number operations. With addition and subtraction, complements are numbers which bond to make a number; 2 and 8 to make 10; 20 and 80 to make 100. For multiplication factors are the complementary numbers; 2 and 8 are factors of 16. Children become familiar with these through practical work and table fact knowledge. Tables provide the pattern of complementary facts collectively.

Table 8.1 Table facts can be collated in a times table square.

	0	1	2	3	4	5	6	7	8	9	10
0	0	0	0	0	0	0	0	0	0	0	0
1	0	1	2	3	4	5	6	7	8	9	10
2	0	2	4	6	8	10	12	14	16	18	20
3	0	3	6	9	12	15	18	21	24	27	30
4	0	4	8	12	16	20	24	28	32	36	40
5	0	5	10	15	20	25	30	35	40	45	50
6	0	6	12	18	24	30	36	42	48	54	60
7	0	7	14	21	28	35	42	49	56	63	70
8	0	8	16	24	32	40	48	56	64	72	80
9	0	9	18	27	36	45	54	63	72	81	90
10	0	10	20	30	40	50	60	70	80	90	100

A key strategy for mental calculations is deriving new results from known facts. The manipulation of what we know to arrive at what is unknown is the malleable mathematical thinking which needs to be engendered in children. Brown describes this as an 'ability to connect known and derived facts through a strategy that can take them comfortably from one to the other' (2003: 57).

Place value

The QCA (1999a) document states it is most important that multiplying by 10 or 100 is not thought of as a case of 'adding noughts': apart from being a very inappropriate expression because adding zero leaves a number unchanged, the rule fails when, for example, 0.2 is multiplied by 10.

A deeper understanding of what is going on is central to real computation as, 'being able to multiply by 10 and multiples of 10 depends on an understanding of place value and is fundamental to being able to multiply and divide larger numbers' (QCA 1999a: 44).

The Sneetches and Other Stories by Dr Seuss

Then up came McBean with a very sly wink.
And he said, 'Things are not quite as bad as you think.
So you don't know who's who. That is perfectly true.
But come with me, friends. Do you know what I'll do?
I'll make you, again, the best Sneetches on the beaches.
And all it will cost you is ten dollars eaches.'

These Sneetches go in and out of a big machine which roars and klonks having stars added or removed, paying a 10 dollar bill each time. The machine is like a function machine, spending 10 dollars each time.

This story can be used to plant the idea of change, relating then to function machines which multiply or divide by 10. Children could create a machine wide enough for two Sneetches creating 2×10 giving 20 and so on. Four Sneetches going in will each pay 10 dollars to have a star imprinted on their chests which means 4×10 giving 40 dollars.

The need to know box for teaching multiplication and division mental calculations

Tips:

Look for patterns

Even number × even number = even number

Even number × odd number = even number

Odd number × odd number = odd number

Which gives a clue that if the answer to a calculation involving an even number is not even, something is wrong (Merttens 1987; QCA 1999a).

Focus on the multiplication facts children can learn and build on these (Chinn 2004). This would include numbers multiplied by 0, 1, 2, 5 and 10.

Provide blank times tables squares which children can complete as they learn more facts (Chinn 2004).

There are 121 facts for 0×0 to 10×10 tables. These can be reduced considerably through realizing connections and patterns (Chinn 2004; Frobisher et al 1999). It is worth knowing this route to reduce the memory load which Chinn is particularly sensitive to in his work with dyscalculic students.

Multiplication obeys three laws

Multiplication is commutative $a \times b = b \times a$

Multiplication is associative $a \times (b \times c) = (a \times b) \times c$

Multiplication is distributive $a \times (b + c) = (a \times b) + (a \times c)$

'without a working knowledge and understanding of the distributive property, either conscious or intuitive, children are unable to develop sophisticated methods of multiplying and dividing large numbers' (Frobisher et al 1999: 147).

Multiplication is commutative but division is not commutative.

Multiplication and division share an inverse relationship

Division is the inverse of multiplication. If $a \times b = c$ then $c \div b = a$ and $c \div a = b$

Multiplication is the inverse of division. If $a \div b = c$ then $c \times b = a$ and $b \times c = a$

If we take 'n' as meaning a number:

$n \div 1 = n$

This aspect needs a greater focus (Frobisher et al 1999); a number 'n' divided by 1 is the number

$n \times 1 = n$

$n \times 0 = 0$ (note that it is not a case of multiply by 0 meaning do nothing)

$0 \times n = 0$

n ÷ 0 = (undefined). We can think of it as the number of zeros that go into the number; this would be as many as you like. It is undefined and therefore not allowed mathematically.

0 ÷ n = 0 (if you have nothing, then however many people you divide it between they will have nothing each)

Strategies for written multiplication and division calculations

It is important to note that QCA guidance states, 'formal written methods should be taught after children have a firm grounding in a range of mental strategies', and they refer to the Framework for Teaching Mathematics recommendation that 'formal written methods should be introduced from year 4' (QCA 1999a). The child of eight years is expected to 'use practical and informal written methods to multiply and divide two digit numbers' (DfES 2006: 76). The emphasis is horizontal multiplication and division number sentences.

Examples:
10 ÷ 5 = 2
30 ÷ 5 = ☐
31 ÷ 5 = ☐ remainder ☐

Brown (2003) advocates an explicit link between speaking and writing mathematics. Frobisher (1999) suggests the use of practical resources running parallel with expressing the calculation in writing. Recording as we go without losing sight of the practical understanding is essential.

Children need understanding of place value and the ability to partition numbers in order to work with written calculations. Haylock and Cockburn (2008) advocate that there is no justification for introducing children to vertical layout before they understand place value. They propose that working with vertical arrangements draws children into working with individual digits rather than seeing the number as it is.

Conclusion

Practical work is essential to teach and learn multiplication and division. This can be facilitated using simple uncomplicated resources such as buttons and boxes. Calculations need to be meaningful, supported with manipulation of materials.

The use of consistent expressions giving full insight will make explicit the different meanings of multiplication and division. When children are familiar with the correct catalytic meaning of words they can then apply the operation.

A dynamic rather than static state is needed to operate mathematically. Promoting economy of thought fully exploits connective thinking (Brown 2003). We achieve this when we take young mathematicians to higher levels, seeing the bigger picture as well as the finer detail.

Pattern paves the way for memory. As educators we can identify patterns which develop children's understanding of multiplication and division. We can start with 0, 2, 5, 10 times tables working out from these. Educators need to interfere to show children how to make links between what they know and don't know, thus circumventing weak knowledge (Chinn 2004).

Problem solving

9

> The future mathematician should be a clever problem-solver: but to be a clever
> problem-solver is not enough.
>
> Polya (1945: 205)

The aims of this chapter are:

- Define different problem types
- Consider difficulties children have with problem solving
- Strategies for problem solving
- Problem posing
- Understand the value of creativity for problem solving
- Consider older children and those with English as a second language

Introduction

Although this chapter focuses on problems, it brings together key ideas relating to play.
Though problems conjure up negative thoughts, the young child is a natural problem
seeker (Pound 2008). This is a good starting point as the practitioner can use this
inherent drive, to advantage. Communication connects the process of problem solving
to the expression of solutions, making this an important skill, especially for children
acquiring English.

A play-based approach is needed for children further along the education system,
as they still need to connect the abstract to the concrete, particularly if unfamiliar with
the language of mathematics. We will explore connections between mathematics and
other curricular areas. Problem-solving challenges children to use what they already
know. This chapter aims to provide a deeper understanding of how to support this area
of mathematics.

> ## Questions to reflect on:
>
> When is a problem not a problem?
>
> How would you support children who are struggling with problem solving?
>
> In what way can a play-based approach benefit older children when presented with problems to solve?

Defining different problem types

When is a problem not a problem? Whether it is a problem or not is determined by the child's experience. Essentially, a problem presents a challenge. A 'mathematics problem for one child may be an exercise for another' (Orton and Frobisher 1996: 24). The child must believe a goal is to be achieved, accept the challenge and search for the way to solve the problem (Orton and Frobisher 1996).

Different types of problem require different strategies to solve them. Children are not necessarily familiar with all the strategies needed, and may not even draw on those they know, to solve problems. The practitioner needs to demonstrate how a range of strategies can be used; and to select the best strategy for the type of problem.

There is a useful document titled *Problem Solving* which classifies problems as follows:

- Finding all possibilities
- Logic problems
- Finding rules and describing patterns
- Diagram problems and visual puzzles
- Word problems/story problems.

(Taken from DfES 2004b Problem Solving)

As this purports to provide a comprehensive list of the types of problems children will be presented with, let's explore each a little further. There is an additional problem, which we will need to examine in order to complete the picture.

Finding all possibilities

This implies openness in the way solutions can be reached. The child's strategy will be to generate lists, organize or record data. The child will need to be shown how to do this in a systematic way, so that all possibilities are found.

Example: a spaceship lands with creatures called tripods and bipods. There are at least two of each type of creature. Tripods have three legs. Bipods have two legs. There are 23 legs altogether. How many tripods are there? How many bipods? Children are asked to find two answers. Ben, seven years old, provides one possibility: five tripods (5 × 3 = 15 legs) and four bipods (4 × 2 = 8 legs) giving 15 and 8, so 23 legs in his drawing (see Figure 9.1).

Figure 9.1 Sketch by child of 'A spaceship lands' for problem solving.

This type of problem concentrates on the mathematics itself and on the thinking processes. Orton and Frobisher (1996) give the example of how many pairs of numbers are there which add up to 475. The goal is defined. There are several methods available arriving at a fixed endpoint.

Logic puzzles

These problems require that one piece of information is held 'in the mind's eye' while interpreting another; the skill of comparison is being used. It is necessary to fix one thing in memory. This problem demands prioritization and comparison of statements.

Example: children use the clues to solve the puzzle in a logical way (see Figure 9.2).

Clues

Red is not next to grey

Blue is between white and grey

Green is not a square

Blue is on the right side of pink

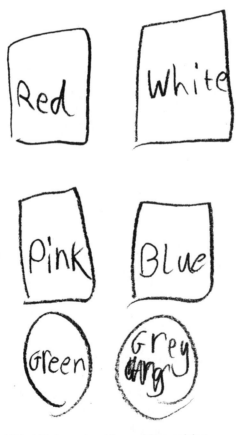

Figure 9.2 Sketch by child of 'Colour clues' for problem solving.

Finding rules and describing patterns

These problems are used to develop reasoning; early work on number pattern pays dividends when tackling them.

Example: one block is needed to make an up-and-down staircase with one step up and one step down. Four blocks make an up-and-down staircase with two steps up and two steps down. The problem is to work out how many blocks would be needed to build an up-and-down staircase with five steps up and five steps down.

This example is particularly good, as it allows bricks to be used in a practical way, connecting the abstract content of the problem to the concrete solution. It also allows bricks to be used by older children and those less familiar with the associated language. This example is described as 'Up and Down Staircases' on the NRICH (2009) website which is managed by the University of Cambridge.

There is a rhythm to the answer as steps increase, so we find a rule for the pattern and this means we can determine the answer for any number of steps. This represents an example of stepping from pattern into algebra through problem solving (see Chapter 6).

Diagram problems and visual puzzles

This requires systematic searching and recording the outcome of the search. Early skills of counting accurately (see Chapter 3) are essential. The skill of remembering what has been already counted is important for this strategy.

Example: draw a triangle. Inside the triangle draw a vertical line from the top straight down. Draw two horizontal lines inside the triangle. How many triangles can you count? There are nine triangles.

Word problems/story problems

These need careful reading to extract information which requires operating on. The child needs to unwrap, operate and ideally, wrap the solution back into words. Again there are strategies which the practitioner can demonstrate. Word problems demand an understanding of the words, the context, the reasonableness of the solution. Orton and Frobisher (1996) call these 'routine problems'.

Example: 'A postman has ninety-four letters in his bag. Twenty-five of them are first class. How many are second-class?' (Orton and Frobisher 1996).

With such problems, children need to understand the context of the problem; in this case they need to understand that stamps can be first- or second-class. The difficulty with such problems is that they make assumptions about experience and prior knowledge (Orton and Frobisher 1996).

Environmental or real problems

An additional category is real problems with an open endpoint. Openness brings the problem into the realm of investigation and 'an investigative approach gives rise to additional problems and other aspects of mathematics to explore' (Orton and Frobisher 1996: 52). The inclusion of 'environmental problems' or 'real problems' is important, as these problems engage children in more creative mathematical thinking. The Rose Report (Rose 2009) advocates that children solve problems in a creative way.

Environmental or real problems relate to mathematics, for example, in determining how much squash is needed for a sports day, or how many coaches are required for a trip to the zoo. The mathematical knowledge employed is a tool rather than an end in itself. Environmental problems lend themselves to more creative thinking, which young children do naturally. Approximation and estimation are more appropriate when solving environmental or real problems (Orton and Frobisher 1996). The defining characteristic is that the goal is not too tightly prescribed (Haylock and Cockburn 2008).

Open-ended tasks and investigations develop the broader skills of problem solving, reasoning and generalizing as described in *Mathematics: Understanding the score* (Ofsted 2009).

The above outline looks at the range of problems children need to work with. Practitioners should develop strategies to show how to address each problem type. For problems with an open end we need to risk not knowing the answer. The open environmental or real type of problem may extend beyond a single lesson, as we may need to 'sleep on it'. One problem may lead to another. A creative approach leads to problem posing as well as problem solving. We will consider problem posing later.

Difficulties children have with problem solving

Orton and Frobisher reassuringly state that, 'no matter how far any one of us has progressed with mathematics, at one time or another all but a very few of us have experienced difficulties in understanding particular abstract ideas' (1996: 2). We will explore 10 potential difficulties children have with problem solving, the first six from Chinn (2004) and the final four from *Problem Solving* (DfES 2004b).

- Short-term memory deficits make problem solving more difficult as the process requires information to be stored and retrieved to solve the problem.
- Poor reading skills make word problems difficult as the child is faced with the added complication of storing the meaning of words so the problem context is understood. Failure to read the problem carefully through hinders the potential to solve it.
- Poor recall of basic facts makes the execution of mathematical operation difficult.

- Recording data needs to be systematic; not recording data carefully leads to an incorrect answer.
- Not checking the answer for reasonableness is not fully completing the problem-solving process. The skill of checking and returning to the problem is a habit which needs to be developed.
- Difficulty recognizing patterns and making generalizations prevents solving certain problem types, for example the stepped brick problem.
- Prerequisite knowledge needs to be secure. Solving problems is applying knowledge previously gained.
- Unfamiliarity with a type of problem means the child may not know what strategies to employ.
- Thinking that there is only one solution hinders the approach to open-ended problems.
- Not talking about the problem with peers eliminates the possibility of sharing strategies.

We need to be aware of these potential difficulties to devise supportive strategies for children. Strategies suggested for children with dyslexia or dyscalculia are suitable for all children, as they are based on multi-sensory work which aids memory.

Strategies for problem solving

For each problem type, a multi-sensory approach works best. The child needs the opportunity to see, hear and do. The practitioner has a key role in modelling how to tackle problem solving. The following 10 suggestions help ensure adult and child achieve a positive approach to problem solving:

- Concrete materials are required to help children move between abstract problems and concrete solutions. Children need to experience problems. Bricks and other resources should be provided for older children beyond reception classes.
- Children acquire problem-solving strategies by modelling how to tackle each type of problem. 'Finding all possibilities' type of problems require adults to practise listing all possibilities, drawing out 'the systematic order of the list as a teaching point for future problem-solving activities' (DfES 2004b, *Problem Solving*). Recording all possibilities needs to be done in a systematic, efficient way.
- Repetition through similar problems, using the same strategies several times, reinforces the approach. Reinforcing is key to mathematical success.
- Checking is a habit which can be demonstrated, incorporating it into the problem-solving process.
- Pictorially representing problems is a strategy which children can observe, appealing to the visual learner.
- Verbally representing problems is appealing to the auditory learner.

- A variety of problems will be needed so that over time children develop a sense of drawing from a bank of approaches.
- Pattern recognition may need to be pointed out so that children make connections, avoiding having to rely on memory.
- Use questioning to develop reasoning and communication skills. Orton and Frobisher suggest, 'sensitive intervention when an impasse has been reached or when frustration is observed', recommending the practitioner to, 'ask a question which will promote construction' (1996: 20). When the solution has been reached, questioning can progress to extending mathematical thinking. What if one of the pieces of information in the problem is changed? Skilful questioning leads to problem posing.
- Check prior knowledge as, 'the focus on problem solving shifts the weight from the acquisition of knowledge and skills to using and applying them' (Orton and Frobisher 1996: 23). Determine and revisit what previous learning is needed before presenting problems which rely on it.

These suggestions will support the problem-solving aspect of mathematics. For each problem type a sequential structure can be used which incorporates them.

Montague-Smith (1997: 157) suggests that children can be supported with problem solving by:

- Identifying the problem and making a plan either verbally or as a picture
- Working at their plan, revising it as they go
- Recalling what has been done

It is worth noting that Suggate, Davis and Goulding (2006) comment that there are two views on providing a routine for problem solving. Some consider that problem-solving skills do not lend themselves to mechanical frameworks. Because problem solving is complex, the author considers a support structure is necessary; it gives direction for those children who need it. Let's consider another structure provided by Polya (1945) who suggests the following steps:

First   Understanding the problem
       (Draw a picture. Separate the various parts of the condition)

Second   Devising a plan
       (Find the connection between the data and the unknown)

Third   Carrying out the plan
       (Check each step)

Fourth   Looking back
       (Examine the solution)

A further suggestion would be to present these processes in a cyclical way with some additions: put the solution back into the context or words of the problem; create a 'what if?' extension problem by changing part of the problem; write one's own problem to give to a peer, teacher or family member.

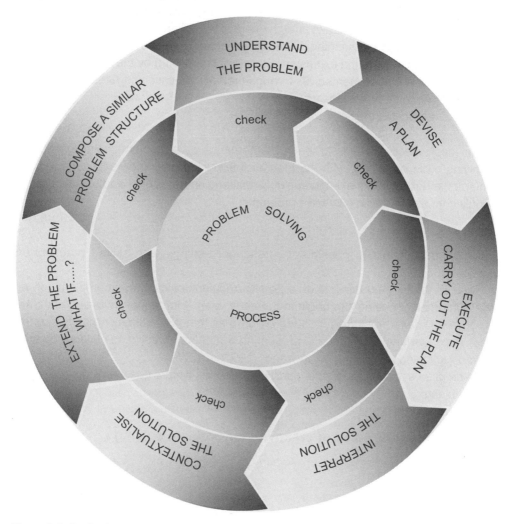

Figure 9.3 Cyclical process for problem solving.

We have looked at the different types of problems children need to learn and considered the difficulties children have and strategies to overcome them; a cyclical structure for the problem-solving process has been presented. With environmental or real problems, the adult becomes a problem solver rather than problem facilitator, as they need to explore the answer to steer the discovery.

Problem posing

Questioning skilfully promotes problem posing. This will be considered in more detail as it impacts on the development of creative thinking. Problem posing presents important challenges. It can be achieved with the youngest child by moving an object further from reach so they need to stretch or crawl. As children acquire language, it can be achieved through questioning. 'What if we change something?' questions open doors to problem posing and extension. Early problem posing by the adult will help the children to problem pose themselves through their own questioning. Creating problems in this way promotes deep thinking.

Brown advocates that:

> The most effective way is to teach mathematics as a problem-posing-problem solving cycle of activity, with the teacher introducing new knowledge and techniques to help children ask increasingly challenging questions, and use increasingly complex processes to solve problems.
>
> (2003: 193)

Brown adds that this is possible in preschool settings with skilled practitioners (Brown 2003).

Marion Walter (1989) in a short report 'Curriculum topics through problem solving' says that problem posing can begin in the early years. Montague-Smith suggests that everyday tasks are problems for young children as they are still making early connections: 'each learning experience is presenting a problem to solve as children connect previous knowledge to the task in hand' (1997: 10). We will consider opportunities within creative activities for problem solving; here the 'what if question?' dovetails play with problems.

Understanding the value of creativity for problem solving

> A great deal of what has been written on creativity is also most applicable to problem solving
>
> Bird (1991: 119)

Play poses problems, which are tested and overcome in a natural way. High-quality play exercises concentration and 'the thinking processes which are part of play are the very ones required for later mathematical thinking' (Pound 1999: 49). In the early stages of a child's educational experience, 'problem solving will be part of every day nursery life. Children should be encouraged to use their growing understanding of number in order to help them solve problems' (Montague-Smith 1997: 44). The art of playing often leads the child to line up and count: 'counting in itself is a problem-solving strategy, which can be used to answer questions' (Montague-Smith 1997: 17). The question 'how many' can lead to the complex question, 'how many more?' We will return to this later; first, we will examine some everyday nursery activities for problem-posing potential.

Junk modelling

Observing a Foundation Degree student brought me to a nursery class where children were working with junk modelling. A particular child who had a disability with one arm was somewhat lost on the edge of the group. I decided to step out of the observer role and spark up a conversation with this child. When asked what she wanted to make she replied, 'a city'. We started by searching for a book that might have a photograph of a city. New York city became the theme and we talked about the yellow cabs and tall buildings. The main problem we had was how to plan the city. It was decided a platform was needed. An opened out cereal box, provided the answer. The next problem was finding a way of sticking the materials down. This is where provision is important; a child-initiated idea cannot take flight if there are inadequate materials to work with. We needed strong brown tape or masking tape. Neither was available.

Bringing a book with a picture of New York City to the junk modelling area promoted detailed discussion, which could otherwise be missed. The activity connected literacy, mathematics, knowledge and understanding of the world through junk modelling.

A small comment can lead to describing a plan, selecting materials, estimating, discussing the progress of the task, evaluating the effectiveness of the outcome (Montague-Smith 1997). It is good practice to compare the original plan, verbal or pictorial to the final product, as this reflection projects the journey taken outwards. This develops the habit of checking or 'looking back' as promoted by Polya (1945). Reflecting in this way allows the child to approach new problems from a stronger base (Suggate et al 2006).

With an open-ended problem the child can see there is more than one way to solve the task. There are situations where a child-initiated activity needs to be shared, in order that the child experiences deep play-based learning. The intervention here was necessary to extend learning opportunities, encouraging the child to set and solve problems for herself, engaging in 'sustained shared thinking'; she can then build other cities in her own way.

What about older children designing cities or towns? After all, people have careers in architecture and town planning. More complex parameters would make for more problems posed, more problems solved creatively. This activity can be presented to older children.

Block play

Through block play, working with construction kits and building models, children will set themselves problems and find ways of solving them.

Montague-Smith (1997: 10)

Building bridges is problem solving. Will you build a bridge? A challenge children respond positively to. Brunel is famous for his bridge building which appeals to older children.

Questions to reflect on:

How could older children use bricks to build more complex bridges?

What would be the value of providing bridge building challenges further up the school?

What variables could be used to pose problems for bridge making?

Small world play

Small world and construction provide many opportunities for children to develop problem-solving skills. We will consider train tracks and farm play. Creating micro worlds affords rich opportunities to solve problems and connects concrete to abstract.

Train tracks

Designing and constructing train tracks exercises complex problem-solving skills. A child as young as two years can make a circular track. This can then be extended to an oval circuit by introducing straight sections of track to the curved pieces. The older child can develop advanced designs, such as figures of eight.

The request to draw a plan first requires that the child visualizes what they will do with the pieces. Alternatively children can look at a picture of the track, construct it and then record.

Children aged seven were asked to represent pictorially the tracks they made so that younger children could use these diagrams to make the same circuits, which presented an unexpected outcome. These seven year olds found it difficult to make the figure of eight and even more difficult to visually represent any of the tracks (Figure 9.4). Their difficulty lay in sectioning the shape with the correct number of pieces pictorially.

The adult can pose new problems by varying the number and type of pieces. Too often a train track is set out by adults or left incomplete. Adult initiation of train track work can move into child-initiated activity, as children become confident connecting pieces of track.

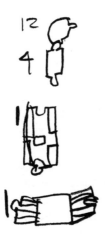

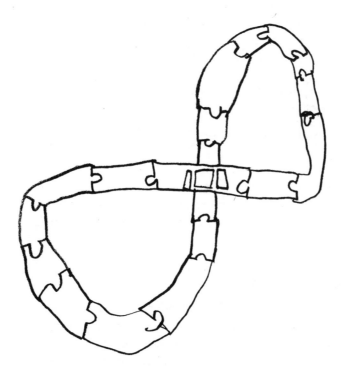

Figure 9.4 Child's sketch of figure-of-eight train circuit.

Farm play

A child playing with sheep on the farm can be presented with the problem of guessing how many sheep will fit into a pen; creating the pens is itself problem solving.

From an early problem of finding how many sheep will fit in pens of different sizes the problem projects to one of sheepdog trials. The problem below is from *Finding All Possibilities* for a year 4 class (DfES 2004b). This problem has been deliberately chosen to show the value of early play where questions posed by adults lead to problem-solving skills further along a child's learning experience.

When you have read the problem, think how the problem could be tailored to fit year two, year one and reception-aged children. Consider the value of the older child using miniature sheep along with pens to work through the possibilities. Consider the value of practical work for the child who is less familiar with English or the child to whom sheepdog trials are unknown.

Sheepdog trials

A farmer and his dog enter a sheepdog trial.
In this event his dog must shepherd 24 sheep into three pens of different sizes.
Each pen must have a different even number of sheep.
The largest pen must have the most sheep and the smallest pen must have the fewest sheep.
How many sheep might the dog try to get in each pen?
Find as many different ways as you can.

(DfES 2004b *Finding All Possibilities*)

Sourcing one dog, 24 sheep, three pens along with a story like *Floss* by Kim Lewis, about a sheep dog, will support the recommendation that for older children, either with no English or not yet fully developed concepts, it is good to support the problem with real materials (DfEE 2000).

Beebot programmable toy

Children were given the freedom to work independently in pairs with Beebots. These small bee-like toys can be programmed to move forwards, backwards, left and right. I asked several children to explain to me how they work and found only one child could precisely programme the toy. Children need to be shown explicitly and then left to experiment.

Figure 9.5 Two children Beebot programming.

Pattern

Possibilities for problem solving with pattern arise as part of children's everyday activities, (Montague-Smith 1997). The importance of teaching pattern was expressed in Chapter 6. We will now consider the relationship pattern has with problem solving. Pattern is the track along which mathematics runs and 'pattern might well sometimes offer a means of generating the construction of mathematics by the children' (Orton and Frobisher 1996: 21).

The stepped brick problem involves searching for a number pattern. The pattern which emerges is: one step, one brick; two steps, four bricks; three steps, nine bricks; four steps, 16 bricks. We can see a pattern; as the step increases by one the difference in the required number of bricks increases as 1, 4, 9, 16 and the difference between these is the clue to predicting the next amount, that is, 3, 5, 7 and so the next increase for five steps will mean nine added to the 16 required for four steps giving 25 bricks. Orton and Frobisher stress that, 'pattern searching is an important mathematical process, which itself depends upon analysis of and reflection upon data, noticing similarities and differences' (1996: 30).

A child threading a pattern of beads can create a symmetrical linear pattern, using say red, blue, green, green, blue, red beads in a row. A mirror can be used to identify reflected symmetry patterns.

This early work involving pattern and mirrors projects forward to the problem presented to year 2 children, as:

Gopal had six squares: two red, two green, two blue.

He put them in a line.

The squares made a symmetrical pattern.

Red-blue-green-green-blue-red.

How many different lines can you make like this?

(DfEE 2000)

This example uses knowledge of pattern making, finding lines of symmetry, and recording systematically six possible ways of doing so. The additional five are:

red, green, blue, blue, green, red

green, red, blue, blue, red, green

green, blue, red, red, blue, green

blue, red, green, green, red, blue

blue, green, red, red, green, blue

This could be supported with beads and mirrors, connecting to early pattern threading. Early learning progressing to later learning through the same principle is evident in the following two examples:

Young children arranging a picnic for teddy bears are presented with ways of changing how the bears are arranged, exploring patterns and relationships. This can be recorded using pictures or photographs. So let's imagine there is one bear who invites two bears for tea. The children can physically arrange the bears to see all the possibilities. This problem lays down experience for later problem solving.

The example below is proposed for a year 6 class.

The objective is that children:

- 'Solve mathematical problems or puzzles, recognize and explain patterns and relationships, generalize and predict'.
- 'Organize the recording of possibilities e.g. in an ordered table or list'.

King Arnold

King Arnold sits at a round table.
There are 3 empty seats.

In how many different ways can 3 knights sit in them?

What if there are 4 empty seats?
In how many different ways can 4 knights sit in them?

(DfEE 2000)

The early work of pattern making may well need to be reinforced for older children before they are expected to solve more complex problems where they need to search for all possible pattern combinations. It is important to return to the origin of the concept before moving forward, avoiding making assumptions about prior learning.

Jigsaws

The universal adult or child activity of completing jigsaw puzzles opens into the search for pattern without reliance on language. Completing a challenging jigsaw is character building. It is good practice to ensure children finish a jigsaw before moving on to something else. Brown states that 'jigsaw puzzles exist for all ages and providing the level of difficulty is not too great, using jigsaw puzzles improves hand-eye co-ordination as well as matching part to whole, and searching for pattern' (2003: 116).

Missing number problems

Familiarity with number bond pattern serves to help children with problem-solving skills. Missing number problems can be introduced using objects or pictures (Frobisher et al 1999) and use the child's knowledge of number bonds, for example, $? + ? = 5$.

Folktales

Stone Soup is a European folktale with French, Swedish and Russian versions. The magical ingredient is sharing. There is a wealth of curricular opportunity in the tale. It would be interesting to explore similarities and differences between cultural versions of Stone Soup. The layering of complexities within the story accommodates all ages. There is a particularly beautiful version of *Stone Soup* retold by Heather Forest and illustrated by Susan Gaber.

Stone Soup by Heather Forest

Two travellers in the mountains come upon a village and ask for food. They are rejected by a woman, a boy and other villagers. They all make out there is nothing to offer. The travellers announce that they are master cooks and suggest that if they had a pot they could make soup. A pot is produced by a curious man and the traveller's promise of delicious soup draws on the will of others. The travellers talk of a magical ingredient which they say they will find in the village. They add a stone into the pot and coax more ingredients with the comment 'it would taste better if ...' A child brings a carrot and one by one villagers bring a potato, a green bean and other ingredients. There is a wonderful use of the repetitive phrase; 'Bring what you've got! Put it in the pot. We're making Stone Soup.'

The villagers see that the travellers have made soup from a stone. The travellers know it to be as a result of the magical ingredient which they did find.

Mathematical opportunity in stone soup recipe

The ingredients can be used to express number, quantity, order. How many ingredients were provided? Which ingredient was added first then last? The problem can be posed as to how the 'magical stone' can be retrieved from the pot.

Other curricular connections

Books can be made with different soup creations. Soup can be made with each child contributing one ingredient. In this version by Heather Forest there is a recipe at the end 'How to Make Your Own Stone Soup.'

There are other stories about Nail Broth or Limestone Broth, all based on the principle of turning selfishness or meanness into generosity by sharing.

Pumpkin Soup by Helen Cooper is a story, for younger children, in a picture-illustrated book. It emphasizes turn taking and avoiding upsetting friends. Problems could be posed along the line of proportion and ratio. If one pumpkin will make soup for six people, what will we do if we want soup for the whole class of 30? Another problem to pose is, what if there are no pumpkins available?

Problem-posing prompts

What if more people than six want soup? What if 12 people want soup?

What if we invite the next-door class for soup?

What if pumpkin is out of season and we can't source any?

What if we don't have enough soup bowls or spoons?

What if there is not enough bread?

What if there is not enough time to make and eat the soup?

What can we do while the soup is cooking?

One grain of rice

Another folktale 'Munna and the Grain of Rice' by Rosemarie Somaiah taken from *Indian Children's Favourite Stories* published by Tuttle also involves shifting attitudes and is rich in mathematics.

'Munna and the Grain of Rice'

Munna, an elephant keeper's daughter, is rewarded for her honesty when the Raja orders that village rice is brought to his stores and she notices and returns some which falls out. The Raja wants to reward Munna but she simply asks for 'one grain of rice on the first day, and on every day following give me only twice what you have given me the day before'. On the first day Munna is given one grain, increasing to 512 on the tenth day. On day 21 Munna has 1,048,576 grains enough to fill a large basket. This story skilfully talks about the increasing numbers of grains of rice and the equivalence in handfuls, bowls, bags and baskets. On the last day the rice grains amount to 28 baskets of rice. Munna has all the Raja's rice. She persuades him to share with the people of his kingdom.

The one grain of rice doubles for 30 days. At 30 days the figure is 536,870,912 which is five hundred and thirty-six million, eight hundred and seventy thousand and nine hundred and twelve grains of rice, enough to feed the village. The intrigue children have for large numbers is satisfied. Older children can calculate the totals at various stages along a calendar (National Council of Teachers of Mathematics 2009). There is great scope for estimating and checking with this story.

The above examples connect story, cooking and mathematics in a cross-curricular way and start with a book or story. There is mathematical opportunity in most books, stories and poems.

Cross-curricular planning

Start inside the book with the story content.

Step outside connecting the story to other curricular areas.

Step back into the story looking for mathematical opportunities both within and beyond the story.

Storytelling

A professional storyteller, Cassandra Wye, was invited to work with Foundation Degree students. Students participated in a creative retelling of a story about a tiger who lost his smile. The experience of listening to a story, partaking in its telling with actions, sounds and emotions, stimulates the imagination. The absence of pictures means we create mental images, like listening to a play on the radio. Repeating words, actions, sounds, stores the sequence of the story in the memory. Retelling a familiar story in this way is creative work. If the practitioner tells a story of their own, this offers children a different experience. Children telling their own stories exercise high-order creative skills.

When listening to a story, particularly a story without a book, we are making connections, imagining, realizing patterns. These processes project into the art of problem solving.

Stories depend on relationships. A story follows a pattern from an opening problem to a conclusion. The parallel between stories and mathematics is perhaps overlooked. Many stories exemplify mathematical concepts. There are obstacles to be overcome, characters to be worked around, and solutions to be found.

Most stories follow a formula, beginning, middle and end, with plot obstacles to overcome. There is a journey taken to arrive at the destination. There are opportunities to use mathematical language repeatedly; 'the tiger climbed up the tree, one, two, three, four. The tiger slipped down to the bottom. The tiger tried again, one, two, three, four.'

In problem solving and investigations, visualization is a required skill. Story telling without a book relies on the imagination. We see the tiger looking into the lake, laughing, finding his smile. Actions, sounds, words, pauses, repetitions, pace, tone, all help with imagining the story.

Considering older children and those with English as a second language

It would seem appropriate to now consider the child who has moved beyond the Early Years Foundation Stage and who is presented with problem-solving challenges. These children may find themselves in play-limited environments. Unless they have acquired problem-solving skills through play, and can work in the abstract context they will struggle with this aspect of mathematics.

Concrete connections

Connections for older children still need to happen through concrete materials. Briggs and Davis (2008: 15) state that 'play activities can be introduced to older children to allow them to explore mathematical ideas through games, puzzles and problems'. Certain activities such as town planning, bingo, farm play, can be presented with greater complexity.

Older children may have memory deficits, particularly if they have dyslexia, dyscalculia, so, 'equipment such as abacus provide a physical dimension to memory' (Pound 1999: 50).

We need to use bricks with all children: perhaps different bricks would bridge later play to earlier memories.

Consciousness of word semantics such as 'more'

There is a need to be aware of mathematical language associated with problem solving. The word 'more' can be particularly troublesome, as it can be used to prompt addition or subtraction (see Chapter 7). Comparison problems containing the word, 'more' can be misleading, as the child may not have had an earlier connection between the word and subtraction. Frobisher et al (1999) suggest that the early skill of comparison needs connecting to appropriate language. They comment that though children compare sets of objects finding out which is more, there is not enough connection made between this word and subtraction. Chinn (2004) makes this point explicit using two examples.

Jon has three toys.

Sam has two more toys than Jon.

How many toys does Sam have?

3 + 2 = 5

> Sam has three toys.
>
> Sam has two more toys than Jon.
>
> How many toys does Jon have?
>
> 3 − 2 = 1
>
> (Taken from Chinn 2004:100)

It is not enough that children acquire vocabulary; they need discourse, which produces understanding. Discourse enables both parties to link their own ideas to speech, action and thought of (at least) one other interested party (Brown 2003).

Contemporary mathematics

Older children can absorb the history of mathematics, 'we can include opportunities for meditative thought within mathematics lessons by studying the use to which mathematics is put in architecture, music and by studying the way different cultures use and have used mathematics in the past' (Brown 2003: 196).

Involving children in thinking about how mathematics has evolved promotes the idea that it is a subject driven by people within the culture they represent. This creates a chance to look at current day mathematicians such as Professor Marcus de Sautoy. What are contemporary mathematicians working on? Prime numbers and symmetry are of particular interest to Marcus, who commented on Desert Island Discs (Radio 4 December 2008) that some of his thinking happens subconsciously on the football pitch. Developing the sense in young mathematicians that mathematics is an evolving force which is driven by people of today brings life to the subject.

> ### Marcus de Sautoy
>
> Born: 26 August 1965 in London. Won a scholarship to Wadham College, Oxford University in 1983. He gained a first in mathematics and won a fellowship at All Souls. He became a professor of mathematics at Oxford. He was made Charles Simonyi Chair in the Public Understanding of Science at the University of Oxford.
>
> He has presented TV programmes such as Mind Games. He has written a book titled *Finding Moonshine* (about mathematical symmetry) and *The Music of the Primes*.
>
> When he started to play the trumpet he fell in love with mathematics realizing that maths and music are connected. He is an Arsenal season ticket holder and plays football as a hobby.

When interviewed he talks of mathematics being a creative subject. For Marcus mathematics is 'a source of joy', 'almost poetic' (Desert Island Discs, Radio 4, December 2008). He also talks of how the work he does, makes his 'head hurt' the concentration is so great.

Context of the problem

Understanding the context of the problem is key to interpreting solutions; the context of the problem will determine the solution. The example below (Haylock and Cockburn 2008) asks children to solve the problem:

How many coaches do we need to book for the school outing to the north Norfolk coast? There were 299 children and 18 adults going on the trip. Coaches with seat belts take 49 people. The number of children (299) is added to the number of adults (18) to give a total of 317. This is divided by 49 (the number each coach can take). Without a calculator:

$6 \times 50 = 300$
so
6×49 will be six less $= 294$
This is 23 short of 317 (our total people)
so
317 divided by 49 will be 6 remainder 23

Using a calculator we get 6.4693877, say 6.5.

The calculation has a remainder of 23 people. This implies you need six and a half coaches. The required answer is seven coaches. The context of the problem dictates that the number is rounded up to seven. Haylock and Cockburn (2008) then change the context of the problem to money. There is a budget of £317 and each coach costs £49. The calculation of how many coaches we can have arrives at 6.4693877 but this time we need to round down to 6.

This example highlights the importance of the fifth stage of the problem-solving cycle. The older child may not have developed the habit of checking solutions. Using an example will give older children insight into the value of this stage in the problem-solving process. There is a need to check the context of both problem and solution.

Creation of problems

Analysis and reflection are reasoning processes, as are clarifying and understanding.

Describing methods is a communication process (Orton and Frobisher 1996). A process becomes a skill when it becomes more automatic. A strategy is a combination of process and skill to solve a problem. Creating problems for others to solve brings strategy to a higher level; one must take a bird's eye view, be aware of flaws inherent in the structure of the problem. The creation of problems is high-level creative work and relates to section seven of the problem-solving process ('compose a similar problem structure' see Figure 9.3).

Children can be encouraged to make books which capture the problem-solving story, 'books made by adults and children together about investigations or problem-solving activities will provide another strategy for sharing children's mathematical successes' (Pound 1999: 86). The book promotes discussion as the journey of the problem is told.

Conclusion

Children need to see adults struggle in their search for solutions. Open, environmental or real problems provoke this opportunity. Polya suggests really looking at the problem. This requires that we look at the big picture rather than being immersed in detail. The answer needs to be tested. If the answer does not work the problem needs to be tackled again. This requires perseverance; Polya offers, 'if today will not, tomorrow may' (1945: 184).

Older children need bricks to solve or pose problems. As Pound says, 'structured apparatus can help children to create mental images and thus support their ability to solve mathematical problems mentally' (1999: 73).

The practitioner holds great influence in the role of problem-solving teacher as 'young children can demonstrate their skills as powerful problem solvers, provided the teacher creates appropriate classroom contexts for learning' and the skill is in the creation of, 'an active web of language and discussion that envelops teacher, learners and context' (Brown 2003: 93).

Problem solving and reflective thought are important not just through childhood but throughout life (Pound 1999), which positions our role delicately as, 'the seeds of such mathematical thinking can be sown at a very early stage' (Suggate, Davis and Goulding 2006: 15).

Conclusion: Reflecting on your learning

10

'It's very good jam,' said the Queen.

'Well, I don't want any to-day, at any rate.'

'You couldn't have it if you did want it,' the Queen said.

'The rule is jam tomorrow and jam yesterday but never jam to-day.'

'It must come sometimes to "jam to-day"', Alice objected.

'No it can't,' said the Queen. 'It's jam every other day: today isn't any other day, you know.'

'I don't understand you,' said Alice. 'It's dreadfully confusing.'

Through the Looking Glass, Lewis Carroll (1832–1898)

The aims of this chapter are:

- To appreciate the magnificence of mathematical thinking
- To expose the importance of reflective thinking
- To connect cross-curricular thinking with creative teaching

Introduction

In this chapter we will bring together the skills of mathematical and reflective thinking. The requirement to be reflective will be promoted as a professional responsibility. We will consider a simple way of doing this and recommend that this becomes part of every practitioner's daily practice.

Through examining mathematics we will review some key connections within the subject, offering this as a model for cross-curricular thinking as promoted by the Rose Report (Rose 2009).

An outcome of the work in this chapter will be to identify a toolbox of essential mathematical resources needed to deliver mathematics in a connected way. We will consider our own mathematical schemas as well as those of the children we teach.

The need for managers to develop systematic encouragement of reflective skills in staff is essential if they are to keep management outcomes in line with government expectations. Finally, the new curriculum, evolving from the Rose Report (Rose 2009), requires a play-based creative thinking approach.

> **Questions to reflect on:**
>
> How would you describe the difference between mathematical and reflective thinking?
>
> What resources would you pack if you were setting off to teach mathematics in an unfamiliar location?
>
> What are the key mathematical ideas to connect with?

Thinking

> Thinking may be creative or reflective, imaginative, convergent, divergent, scientific, visual, mimetic or somatic.
>
> Pound (2008: 56)

The word 'mimetic' relates to 'mime' or 'show' and the word 'somatic', expresses physical thinking such as children dancing, moving, engaging in gymnastics. Mathematical thinking is a combination of these thinking types. Then there is thinking about thinking, meta-cognition.

Mathematical thinking

To think in a mathematical way we hook up what we know to what we don't know with varying degrees of ease; 'all thinking involves both pain and pleasure: the pain of incomprehension and struggle to understand, and the pleasure of insights and convincing arguments' (Mason, Burton and Stacey 1982: 159). Thinking can be difficult, even uncomfortable.

As we become more familiar with a procedure, the pressure of thinking eases as repetition brings us closer to practical application, provided understanding is secure. Repeating what is not understood exposes fears and anxieties which result in a paralytic lack of thinking, 'feel sick, can't think.'

With mathematics we first need to make connections either by finding new understanding or realizing explicitly what is understood and is automatic. Unless we undo the complexity of counting for example, we cannot put emphasis on the correct components or watch out for important connections children arrive at. Thomas aged 4, made the connection that $3 + 2 = 2 + 3$ and allowing time for this to click into place, like the last piece of a jigsaw, was important.

Praising children who touch items as they count makes explicit the advantage of employing this technique. Rowland et al say of making connections that, 'in order to do so, teachers must have sufficient foundation knowledge of their own to plan for connection-making with their pupils' (2009: 102).

Our role is twofold: building bridges then dismantling to rebuild with children. The challenge for the educator is knowing what they know well enough to dissect it; sensing what they don't know so they can find it out; bringing children backwards then forwards along a learning continuum (see Chapter 4).

It is as if we have to create our own schemas of thought first. Reflect back on questions posed at the start of various chapters, and think now about the possibility of providing answers. What connections have you made which strengthen your understanding? Take, for example, pattern. Were you aware of how pattern underpins so much mathematics? Take another example, addition. Were you aware of how complex this is, with five possible meanings? How do you view the point about the importance of zero being visible or not? Or the importance of children understanding place value?

The projection of these thoughts outwards to make other connections is potentially developing your own mathematical schemas. The projection of this in teaching will allow children to make connections in their thinking. We need to scaffold our own learning, building schemas connectively. The provision we choose can spark child-initiated or indeed adult-led schemas for children. The little girl, Charlotte in Chapter 2, embarked on a child-initiated wrapping and then sharing out experience with the stones in the fabric, but only because Nina had used such inviting objects.

Out of our thinking come questions, steering children's thoughts. The language within questions needs to be carefully considered, as this in itself is complex and sensitive to variations in meaning.

With mathematical thinking we will experience pain when we allow ourselves to venture into unfamiliar applications or challenges. This extends our thinking, bringing tension if we find we cannot see our way through. We need to manage this state, as too much tension impedes thinking (Mason, Burton and Stacey 1982). Our skill is offering challenge to young mathematicians as well as strategies to manage the pain of not immediately knowing what to do. This was exemplified when we looked at solving problems in Chapter 9, and the cyclical system which includes checking outcomes. Children need to observe adults struggle, not always knowing the answer. The professional mathematician needs to walk away sometimes, finding the answer later. We need to place ourselves beyond a state of comfort, demonstrating perseverance. This requires a willingness to think mathematically rather than have answers pre-prepared.

Awareness of what we don't know is a bridge worth walking across, as it helps us build other bridges. Maybe we should accept mathematics as a world beyond absolute reach, spinning out the unexpected, depending on the children we teach. It is safe to assume we never arrive at fully knowing everything but that we can think mathematically. It is the quality of this underlying thinking which matters.

We have, through the course of this book, made the connection that mathematics relies on experiences that draw out pattern, problem solving and problem posing, that support abstract thinking through working with physical materials, stories, poems and play, all of which feed the imagination. We have also considered the association of stories for storing facts for recall in the memory, applying this to number formation in Chapter 3.

Place value can be experienced through the exchange game. Before this, the idea of grouping and exchange can be played using the egg box idea. The exchange game idea can be linked to money, to more complex numbers, to structured apparatus such as Dienes or Cuisenaire rods.

We considered how it is important to avoid assuming that children know what went before. We need to go back to early mathematical ideas, such as grouping, before working on an age- or stage-related slice of the curriculum. Rowland et al state, 'the idea of making mathematical connections by building upon what is already familiar to the class is clearly vital' (2009: 107). The challenge is making the 'already familiar' common to all in the group.

Askew et al (1997) consider the 'connectionist' style of teaching to be the most beneficial for children's mathematical learning. The curriculum resulting from the Rose Report (Rose 2009) highlights the importance of making connections and of sustained shared thinking, previously promoted by Pound (2008).

Thinking of mathematical provision

A question posed at the start of this chapter relates mathematical thinking to planning for teaching and in particular to thinking about provision. A Special Educational Needs Coordinator recently expressed the thought, 'there is just so much out there, how does anyone know what to choose?'

If we now take this on as a challenge; what would you put in a box that was to be transported abroad, where you are to teach children aged from birth to eight who do not speak English? This is based on my own real life experience of working abroad.

A first year student also asked what she should bring to Kenya to work with young children. The group divided the task into the six curriculum areas, drawing the outline of a suitcase on a large piece of paper, using their imagination along with the EYFS (DfES 2008) 'planning and resources' section to generate ideas. Sand and water are available in abundance at the location!

Table 10.1 Toolbox
Books could extend to those listed in the Bibliography and beyond to include narrative stories which offer a different experience to the child.

Resource	How it will support teaching
This Little Puffin by Elizabeth Matterson	Comprehensive collection of songs and rhymes to support sequencing and rhythm of language across themes e.g. 'Time and Weather', 'Animals', 'Baby Games'.
PEEPO! by Janet and Allan Ahlberg	Pattern of the day.
Rosie's Walk by Pat Hutchins	Positional language.

Resource	How it will support teaching
The Very Hungry Caterpillar by Eric Carle	Counting, days of the week, science.
Music	Movement, rhythm, motion, pattern.
Recipes for biscuits and cakes	Measurement of ingredients, mixing, timing, sequencing.
Play dough ingredients with black food colouring for making spiders (see Exchange Games Chapter 3). One cup of flour. Half a cup of salt. One cup of water. One tablespoon of oil. Two tablespoons cream of tartar. Black food colouring. Heat all ingredients in saucepan and mix until mixture leaves side of saucepan.	Hand eye coordination. Measurement and mixing of ingredients. Understanding concept of grouping and exchange.
Pipe cleaners (To make eight legs for each spider Chapter 3)	Understand concept of grouping and exchange.
Wooden bricks and blocks	To build steps, bridges, small worlds. To develop spatial skills. Note: large blocks offer a different experience.
Wooden train track with train and carriages	Problem solving: problem posing. Planning. Topology.
Skittles and balls	To see repeatedly the regular pattern of the total set and the change which each successful throw brings.
Snakes and Ladders	To promote turn taking. To experience counting on.
Velvet feely bags	To allow sensory work relying on touch. To develop memory; matching without looking at numbers, shapes or objects.
Buttons of different shapes and sizes. Note: buttons without holes will be less distracting for some children.	Sorting and categorising. To allow representation of quantities. Pattern: buttons arranged in pairs to show the odd and even feature of numbers.
Cuisenaire rods, Dienes blocks, Unifix cubes, Numicon	To experience number bonds, fractions, place value, odd and even number work.
Compare Bears	To promote sorting by colour and size; counting.
Coloured trays, hoops, small stretches of fabric	To promote sorting, counting in groups.
Weighing scales or balances	To support comparative weighing.

Resource	How it will support teaching
Measuring tapes, rulers, string	To allow children to measure.
Abacuses of different styles: horizontal, Slavonic (bead colour pattern of fives) and vertical	To allow counting in ones to 100; to allow counting in tens to 100; to encourage one-to-one correspondence with the 'Catch me out game', see chapter 6.
Dice with dot patterns Dice with numerals	To promote number and numeral recognition.
Number tracks with and without zero Number lines with and without zero Horizontal and vertical representations of number tracks and lines Sets of number cards to fit over number track spaces (see paired game, Chapter 6)	Children experience the pattern of numerals with and without zero. Children recognise and match numerals.
Hundred squares with zero Hundred squares without zero	To allow number recognition from zero to one hundred. To see the pattern as a result of including or excluding zero.
Pegs and peg boards Threads and beads	To encourage pattern creation and pattern replication. Pattern created on peg boards can be recreated with bead threading; crossing between materials with the one pattern.
Chalk (range of width and colours) Pencils (range of widths including triangular), pens, crayons, charcoal, paint	To allow children to express mathematical ideas.
Small and large white wipe boards Small and large blackboards Paper cut into various shapes and sizes Card or heavy-weight paper Art easels	Children will be encouraged to express themselves graphically. Fine motor control.
Junk modelling boxes Glue, sticking tape of a range of strength, tape dispensers Scissors (left and right handed; double barrelled to support cutting)	Model making develops spatial skills. Problem solving: problem posing.

Resource	How it will support teaching
Wrapping paper Wallpaper Fabric Boxes	Encourages wrapping of objects. Children select the most size appropriate to contain items.

This toolbox also represents all you need in your current location. Additional materials can be critically checked to see how they contribute to mathematical teaching. Sometimes, less is more. Too much choice can get in the way of choosing. Every mathematics teaching session needs materials so that children are learning in a concrete way. Abstract thinking is remote and difficult to connect with until ideas are set in the mind. Consider the example of a student teaching odd and even numbers in Chapter 4. The children needed structural materials to feel the symmetry and asymmetry of even and odd numbers.

Reflective thinking

To think is to have one's mind at work; to reflect is to reproduce to the eye or mind (based on the Oxford English Dictionary). Reflective thinking is an important attribute for an effective practitioner. We will consider why this is so, what it entails and how best to do it without creating more demands on what is already a complex role.

Why reflect?

Caroline Leeson describes how, 'reflective practice should be seen as an integral part of developing competent professionals in early years care and education' (2004: 172). The skill of reflecting gives potentially deeper insight into practice. Reflection is a route to decision-making. Reflecting accurately impacts on decision-making.

Reflection about practice allows us to be self-critical, realizing why we got it wrong or right. It allows one to separate personal self from teaching self. Smith explains that, 'reflection has an important part to play in helping us resolve the part the self plays in teaching and in helping us to identify the blind spots and troublesome areas which make our teaching less effective for some children' (2001: 141). We cannot be experts in all curricular areas. We are general practitioners with possible specialist interests.

The trainee practitioner is in the best position to connect theory to practice. With their fresh, raw consciousness this can be deeper, stronger, more critical. Through their studies and practical experience trainees are connecting theoretical subject knowledge to practical application. They are looking for ways of delivering clear messages. Mathematical thoughts can therefore mirror reflective thinking and cross-curricular teaching.

The demands of working with children as a social worker, paediatric nurse or early years practitioner are immense. The child is our responsibility whilst in our care. Events within and beyond the immediate need to be thought about. At times this thinking is factual, 'bad nights sleep', 'child's parents are divorcing', 'death of grandparent' and at other times intuitive, 'a hunch', 'a feeling', 'something has changed'.

Reflecting on intuition is important; allow for your instinct to take shape and carry thoughts forward. This is harder when in the challenging role of student or newly qualified practitioner as there is a sense of, 'what do I know?' The irony is that you may know more than you think, or that your instinct is absolutely correct. Instinct is based on more than experience.

The role of working with young children is exhausting. At times you are depleted, emotionally, intellectually and physically. Thinking in a reflective way for a predetermined amount of time allows you then to put work to one side and concentrate on restoring yourself. The art of thinking reflectively can offer protection against this depletion, 'a journal can bring a sense of perspective to some things that can feel potentially overwhelming as you begin to work in a classroom' (Smith 2001: 147).

What to reflect on?

To a certain extent we are continually thinking and reflecting in and after action (Schon 1991). There is also the need to reflect on interactions. We need to interact in different ways with different people. A student placed in a children's centre upset members of staff unintentionally with her abrupt communication style. As part of an assessment visit this was discussed and she became aware of how to modify interactions.

A difficult interaction with a parent may need to be thought about in order to resolve it. Realizing that a different time or place is needed when they will have your undivided attention can bring out other issues hiding behind an outburst. Other examples often requiring hard thinking concern managing behaviour; a strategy chosen once may not work the second time, leading to a sense of dissatisfaction. This needs reflecting on to move forward. Why did this strategy not work? What other strategies could be employed? What will happen if these alternatives fail?

It is more difficult to reflect on successful activities or practice. The essence of what makes it good can be more elusive. How easy is it to reflect in detail on our strengths? Students remind me that they find this difficult, needing prompts for what they can write in the empty box on the paperwork. The benefit of pinning down positives is that we can capitalize on them. The advantage of knowing our weaknesses is that we can work on our 'blind spots'.

How to reflect?

As individuals

The Foundation Degree along with other courses promotes the use of reflective journals. Over the course of a two-year programme the focus of reflection changes. Initially these reflections tend to be on routines, moving on to more specific events. This reflection of experience can also be captured through poetry or drawings.

Planning, implementing and evaluating activities involve reflecting on the children, the curriculum and provision. Discussions in lectures offer opportunities to think about academic content and how this relates to practice. We reflect on our own practice by listening to or observing others. Students who bring accounts of good and poor practice into discussion make a difference to the learning experience of a group, providing ideas for professional conversation. It may be that they thought about this on the bus on the way home from placement, but their generosity of spirit to share drives practice forward.

When qualified it is advisable to have a sounding board, perhaps a student in the group with good reflective skills who will listen in more than a sympathetic way. With practice, the skill will become more automatic, not always needing to be written. It might be on the bus, in the shower, or listening to music. Some aspects of thinking are more appropriately reflected upon if written.

We think differently in different places, such as on trains, in parks, near running water. Time away either as individuals or as teams generates a very different thinking experience. In certain cases, the greater the distance from the writing on the board the clearer the words. Standing close up to a painting in an art gallery then moving back creates a changing impression on the mind.

As teams

The role of an early years practitioner brings with it exceptional emotional demands (Elfer and Dearnley 2007). We talked in Chapter 2 of the importance of creating a positive emotional environment. We identified this as intangible, resulting from attitudes of individuals. As well as individual positive attitude, it is necessary that 'staff first strengthen their own professional relationships together' (Elfer and Dearnley 2007). The positive attitude then impacts on children, parents, carers and other professionals.

The reflective aspect of the role needs to be given greater status as it determines so much. Management should support reflective practice in a systematic way. Staff need to be encouraged and required to think about individual feelings and thought processes evoked by their emotional work with children. Elfer and Dearnley (2007) consider, 'reflective practice as an entitlement of staff, both legitimate and necessary, if changes in professional practice are to be facilitated and sustained'.

A daybook

With the demands of the role intensifying there is a greater need to respond accurately. The role involves exchanges with other professionals, for example, speech therapists, parents, forest school leaders. Communication modes have widened with emails, blogs and mobile phones. The pressures are great both for staff and parents. There is a need to keep a record or track of work.

It is advisable to keep a daybook. This is standard with other professions such as engineers, project managers, architects; a functional A4 size book to record the date, make notes of phone calls, things to action, training events attended, outcomes of meetings, resources required for activities and so on. There is scope for the content to become deeply reflective or creative. It is a place where ideas are recorded, returning to them at a later time for developing. Lists can be made, checked, rewritten. It is a working tool, which tracks the daily happenings in your job.

It provides a sense of control over what is a complex role. It assists in achieving quality practice. It can be as brief or as detailed as you wish. If embarking on independent study it can help to set out aims giving self-direction. It is interesting to flick back and note what you have achieved over the course of time, whether studying or in employment.

Operating a daybook allows for reflection on many levels. It is a way of continually referencing where you are, and where you are going. There is something different about keeping the whole story together in one book rather than on separate pieces of paper; the experience is contained in chronological date order.

> Mel, a Foundation Degree student was finding it all a chaotic, unmanageable experience, losing ground, becoming stressed. On a visit just before Christmas, we discussed the need to write things down (which we had discussed before). Feeling generous I gave her a blank pink book. She did use it, bringing it to tutorials!

Reflecting makes more confident, more responsive, more creative practitioners who can positively influence the world of early years education (Leeson 2004). The practice of keeping a daybook, gives a professional dimension to your work.

Sharing practice

In 2003 Carruthers and Worthington established the Children's Mathematics Network (CMN at www.childrens-mathematics.net) and are keen to extend this. Professional development maintained through regular contact with colleagues sharing the same interest arguably impacts more on practice than one-off training events (Carruthers and Worthington 2009).

Cross-curricular thinking

New curriculum

The Rose Report (Rose 2009) recommendations lead to a new primary curriculum from September 2011. The curriculum will have six areas, of which some will be taught discretely and others in a thematic, cross-curricular way. The implication is that practitioners will need to think creatively. A creative approach will be required so that children get a good bite of the curriculum sandwich.

Creative teaching in a cross-curricular way

We can start with a story like *The Giant Jam Sandwich* by John Vernon Lord and Janet Burroway, looking at the content first. Then we look for mathematical opportunity. Finally we consider how this could serve to teach other curriculum areas, such as science. What about making the jam and the bread? We can put this beside *The Door Bell Rang* by Pat Hutchins which we used in Chapter 8. Using the simple model below we can start to plan how either can be used.

Table 10.2 Exploring the content, opportunities and cross-curricular connections.

The Doorbell Rang by Pat Hutchins	Book	*The Giant Jam Sandwich* Story and pictures by John Vernon Lord Verses by Janet Burroway
Ma makes 12 cookies and gives them to Victoria and Sam; six cookies each. *The doorbell rings and is opened to two children. Twelve cookies shared between four children gives three cookies each. The doorbell rings and is opened to two more children. Twelve cookies shared between six children gives two cookies each. The doorbell rings and is opened to six children. Twelve cookies shared between 12 children gives one cookie each. The doorbell rings. Ma suggests the children eat the cookies before it is opened. Sam overrides this and the door is opened to Grandma with a tray of cookies.* *The doorbell rings again.*	**Content**	*Four million wasps fly into a town. The villagers must think what they can do. They call a meeting in the village hall, and Bap the Baker leaps to his feet with an idea. 'What do wasps like best to eat? Strawberry jam!' He proposes they make a giant jam sandwich to trap the wasps. Bap gives instructions for the making of the dough: 'Mix flour from above and yeast from below. Salt from the seaside, water from the spout. Now thump it! Bump it! Bang it about!' The loaf rises to mountain size. Using 50 cookers in an old brick mill, they let it bake for hours and hours. They use eight fine horses to pull the bread to a field where the picnic cloth is spread. Four million wasps come to the trap. There are only three that get away. The birds have a feast for a hundred weeks.*

Language:		**Problem solving:**
Share them Six each Plenty Comparison 'like Grandma's' Door bell rings six times		How could we solve the problem of four million wasps? What quantities would be needed to scale the bread recipe up? How would you dispose of such a large sandwich? What other ways could the loaf be transported?
Addition:		
2 children 2 + 2 = 4 children 2 + 2 + 2 = 6 children 2 + 2 + 2 + (6) = 12 children		**Subtraction:**
		4,000,000 wasps subtract 3 leaves 3,999,997 wasps. Children age seven enjoy reciting this number.
Division:		
12 divided by 2 = 6 each 12 divided by 4 = 3 each 12 divided by 6 = 2 each 12 divided by 12 = 1 each		**Number names:**
		Four million wasps Fifty cookers
Problem:	**Mathematical opportunities**	Six strong men
If there are more than 12 children there will be less than one biscuit each. What if instead of Grandma there is another child at the door?		Slice two Eight fine horses Six flying machines All four million Three got away One hundred weeks
It is difficult to count but suppose there are 58 cookies on the tray. Along with the 12 on the plate that gives 58 + 12 = 70.		**Other time references:**
		Hours and hours, Wait, Day, Weeks
This number could be shared between the twelve children or 14 people if Grandma and the children's mother decide to be part of the share.		**Division:**
		How many months equate with 100 weeks?
Chairs:		How many jars of jam were required?
There are eight chairs. Four chairs have two children sharing.		How many blocks of butter?
Plates:		
How many will they need?		

Design and technology:		Design and technology:
The tablecloth and the floor are chequered. Could children design their own chequered pattern? Where else do we see this type of pattern? e.g. chess boards.		How would you set about designing a tablecloth the size of a field?
		Science:
Science:	**Cross-curricular learning**	Making dough and bread; the mix of flour, yeast, salt and water. The sequence of mixing, heating and cooling.
Cooking cookies. Scaling recipes up to cater for larger groups of people. Doubling up or multiplying ingredients.		
		The difference between wasps and bees.
Footprints. The floor needs mopping as more people walk across from door to table.		
Steam. There is a kettle and a point where it comes to the boil as the story reaches a climax.		

We talked about stepping inside a story, looking for mathematical opportunity and stepping beyond to link with other learning. This model can be used with any resource.

The same three-step approach can be used with creative ideas, songs, music, and cookery. We are 'thinking like spiders' (reception class teacher comments in Chapter 8 of 'Children's Thinking') as we move from the centre of an idea out.

To arrive at cross-curricular creative teaching

Start inside a story, enjoy the story for what it is

Examine the content for mathematical opportunity

Step outside the story to connect to other learning

Other environments

The Rose Report (Rose 2009) promotes the idea of children going beyond the classroom out into the community. A great opportunity, which we considered in an earlier chapter, was that which a forest school experience presents.

To use such a different environment to link cross-curricular teaching we could ask two questions: what aspect of the curriculum cannot be experienced? How can particular focus points be emphasized while allowing the advantage of child-initiated learning?

The exciting opportunity is that most of the curriculum and more can be learnt outside: the challenge is including adult-led teaching in a place rich for children's imagination. The answer may be that we only sometimes intervene and that will then be in a concentrated way. Children will make greater connections with the world if given the experience of learning somewhere else.

Conclusion

Mathematical thinking is magnificent. There is a great satisfaction in understanding how what seems simple is complex, finding ways of defining it for children we teach, ways which make sense. There is little surprise that we might struggle with such a deceptive subject.

There is a real need for educators to bore down into detail, understand complexities, and see ahead to where learning progresses. A solid understanding of what we are working with allows for connective learning. We need our own schemas, which we can then project out through teaching. This thinking extends to selecting provision, which represents the intended mathematical meaning, giving an essential toolbox. We can work out from this selection, adding resources.

Reflective thinking is a professional responsibility. If we record why a mathematical lesson went well or did not work out, we are evaluating our practice in a constructive way, leading to progress. The habit of recording on many levels can be achieved by maintaining a daybook.

Children will learn with concrete materials in a 'playful way', regardless of age. Why would we not provide for kinesthetic learning at any age? A play-based approach allows for mathematics to happen naturally. Thinking reflectively, mathematically, connectively, will influence the creativity of our young children. The characteristics of creative people are competence in identifying patterns, making connections and risk taking (Pound 2009). We are the creative people children mimic and rely on to nurture their own creativity. Creative teaching of mathematics starts with a positive attitude, enthusiasm and openness to not knowing the answers. Enjoy teaching and crafting mathematics.

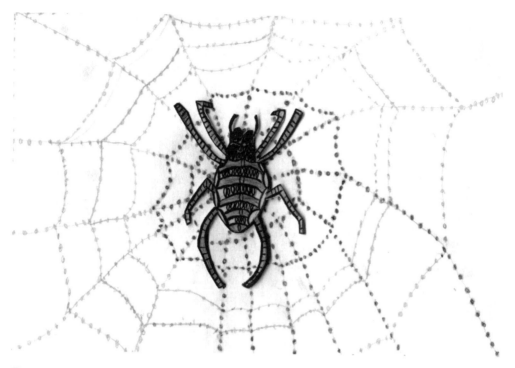

Figure 10.1 'Spider finishes web'.

Appendix

Learning objectives/Goals (Identify Early Learning Goals, National Curriculum)	**KEY WORDS**
Topic/Theme	
Children involved (Number of children, age, gender)	
Resources	
Health and safety considerations	

Session/Activity

Introduction

Content
(What will you do? What will the children do? What questions will you ask?)

Conclusion
(How will you finish the activity and reinforce the learning goals?)

Differentiation

● How will you support low achievers?

● How will you extend high achievers?

Assessment

How will you assess the children's learning?

Detailed analysis and evaluation

What went well? Why?

Were the learning objectives/goals achieved or did you work towards them?

What would you do differently if you carried out the activity again?

How could you extend the activity to increase learning?

Reflect on your learning.

References

Anghileri, J. (1991) 'The language of multiplication and division' in K. Durkin and B. Shire (eds), *Language in Mathematical Education: Research and Practice*, Milton Keynes: Open University Press.

Anghileri, J. (1995) 'Making sense of symbols', in J. Anghileri (ed.), *Children's Mathematical Thinking in the Primary Years: Perspectives on Children's Learning*, London: Continuum.

Anghileri, J. (1997) 'Uses of counting in multiplication and division', in I. Thompson (ed.), *Teaching and Learning Early Number.* Buckingham: Open University Press.

Anthony, G. and Walshaw, M. (2007) *Effective Pedagogy in Mathematics/Pangarau Best Evidence Synthesis Iteration* (Online). Available at: www.educationcounts.govt.nz/publications/series/2515/5951 (Accessed 23 March 2009).

Askew, M., Brown, M., Rhodes, V., Johnson, D. and Wiliam, D. (1997) Effective teachers of numeracy – final report (February 1997): report of a study carried out for the Teacher Training Agency 1995–96 by the School of Education, King's College London. London: King's College.

Association of Teachers of Mathematics (2009) *Slavonic Abacus* (Online). Available at: www.atm.org.uk/resouces/slavonicabacus.html (Accessed 17 October 2009).

Athey, C. (1990) *Extending Thought in Young Children: A parent–teacher partnership.* London: Paul Chapman.

BBC News (2009) *Call for Lessons to Begin at Six* (Online). Available at: http://news.bbc.co.uk/1/hi/education/8309153.atm (Accessed 19 October 2009).

Bird, H. (1991) *Mathematics for Young Children: An active thinking approach.* London: Routledge.

Boaler, J. (2009) *The Elephant in the Classroom: Helping children learn and love maths.* London: Souvenir Press Ltd.

Briggs, M. and Davis, S. (2008) *Creative Teaching: Mathematics in the early years and primary classroom.* Routledge: London.

Brown, T. (2003) *Meeting the Standards in Primary Mathematics: A guide to the ITT NC.* London: RoutledgeFalmer.

Butterworth, B. (2005) *From Fear of Fractions to the Joy of Maths.* Chapter 10 provided as part of material for the Inaugural Conference on Dyscalculia and Maths Learning Difficulties, June 2009. Available at: www.mathematicalbrain.com/pdf/ (Accessed 6 January 2010).

Buzan, T. (1986) *Use Your Memory: Understand your mind to improve your memory and mental power.* Harlow, Essex: Educational Publishers LLP.

Cambridge Primary Review (2009) *Final Report from the Cambridge Primary Review* (Online). Available at: www.primaryreview.org.uk/Downloads/Finalreport/CWE-briefing.pdf (Accessed 19 October 2009).

Carruthers, E. and Worthington, M. (2006) *Children's Mathematics: Making marks, making meaning* (2nd edition). London: Paul Chapman.

Carruthers, E. and Worthington, M. (2009) 'The inter-relationship between an Early Years' CPD initiative for mathematics and young children learning mathematics: the power of grassroots learning', paper presented at the British Society for Research into Learning Mathematics (BSRLM) Day Conference, University of Cambridge, 28 February 2009.

Chinn, S. (2004) *The Trouble with Maths: A practical guide to helping learners with numeracy difficulties*. London: RoutledgeFalmer.

Chinn, S. (2009) *Mathematics anxiety in secondary students in England* (Online). Available at: www.interscience.wiley.com (Accessed 6 January 2010). Published in *Wiley Interscience* on 16 December 2008.

Clausen-May, T. (2009) 'Seeing and doing mathematics', Lecture at Inaugural Conference London Dyscalculia and Maths Learning Difficulties. Also personal communication with the author, 19 June 2009.

Coffield, F., Edward, S. (2008) 'Rolling out "good", "best" and "excellent" practice. What next? Perfect practice?', *British Educational Research Journal*, 99999:1, 1–20.

Cole, J. (2008) 'Our role as adults in enabling independent learning', in S. Featherstone and P. Featherstone (eds), *Like Bees, not Butterflies Child-initiated Learning in the Early Years*. London: A and C Black.

Cooke, H. (2000) *Mathematics for Primary and Early Years: Developing subject knowledge* (2nd edition). London: SAGE Publications.

Copley, V. (2000) *The Young Child and Mathematics*. Washington, D.C.: National Association for the Education of Young Children.

Craft, A. (2002) *Creativity and Early Years Education. A lifewide foundation.* London: Continuum.

De Corte, E. and Verschaffel, L. (1991) 'Some factors influencing the solution of addition and subtraction word problems' in Durkin, K. and Shire, B. (eds), *Language in Mathematical Education: Research and Practice*, Milton Keynes: Open University Press.

Desert Island Discs (2008) BBC Radio 4, December.

DfEE (2000) *Mathematical Challenges for Able Pupils in Key Stages 1 and 2* (Online). Available at:http://publications.teachernet.gov.uk/eorderingDownload/DfES-0083-2000.PDF(Accessed 17 October 2009).

DfES (2004a) *Finding all Possibilities Foundation Stage*. Primary National Strategy (Online). Available at: www.edu.dudley.gov.uk/numeracy/primary/dfes%20problem%20solving/problem-solving%20packpdf (Accessed 17 October 2009).

DfES (2004b) *Problem Solving: A CPD pack to support the learning and teaching of mathematical problem solving* (Online). Available at: www.lgfl.net/lgfl/leas/greenwich/accounts/subjects/mathematics/web/information/menu%202%20files/problem%20solving%20CPD.pdf (Accessed 19 October 2009).

DfES (2006) *Primary National Strategy; Primary Framework for Literacy and Mathematics.* Norwich: DfES Publications.

DfES (2008) *Practice Guidance for the Early Years Foundation Stage.* Nottingham: DfES Publications.

Edgington, M. (2009) '"Let's be kings" – facilitating high quality, child initiated learning' [lecture for Early Education at Southdown Infant School, Bath, and personal communication with Caroline McGrath] 6 June 2009.

Einstein, A. (1954) *Ideas and Opinions.* London: Alvin Redman Ltd.

Elfer, P. (2006) 'Exploring children's expressions of attachment in nursery', *European Early Childhood Education Research Journal*, 14:2, 81–95.

Elfer, P. and Dearnley, K. (2007) 'Nurseries and emotional well being: evaluating an emotionally containing model of professional development', *Early Years,* 27:3, 267–279.

Emmerson, J. (2009) 'Making Maths Real ... What Works?' [lecture at the Inaugural Conference London Dyscalculia and Maths Learning Difficulties] 19 June 2009.

Every Child a Chance Trust (2009) *The Long Term Costs of Numeracy Difficulties* (Online). Available at: www.everychildachancetrust.org/pubs/ECS_long_term_costs_numeracy_difficulties_final. pdf (Accessed 14 October 2009).

Eves, H. (1911) *Return to Mathematical Circles.* Boston: PWS-Kent Publishing Company.

Eye of the Storm: Blue Eyes Brown Eyes (no date). [Videocassette]. Ipswich: Concord Video & Film Council Ltd.

Featherstone, S. and Featherstone P. (eds) (2008) *Like Bees, Not Butterflies: Child-initiated Learning in the Early Years.* London: A and C Black.

Frobisher, L. (1999) 'Primary school children's knowledge of odd and even numbers', in A. Orton (ed.), *Pattern in the Teaching and Learning of Mathematics.* London: Cassell.

Frobisher, L. and Threlfall, J. (1999) 'Patterns in processing and learning addition facts', in A. Orton (ed.), *Pattern in the Teaching and Learning of Mathematics.* London: Cassell.

Frobisher, L., Monaghan, J., Orton, A., Orton, J., Roper, T., Threlfall, J. (1999) *Learning to Teach Number. A handbook for students and teachers in the primary school.* Cheltenham: Stanley Thorne.

Garrick, R., Threlfall, J. and Orton, A. (1999) 'Pattern in the Nursery' in Orton, A. (ed.) *Pattern in the Teaching and Learning of Mathematics.* London: Cassell.

Gifford, S. (2004) 'A new mathematics pedagogy for the early years: In search of principles for practice', *International Journal of Early Years Education*, 12:2, 99–115.

Gifford, S. (2005) *Teaching Mathematics 3–5: Developing learning in the foundation stage.* Maidenhead: Open University.

Goddard, P. (2009) Notes to Caroline McGrath, 1 September 2009.

Griffiths, R. (2005) 'Mathematics and play', in J. Moyles (ed.), *The Excellence of Play* (2nd edition). Maidenhead: Open University Press.

Haylock, D. (2006) *Mathematics Explained for Primary Teachers* (3rd edition). London: SAGE Publications.

Haylock, D. and Cockburn, A. (2003) *Understanding Mathematics in the Lower Primary Years*. London: Paul Chapman

Haylock, D. and Cockburn, A. (2008) *Understanding Mathematics for Young Children*: A guide for Foundation Stage and Lower Primary Teachers. London: SAGE Publications.

Haylock, D. and Thangata, F. (2007) *Key Concepts in Teaching Primary Mathematics.* London: SAGE Publications.

Hill, J. (2009) 'Escape to the Forest. Discover the impact for our forest therapy group!' [Third National Annual Conference Redcliffe Children's Centre RESEARCH = Freedom, Reflective Practice, Possibilities and a Deeper Understanding of Children and Families] 1 May 2009.

Hughes, M. (1986) *Children and Number: Difficulties in learning mathematics.* Oxford: Blackwell.

Isaacs, S. (1932) *The Children We Teach.* London: University of London Press.

Kiely, R. (2009) *Teaching as Craft-theory, Policy and Practice Perspectives* [City of Bristol College Research Conference] 6 July 2009.

Kline, M. (1953) *Mathematics in Western Culture: A fascinating assessment of a science that has contributed immeasurably to our civilization.* London: Penguin.

Lafferty, P. (2008) 'Child-initiated learning – a view from High/Scope', in S. Featherstone and P. Featherstone (eds), *Like Bees, Not Butterflies: Child-initiated Learning in the Early Years.* London: A and C Black.

Learning and Teaching Scotland (2005) *Birth to Three: Supporting our youngest children.* Scottish Executive.

Learning and Teaching Scotland (2009) *Curriculum for Excellence: Numeracy and mathematics.* Scottish Executive.

Leeson, C. (2004) 'In praise of reflective practice', in J. Willan, R. Parker-Rees, J. Savage (eds), *Early Childhood Studies* (2nd edition). Exeter: Learning Matters Ltd.

Liebeck, P. (1984) *How Children Learn Mathematics: A guide for parents and teachers.* London: Penguin.

Lindon, J. (2008) 'Child-initiated learning: what does it mean, where does it fit and why is it important for young children? Key messages from the Early Years Foundation Stage', in S. Featherstone and P. Featherstone (eds), *Like Bees, Not Butterflies: Child-initiated Learning in the Early Years.* London: A and C Black.

Mason, J., Burton, L. and Stacey, K. (1982) *Thinking Mathematically* (revised edition). London: Prentice Hall.

May, P., Ashford, E. and Bottle, G. (2006) *Sound Beginnings: Learning and Development in the Early Years.* London: David Fulton.

Maynard, T. (2007) 'Encounters with Forest School and Foucault: a risky business?' *Education, 3–13,* 35:4, 379–391.

Merttens, R. (1987) *Teaching Primary Mathematics.* London: Edward Arnold.

Merttens, R. (2009) *Ruth Merttens Describes the New Maths Teaching Sequence* (Online). Available at: www.hamilton-trust.org.uk/standard.asp?id=8995 (Accessed 14 October 2009).

Montague-Smith, A. (1997) *Mathematics in Nursery Education* (2nd edition). London: David Fulton Publishers.

Moyles, J. (2008) 'Empowering children and adults: play and child-initiated learning', in S. Featherstone and P. Featherstone (eds), *Like Bees, Not Butterflies Child-initiated Learning in the Early Years.* London: A and C Black.

National Council of Teachers of Mathematics (NCTM) (2009) *One Grain of Rice* (Online). Available at: http://illuminations.nctm.org/lessons/OneGrainRice-AS-OGR.pdf (Accessed 17 October 2009).

NRICH (2009) *Up and Down Staircases* (Online). Available at: http://nrich.maths.org/2283 (Accessed 17 October 2009).

O'Brien, L. and Murray, R. (2006) *A Marvellous Opportunity for Children to Learn: A participatory evaluation of Forest School in England and Wales* (Online). Available at: www.forestry.gov.uk/pdfreport.pdf/$FILE/fro112forestschoolsreport.pdf (Accessed 14 October 2009).

Ofsted (2009) *Mathematics: Understanding the score: Improving practice in mathematics teaching at primary level* (Online). Available at: http://www.ofsted.gov.uk/content/download/9168/101182/file/mathematics%20understanding%20the%20score%20-%20primary.pdf (Accessed 17 October 2009).

Orton, A. and Frobisher, L. (1996) *Insights into Teaching Mathematics* (2nd edition). London: Continuum.

Orton, A. (1999) *Pattern in the Teaching and Learning of Mathematics.* London: Cassell.

Papatheodorou, T. (2006) *Seeing the Wider Picture: Reflections on the Reggio Emilia Approach* (Online). Available at: http://www.tactyc.org.uk/pdfs/Reflection_Papatheodorou.pdf (Accessed 28 April 2010).

Polya, G. (1945) *How to Solve it: A new aspect of mathematical method* (2nd edition). Princeton, New Jersey: Princeton University Press.

Pound, L. (1999) *Supporting Mathematical Development in the Early Years*. London: Routledge.

Pound, L. (2008) *Thinking and Learning about Mathematics in the Early Years*. Oxon: Routledge.

Pound, L. (2009) 'The genius of creativity', *Early Years Educator (EYE)*, 11(1): 14–16.

Pratt, N. and Woods, P. (2007) *Changing PGCE Students' Mathematical Understanding through a Community of Inquiry into Problem Solving. Research in Mathematics Education*, 9:79–94.

Qualifications and Curriculum Authority (QCA) (1999a) *Teaching Mental Calculation Strategies: Guidance for teachers at key stages 1 and 2*. London: QCA, for the National Numeracy Strategy. Part 3 Teaching addition and subtraction strategies (Online). Available at: http://fp.sprisheffsch.f9.co.uk/n/s/docs/MathsPubs/ (Accessed 15 October 2009).

Qualifications and Curriculum Authority (QCA) (1999b) *Teaching Written Calculations: Guidance for teachers at key stages 1 and 2*. London: QCA, for the National Numeracy Strategy. Part 3 Teaching addition and subtraction strategies (Online). Available at: http://fp.sprisheffsch.f9.co.uk/n/s/docs/MathsPubs/ (Accessed 15 October 2009).

Rose, R. (2009) *Independent Review of the Primary Curriculum: Final report*. Nottingham: DCSF Publications.

Rousham, L. (1997) 'The empty number line: a model in search of a learning trajectory?' in I. Thompson (ed.), *Teaching and Learning Early Number*. Buckingham: Open University Press.

Rowland, T. (2006) 'Subtraction-difference or comparison?' *Mathematics in School,* 35(2): 32–35.

Rowland, T., Turner, F., Thwaites, A. and Huckstep, P. (2009) *Developing Primary Mathematics Teaching*. London: SAGE.

Sammons, P., Sylva, K., Melhuish, E., Siraj-Blatchford, I., Taggart, B., Grabble, Y., Barreau, S., (2007) *Effective Pre-school and Primary Education 3–11 Project (EPPE 3–11) Influences on Children's Attainment and Progress in Key Stage 2: Cognitive outcomes in year 5* (Online). Available at: http://publications.dcsf.gov.uk/eorderingDownload/RB828.pdf (Accessed 14 October 2009).

Schon, D. (1991) *The Reflective Practitioner: How Professionals Think in Action*. Aldershot: Avebury.

Sennet, R. (2008) *The Craftsman*. London: Penguin.

Siraj-Blatchford, I. (2004) 'Quality teaching in the early years', in A. Anning, J. Cullen and M. Fleer (eds), *Early Childhood Education*. London: SAGE.

Siraj-Blatchford, I. and Sylva, K. (2004) 'Researching pedagogy in English pre-schools', *British Education Research Journal*, 30:5, 713–730.

Smith, J. (2001) 'Reflective practice', in A. Cockburn and G. Handscomb (eds), *Teaching Children 3 to 11* (2nd edition). London: Paul Chapman Publishing.

Stevens, J. (2008) 'Count us in! – the importance of child-initiated learning in problem solving, reasoning and numeracy', in S. Featherstone and P. Featherstone (eds), *Like Bees, Not Butterflies: Child-initiated Learning in the Early Years*. London: A and C Black.

Straker, A. (1993) *Talking Points in Mathematics*. Cambridge: Cambridge University Press.

Suggate, J., Davis, A., Goulding, M. (2006) *Mathematical Knowledge for Primary Teachers* (3rd edition). Oxon: David Fulton Publishers.

Thompson, I. (1997) *Teaching and Learning Early Number*. Buckingham: Open University Press.

Thompson, I. (2001) 'Issues for classroom practices in England', in J. Anghileri (ed.), *Principles and Practices in Arithmetic Teaching*. Buckingham: Open University Press.

Threlfall, J. (1999) 'Repeating patterns in the early primary years' in Orton, A. (ed.), *Pattern in the Teaching and Learning of Mathematics*. London: Cassell.

Tucker, K. (2005) *Mathematics Through Play in the Early Years*. London: Paul Chapman.

Walter, M. (1989) 'Curriculum topics through problem posing', *Mathematics Teaching*, 128, 23–25.

Welsh Assembly Government (2008a) *Flying Start Guidance* (Online). Available at: http://wales.gov.uk/topics/educationandskills/policy/104009-wag/flyingstart/?lang=en (Accessed 17 October 2009).

Welsh Assembly Government (2008b) *Foundation Phase Framework for Children's Learning for 3 to 7-year-olds in Wales*. Cardiff: Department for Children, Education, Lifelong Learning and Skills.

Welsh Assembly Government (2008c) *Key Stages 2–4 Mathematics in the National Curriculum for Wales*. Cardiff: Department for Children, Education, Lifelong Learning and Skills.

Wright, R., Martland, J. and Stafford, A. (2006) *Early Numeracy: Assessment for teaching and intervention* (2nd edition). London: SAGE Publications.

Yackel, E. (2001) 'Perspectives on arithmetic from classroom-based research in the United States of America', in J. Anghileri (ed.), *Principles and Practices in Arithmetic Teaching*. Buckingham: Open University Press.

Bibliography

Aubrey, C. (1997) *Mathematics Teaching in the Early Years: An investigation into teachers' subject knowledge*. London: Falmer Press.

Burgess, D. (2008) 'More than a numbers game', *The Times Educational Supplement*, June, p.27.

Burgess, H. and Mayes, A. S. (2008) 'Using e-learning to support primary trainee teachers' development of mathematical subject knowledge: An analysis of learning and the impact on confidence', *Teacher Development*, 12:1, 37–55.

Calder, P. (2008) 'Early childhood studies degrees: the development of a graduate profession', in Cable, C. and Miller, L. (ed.), *Professionalism in the Early Years*. London: Hodder Education.

Denscombe, M. (2003) *The Good Research Guide: For small-scale social research projects* (2nd edition). Maidenhead: Open University Press.

DfES (2001) *Guidance to Support Pupils with Dyslexia and Dyscalculia*. NNS: DfES 0512/2001.

DfES (2002) *Mathematical Activities for the Foundation Stage Reception*. NNS: DfES 0188/2002.

DfES (2002) *Mathematical Activities for the Foundation Stage Nursery*. NNS: DfES 0187/2002.

McNiff, J. and Whitehead, J. (2002) *Action Research: Principles and practice*. Oxon: RoutledgeFalmer.

Nunes, T. and Bryant, P. (1996) *Children Doing Mathematics*. Oxford: Blackwell.

Poulson, L. (2001) 'Paradigm lost? Subject knowledge, primary teachers and education policy', *British Journal of Educational Studies*, 49:1, 40–55.

Sfard, A. (1998) 'On two metaphors for learning and the dangers of choosing just one', *Educational Researcher*, 27:2, 4–13.

Shulman, L. (1986) 'Those Who Understand: Knowledge growth in teaching', *Educational Researcher*, 15:2, 4–14.

Thompson, I. (ed.) (1997) *Teaching and Learning Early Number*. Buckingham: Open University Press.

Woods, P. (1996) *Researching the Art of Teaching: Ethnography for educational use*. London: Routledge.

Children's books referred to in the text

Ahlberg, J. and Ahlberg, A. (1981) *PEEPO!* London: Penguin.

Carle, E. (1970) *The Very Hungry Caterpillar.* London: Penguin.

Carle, E. (1993) *Today is Monday.* London: Penguin.

Cooper, H. (1998) *Pumpkin Soup.* London: Transworld Publishers Ltd.

Forest, H. (1998) *Stone Soup.* Arkansas: August House LittleFolk.

Gardner, M. (1996) *The Universe in a Handkerchief: Lewis Carroll's Mathematical Recreations, Games, Puzzles, and Word Plays.* New York: Copernicus.

Hendra, S. (1996) *Oliver's Wood.* London: Walker Books.

Hutchins, P. (1968) *Rosie's Walk.* London: Penguin.

Hutchins, P. (1986) *The Doorbell Rang.* New York: Greenwillow Books.

Inkpen, M. (1989) *The Blue Balloon.* London: Hodder Children's Books.

Landström, O. and Landström, L. (1996) *Boo and Baa in a Party Mood.* London: Rand S Books.

Lewis, K. (1992) *Floss.* London: Walker Books.

Lord, J. V. and Burroway, J. (1972) *The Giant Jam Sandwich.* Basingstoke: Macmillan Children's Books.

Martin Jr., B. (1983) *Brown Bear, Brown Bear, What Do You See.* New York: Henry Holt.

Matterson, E. (1991) *This Little Puffin.* London: Puffin.

Rosen, M. (1996) *Poems for the Very Young.* London: Kingfisher.

Rosentein, R. (1998) *One, Two ... Where's the Shoe?* Edinburgh: Floris Books.

Somaiah, R. and Somaiah, R. (2006) *Indian Children's Favourite Stories.* Singapore: Tuttle Publishing.

Index